P9-DMG-469

PRESSURE GROUPS IN AMERICAN POLITICS

JK
1118
.M3

Pressure Groups in American Politics

H. R. Mahood
Memphis State University

CHARLES SCRIBNER'S SONS
New York

11546   138 (blue)

147606

Illustrations on pages 105-117 courtesy of *Harvard Business Review*.

COPYRIGHT © 1967 CHARLES SCRIBNER'S SONS

THIS BOOK PUBLISHED SIMULTANEOUSLY IN THE UNITED STATES OF
AMERICA AND IN CANADA—COPYRIGHT UNDER THE BERNE CONVENTION

ALL RIGHTS RESERVED. NO PART OF THIS BOOK MAY BE REPRODUCED IN
ANY FORM WITHOUT THE PERMISSION OF CHARLES SCRIBNER'S SONS.

A-1.67 [Col.]

PRINTED IN THE UNITED STATES OF AMERICA

LIBRARY OF CONGRESS CATALOG CARD NUMBER 67-10457

4/7/67   B & T   2.61

Dedicated to the memory of my father

CONTENTS

III. PRESSURE GROUPS AND GOVERNMENT

IV. PRESSURE GROUPS AND REGULATION

PREFACE

The purpose of this volume is two-fold: to bring to the attention of the college student the role of formally organized pressure groups in public policy formation and to emphasize the existence of a group theory of politics. However, a word of caution is in order. Although the importance of groups in policy-making is stressed here, they are not the only actors on the political scene. To be sure, the political environment, values, attitudes and the political system have an impact along with pressure groups. Further, group theory is not an all-inclusive concept. It has, for example, excessive concern with group conflict and over-emphasizes the importance of politically-oriented groups as opposed to those of socialization. More positively, group theory provides the student with a methodological tool which allows him to take advantage of the latest techniques of scientific inquiry. Also, it provides him with a theoretical framework for viewing politics as a continuous association of men with other men attempting to secure some type of political objective.

The author wishes to acknowledge the various writers upon whose work he has drawn. An attempt was made to choose selections from diversified writers and sources. As far as possible, the selections are printed in full. This anthology, obviously, does not exhaust the field of pressure groups group theory. Hopefully, these articles will stimulate in the student the desire to explore the growing literature on pressure groups.

Grateful acknowledgment is due the various publishers who generously granted permission to reprint the articles used. And, a very special debt of gratitude to Professor Phillip Monypenny of the Department of Political Science, University of Illinois, who graciously contributed the Introduction to this volume.

H. R. M.

PRESSURE GROUPS IN AMERICAN POLITICS

Introduction

PHILLIP R. MONYPENNY

The essays and papers presented in this volume provide an introduction both to the development of interest groups, or pressure groups, as a part of the structure of politics in the United States and to the theoretical outlook which stimulated the attention of political scientists to this relatively new political phenomenon. The ready acceptance of the term "pressure group" and the widespread recognition of the importance of the entities indicated by that name in the work of politics has obscured somewhat the underlying ideas about the study of politics embodied in it. This is developed in both Professor Golembiewski's and Professor Latham's essays which call attention both to the ambitious character of Arthur Bentley's original manifesto in *The Process of Government* and to the widening vistas in the study of politics which were implicit in his introduction of the concept of "group" as the primary unit in political life.

The introduction of the idea of "groups" rather than "persons" as the basic unit of politics encountered and still encounters considerable resistance. The general tradition of political thought is individualistic, just as the rhetoric of politics is individualistic outside the countries of the Communist bloc. In the study of politics as in psychology the individuals as a self-acting, autonomous, decisional unit has been the usual starting point of analysis. In the tradition of political thought he is treated as rational, deliberately selecting means to achieve deliberately chosen ends. He has the attribute of free will. He joins parties and attempts to use them to promote ends which he values, whether these be selfish or altruistic. If he gains power, he attempts to maintain it, for power is an important independent motive and he attempts to use power to achieve his ends—personal or social. Those who have power can be controlled by the threat of the loss of power or by manipulating the conditions under which they can achieve their ends. In turn, those who have power manipulate the sanctions of rewards and penalties which power gives them to control those who are their subjects. The great example of this kind of analysis is Machiavelli's *The Prince*.

This train of thought produces a political analysis in which the structure of government can be deliberately planned, almost without regard to time or place, to provide opportunities for action and means of control, and to permit quick and decisive action. Individual men, calculating their own interests, will concert their action with like-minded men, taking account of the rewards and penalties which the political structure provides, including the opportunities of holding office and using the powers of office to achieve their ends. The *Federalist Papers* are a magnificent example of this kind of analysis. Except in terms of the deliberate calculation of individuals of their own interests, moral and material, in the light of the choices open to them under prevailing governmental policy, there is little in such analysis to indicate the terms of relationship between the office holder and the general population over whom he exercises some formal power.

The general outlook which took for granted the rational and moral autonomy of the individual—at least of the individuals judged fit to participate in politics—was not peculiar to politics. It was obviously supported by religious and ethical outlooks and the whole course of formal philosophy. When it was challenged in some social science areas, such as the study by German scholars of the history of legal institutions, the formulation of society as an organism rather than as a collection of separate persons was cast in terms so allegorical and mystical, that it seemed absurd to English and American scholars brought up in the Lockean and Benthamite traditions.

In the nineteenth century, however, the growing body of work on the history and contemporary character of human society provided a basis for shifting the standpoint from which to study politics from the self-acting individual to the individual or collection of individuals in a social setting. The most emphatically argued effort of this kind in the United States was Arthur Bentley's *The Process of Government*. It argued both for the acceptance of politics as social and not individual and for shaping the conceptual apparatus for the study of politics from direct observation and not speculation. It strongly assailed the idealistic tendencies of philosophy which saw reality as inhering in the ideal form traced by philosophical symbol, not in the object as immediately experienced.

In the contemporary study of politics the interest in Bentley's work is less in his argument over method than in the much more comprehensive view of the relation of government and politics to the total society to which his view of method led him. If the position that politics is social is accepted, then the individual man does not respond to politics as an isolated being. He responds according to his social conditioning—his "socialization" as the contemporary jargon puts it—and according to his current linkage with other men. Even his perceptions of what is around him is not that of a single pair of eyes, but of his eyes and his mind linked with the mind and eyes of other men so that sometimes despite himself he sees what they see and not what he might see if he were truly alone and able to make a separate judgment. The course of politics is not then determined by the action of single men, be they great or small, but the action of particular men who take other men with them as they move and who in turn are influenced by those whom they take with them. The audience shapes the actor's style, even as the actor's style moves the audience. So that in any comprehensive view, one never deals with men as individuals, but men related to other men—a group.

Given that standpoint, the relationship between rulers and the ruled, between officials and those in whose name they act, cannot be reduced purely to the legal bases of action, to the legal authority of the officials over the populace, or to the control of officials by the populace. In the conduct of government, the formal actions of officials and the behavior of populations or parts of populations are congruent; which depends on the other is not too clear. Did Franklin D. Roosevelt take the people to war or was he taken to war by the Committee to Defend America by Aiding the Allies which changed his opinion as it changed the opinion of many people in the general population?

Given social constraints and uniformities which override disparate individual tendencies, we may expect to find limitations on the extent and clarity of official action which cannot be found in the pure law which applies to the action. There will be classifications of people, in fact, which cannot be justified by the law. There will be differences of treatment for Negro and white, for native and immigrant, for mountain people and urban dwellers which may not rest on law, but which are deeply ingrained patterns of thought and action. The group approach to politics requires that a simple mechanical account of government be modified to take into account the actual practice of government as it may be revealed by direct observation. Since it implicitly refers to psychological variables, it suggests the appropriateness of charting bodies of belief and attitude which appear to give rise to groupings which have an effect on political and governmental action. It also implies enlarging the account of governmental institutions to include the continuous existence of extra-governmental bodies which participate in governmental decisions.

Direct observation of the interests or political purposes which were actively contending at a given time apparently appealed the most to Bentley. He would have recast the study of politics as a study of forces with each identifiable "interest" as a separate force. (This is the origin of his use of the term "pressure.") He proposed dealing with these forces as they were displayed in visible human behavior and suggested that forces might be described by the interest they embodied, by the number of persons acting on behalf of this interest, by their intensity and by their technique. These are terms easily applied to the organized groups whose participation in politics is set forth in this volume even though they apply as well to groups without visible organization. Since Bentley's time, political behaviorists have attempted to account for voting and for other forms of political participation and to sketch the prevalence in the population largely substituting psychological data and concepts for the older legal categories. The third possibility set out above, and the most modest, that of extending the conception of political institutions to include extra-governmental organizations, has been widely accepted and has been the most influential outcome of Bentley's insights. It should be noted that the organized groups which have largely been substituted as units for analysis for Bentley's interests embody multiple interests, including one in the survival of the reorganization itself. Nevertheless much of Bentley's thought can be transferred to the organized groups so evident in politics in the United States. Their effectiveness or lack of it can certainly be accounted for in some part by the number of their adherents, the intensity of their activity, and their technique in mobilizing their members and presenting their case.[1] The recognition of the part played by organized groups also permits the recognition of the fluidity of the practice of politics as opposed to the formal rigidity of governmental institutions. The essays in this book show that pressure groups may operate in the courts, in the halls of Congress, through the presidency, in the administrative agencies, and may, if they are sufficient masters of technique, move between them. They may operate at various governmental levels— national, state, and local—finding the one most responsive to them. Governmental bodies and agencies themselves may act as pressure groups which attempt to influence other governmental bodies and other governmental levels.[2]

The papers in this collection reflect almost exclusively the work of groups which are well organized with contributors or members,

[1] The papers by Scoble and Masters in this volume illustrate these considerations with respect to organized labor, pp. 121-145 and pp. 146-165 respectively.

[2] Note in particular the paper by Morgan on resources administration, pp. 244-267 infra.

budgets, paid secretariats and publications and able to maintain permanent staffs at various seats of government. This is characteristic of the studies which have been done on pressure groups. A more penetrating view would recognize that organized groups have more or less effect as they become the center for bodies of like-minded persons who have no organizational connection with them, but quietly or more actively make common cause with them.[3] One of the curiosities of politics is the effectiveness on particular fields of policy of apparently small organizations. Wildlife conservation, the conservation of natural beauty, prison reform, and opposition to British rule in Northern Ireland are examples. The opposite is true. Groups may be large and well-organized and ineffective, as is organized labor in the case of some of its most cherished objectives. Here the explanation seems to lie in very well-organized and determined opposition, and in the apparent indifference of much of the membership of labor unions to the explicit political programs of the labor movement. Small and well organized movements may face opposition from widely-held though largely unorganized opinions, as in the case of the movement to abolish capital punishment, whose membership is small and articulate, but usually ineffective.

Another variable in the effectiveness of groups, not easy to assess as an independent factor, is the skill of their officers and their secretariats, a matter related to, but not wholly dependent on, the size of membership and financial resources. The organizations advancing the particular interest of Negroes in escaping the barriers of segregation have apparently been exceptionally fortunate in the ability and sheer legal and organizing skill of their officers and staffs.[4]

In the general study of politics the conditions of the organization of pressure groups is important, or at least, their coming into being as an identifiable aggregation of people, whether organized or not. The conditions under which they extend their membership and

---

[3] This would seem to explain in part the successes and the failures of the business groups discussed by Hacker and Aberbach, and Reagan, pp. 81-101 and pp. 102-120 in this volume.

[4] See the essay in this volume by Rich, pp. 196-203 *infra*.

thereby their influence are also of importance. This concern leads in two directions. On the one hand is the study of the history of particular groups, represented in this volume by the papers of Fite and Johnson.[5] On the other is the study of the streams and patterns of communication, formal and informal in which members of interest groups participate and by which apparently unconnected persons can concert their efforts and regulate their relationships. Streams of communication are also means of adding members and influencing the opinion of governmental officials. Unfortunately this is a difficult matter to study and published studies, from the standpoint of a political scientist, have been suggestive rather than conclusive. The fortunes of particular groups in the political struggle are probably as often determined by shifts, difficult to detect, in public opinion, or what is regarded as public opinion by those who have the responsibility for making official decisions as by the immediate maneuvers of themselves and their opponents.

It is obvious then that the detailed studies of group action presented in this volume have a significance beyond the events of the particular case. Each illustrates the extent to which a complete catalogue of governmental machinery must include many organizations which are not ordinarily considered governmental.[6] Each indicates that means exist of putting checks on governmental agencies which could not be guessed from the legal and statutory powers and limitations under which particular agencies work. Each illustrates how the formal limits on the jurisdiction of governmental agencies, such as the Corps of Engineers, or the Bureau of the Reclamation may be evaded by a unity of action between governmental agencies and supporting outside groups. The latter are not inhibited by law or custom in exploring the whole machinery of government and the possibility of cooperating with other organized groups to get laws changed. They may negotiate understandings by which the agencies will divide their fields of action laying a base for inter-agency cooperation. Each case study illustrates that the separation of powers does

[5] Pp. 166-193 *infra*.
[6] See Celler's comments on the essentiality of lobbies to legislation, pp. 231-243 *infra*.

not prevent legislatures in general and Congress in particular from influencing administrative action by direct representations to agencies nor prevent agencies from getting legislative proposals into Congress, and acted on favorably, despite opposition from the President's office. One of the most fascinating accounts of the operation of unofficial organizations in determining governmental policy is the story of the farm organizations and farm legislation of 1932 and 1933.[7] Each raises questions about the means whereby influence is exercised. Is it merely a close calculation of the costs of accepting or denying the demands of a particular group? Or is it something like role theory at work which postulates that in a stable social situation the mutual expectations of participants define the acceptable and necessarily complementary conduct of members of the group of participants or actors? Is there a role for the spokesmen of organized farmers, or organized labor, or organized business, which with its complementary congressional and administrative roles, better explains what is asked and what is given than the abstract ideas of power or influence, or even David Truman's idea of access?

The recognition of the importance of interest and pressure groups has raised a number of normative or moral issues both inside and outside political science. What happens to the obligation of government to pursue a general public interest if all politics becomes a competition of particular interests with a preponderance among mutually supporting, or at least not incompatible, interests determining the outcome? One answer is that the recognition of the phenomenon of interest groups as a major aspect of any political system does not constitute an endorsement of the situation.

However, most students of interest group participation in politics are not unduly disturbed by what they find. Their relative tolerance is based on a belief that general public interests rarely exist which do not include to a substantial degree the interests of particular groups and that all groups have some claim to have their interests regarded at least potentially as an element in a more general public interest. The prescription of interests to other people, that is deciding

[7] See the paper by Johnson, pp. 179-193 *infra*.

for them what their interests are and taking action accordingly, is tyrannical, however well motivated it may be. It is also likely to be grounded on imperfect knowledge and thus to have unintended consequences. It is not easy for advantaged persons to have a clear understanding either of the situation or the desires of those in subordinate social positions. It has always been easy to say of subordinated peoples, whether Negroes in the United States, Jews in Slavic countries, Slavs in German and Magyar countries, Gaels in the British Isles at the times of Saxon dominance, that they were happy in their lot and that *their* best interests as well as those of society required their subordination. Parallel is the argument that the poor are poor because they want to be and that action to improve their lot is therefore a waste of resources. Any general public interest must take into account the particular interests of parts of the population and each part of the population is the best source of advice as to what its interests are.

Second, interests so widely shared that they may be described as general interests, such as the tradition-honored belief that the maintenance of public order and the security of life and property is the first obligation of government, will in fact be generally perceived interests for which nearly everyone will displace particular interests in opposition to them. It is not merely fear which leads to the acceptance of military service. In New York City during the Civil War there were serious riots growing out of efforts to enforce compulsory military service. The acceptance of the legitimacy of such service is far more widespread now. The problem of general public interests which are defeated by wicked special interests generally arises because some apparently important interests, in their nature general as to the extent of area and population affected, have a relatively small number of vocal advocates. This has been characteristic of the efforts to conserve natural beauty, to avoid the waste of scarce resources such as water, and control private land development in our cities so as to produce a harmonious whole. However well-reasoned and correct the ideas of the proponents of these interests, there is still only a limited public which is committed to them. Another situation in which public interest seems to suffer is one in which certain interests, such as the protection of women and children at work in the more ruthless days of industrialization, the elimination of racial discrimination, or the varied interests of the remaining Indian population, although they seem to be the proper obligations of all of society, are in fact the particular concern only of those subordinate people whose subordination permitted injustice in the first place. When very great damage has been done as in the case of water pollution or when the conscience of the nation is finally aroused as in racial discrimination, then sufficient support can be won to get action. Then perhaps, as in the case of water pollution, those who once contributed greatly to the problem, the industries polluting streams with their wastes, may be willing to undertake considerable expense to remedy the situation. Those public interests which are established as public interests only by reason of disinterested thinkers become politically viable public interests only when there is considerable support for or at least great acquiesence in, their realization.

There is another normative aspect implicit in all accounts of interest group activity in politics. Studies of interest groups always disclose the very unequal distribution of political power and influence which exists in a society formally committed to political egalitarianism. They provide support for the old observation that politics and political decision are essentially the province of a small elite, whatever the formal opportunities for political participation may be. Even worse, they show the ability of persons who do not even hold elected office to have a decisive role in the shaping of policy. The only simple answer to the charge that power is unequally distributed is to grant that this is so.

However, observations may be made which condition this simple and unwelcome conclusion. One is that broadly representative government, buttressed by consent, is not possible if significant numbers of persons bitterly resist policies imposed on them by large numbers of persons who act in the name of a majority. Government which is not tryrannical normally requires that strongly advocated and incompatible interests be adjusted in some way more complicated than the simple overriding of one by the other. The mere fact of majority support does not make a policy workable, though it may give it legitimacy. However, if majorities draw back in the face of the determined resistance of minorities, as in the disposition in Canada to make some concessions to the claims of French-speaking citizens, then clearly the member of the minority has, per capita, more power than members of the majority with respect to that particular issue.

Another observation which must be balanced against the conclusion that power is unequally divided is that on relatively few questions on which governments must decide is there any clear majority position. The daily business of government is not the invention of major new tax schemes or even grand decisions about peace and war, ubiquitous as this issue now is. It is not often that one decides to nationalize the railroads or the steel industry, or not to nationalize them, or even to institute Medicare. The first official proposals which could be labelled Medicare were made twenty years before the legislation passed Congress. As these case studies show, group conflicts are not apt to be about such general issues as the desirability of some federal aid to agriculture, but about its particular form (in 1933 at least); not about the need to provide some protection for labor's right to organize, but what to regard as a proper limit to that right. On the particulars, as against the general issues, only those particularly informed are able to be active and they are the ones who have a direct interest in the decisions being made and are therefore subject to the charge of having special interests, whether the constituencies they represent have a few dozen members or a few million. The only offset to this practice of deciding the vast bulk of governmental questions among numbers of participants who are small compared to the whole population is that there are periodic elections in which discontent can be shown, whatever its cause. Even if an election is won, a shift of a small percentage point in votes received is a warning that an incumbent officer or party will not ignore.

Nevertheless, questions can be asked as to how well informed the public and even the government itself is about some of the organized effort to influence decisions. It is questionable whether some of the uses of an easily-mobilized membership, and of tactical skill and great sums of money to influence opinion and create the appearance of general public support for particular positions do not give some groups an excessive advantage. There is a question as to the adequacy of the flow of information about things of potential interest to parts of the population that are not well-organized and provided with professional staffs to keep them alerted to matters of interest; there is an obvious dearth of leadership for many groups which puts them at a disadvantage as compared with others.

Whatever questions may be asked, and however little cause for complacency the answers may reveal, the phenomenon of interest groups would seem to be unavoidable and to a considerable degree a necessary complement to the traditional politics of the control of government by two major parties, each seeking to win a majority of votes at an election.

From a purely academic standpoint, the vitality of the conception of interests and interest groups as important factors in all politics is shown by the use of interest group conceptions by those who study the politics of countries other than the United States. Even theorists of the governments of developing countries where there are no strong traditions of popular government based on open and competitive elections, talk of interest "aggregation" and "articulation," noting that intermediate groupings between the individual, the family, or the rural village and the state, are far less extensively developed than they are in long-industrialized and urbanized countries in Western Europe and the United States. There have been several studies of interest groups in Great Britain, on the European continent, and recently, studies of interest groups in Japan. It has been particularly striking that in Britain, where the formal political system is majoritarian and based on coherent and responsible political parties which have the full power of government while they govern, interest group activity has been documented as having a similar effect on policy as that found in the United States. However, it is harder to trace since there are no semi-autonomous legislative committees holding public hearings, before which such groups appear, nor the extensive reporting, official and unofficial, of the course of decision within administrative agencies.

The studies in this volume are a contribution to political understanding and supply an important element in the analysis of politics which would be left out if one looked at government as only a matter of executives, legislative bodies, parties, elections, and general public opinion. Behind it lies sixty years of effort to create a more comprehensive and adequate science of the study of politics and a gradual widening of popular awareness of the detailed machinery of the governmental system of the United States. Whether one is attempting to understand politics as a matter of pure science, to assess the character of democracy in America, or attempting to mount a campaign for governmental action on a favorite project, these essays are of interest.

BIBLIOGRAPHIC NOTE

The most useful discussion of the different types of theory and explanation which arise from starting either with the individual or the group as the unit of social analysis are in two essays, one by E. R. Hilgard, "The Individual," and, the other by Edward Shils, "The Group" in *The Policy Sciences*, edited by Harold Lasswell and Daniel Lerner (Stanford, 1951).

The classic presentations of the central importance of the political elite in the development of political institutions are in the works of Pareto and Mosca, an introduction to which is provided by J. H. Meisel, *Pareto and Mosca* (Englewood Cliffs, 1965). Roberto Michels developed the "iron law of oligarchy" from his study of European Socialist parties in the period before 1914. His observation that voluntary organizations tend to be dominated by their salaried officials has a direct relevance to the question of who develops policies within pressure groups. The existence of a political and economic elite which makes all significant decisions in the United States has been asserted by C. Wright Mills in *The Power Elite* (New York, 1956). This work provides a very different account of the operation of interests in the politics of the United States than is provided by the usual interest groups studies.

The topic of public interest as a standard of governmental policymaking is most thoroughly reviewed in an article by Glendon A.

Schubert, "The Public Interest—," in *American Political Science Review*, LI (June, 1957) pp. 345-368. A general review of the place of interest groups in American politics is provided in "Unofficial Government Pressure Groups and Lobbies," *The Annals*, CCCXIX (September, 1958), from which an article by Rep. Emanuel Celler is reproduced in this volume.

The interest group approach to the study of politics has been applied to foreign governments. Examples include Harry Eckstein and David Apter, eds., *Comparative Politics: A Reader* (Glenco, 1963), Sec. VI, "Pressure and Interest Groups," especially the essays by Eckstein and Gabriel A. Almond; Harry Eckstein, *Pressure Group Politics: The Case of the British Medical Association* (Stanford, 1960); Joseph La Palombara, *Interest Groups in Italian Politics* (Princeton, 1964); H. W. Ehrman, ed., *Interest Groups on Four Continents* (Pittsburgh, 1958).

The essays by Robert T. Golembiewski, H. R. Mahood and Earl Latham in this volume provide a good listing of the principal works which deal with the general theory of interest group analysis and its impact on the study of politics in the United States.

I
THEORY OF GROUPS

Foreword

Since World War II, political research has come to focus more and more upon the *group* concept. Prior to this time, political analysis was largely concerned with forms of government, political theory, and law. The reason for this shift in emphasis was the publication of the book, *The Process of Government*. This book, published in 1908 by Arthur F. Bentley, counseled a reorientation in political analysis toward the *activity* of the individual as a more realistic way of viewing and understanding political and social action. According to Bentley, men came together because of a *common activity* and, in turn, were thrown into competition with the activity of other men. This activity produced a mass of purposeful action or a group. For Bentley, group and activity were equivalent terms. Through groups, masses of individuals were able to achieve political, economic, and social satisfactions. Therefore, by studying groups, one would also be studying politics.

Bentley's "attempt to fashion a tool," as he called his book, was not of immediate import for political research or theory-building. However, other studies were later published which ran parallel to certain Bentleyan postulates. Peter Odegard's book, *Pressure Politics* which appeared in 1928, was an exhaustive analysis of the origins and tactics of the Anti-Saloon League. Professor Odegard traced the origins of the movement from the time it was a mere abstraction to its establishment as a national pressure group. In the following year, Pendleton Herring examined the activities of over a hundred formal pressure groups which were operating before Congress. Herring's book, *Group Representation Before Congress,* was not only an analysis of various pressure groups before government, but was also an attempt to theorize about the role of groups in the political process.

To Professor David Truman must go the credit for the resurrection of Bentleyan concepts and their applicability to present-day politics. Professor Truman is one of the most authoritative interpreters of Bentley today. His publication, *The Governmental Process,* is both an explanation of Bentleyan thought and terminology and a guide to the study of politics through the group concept. Truman modifies some of Bentley's thought but only with the idea of making it more applicable for contemporary studies and for understanding the political process. For example, he sees the individual more important, politically speaking, as a bearer of certain attitudes rather than as an intersection of political activity. The collective attitudes brought to a group by its members gives that group its orientation toward specific political goals and objectives. Truman also redefined Bentley's group concept to be "any group that, on the basis of one or more shared attitudes, makes claims upon other groups in the society for the establishment, maintenance, or enhancement of forms of behavior that are implied by the shared attitudes."

Truman's contributions, plus those of Earl Latham, Robert T. Golembiewski and others, have helped establish a basis for a group theory of politics. Bentley laid out only a general theme for political analysis, not a substantive theory. Data from various group studies has helped underpin a theory which is not yet complete. These studies have shown, among other things, that groups (or pressure groups) are concerned with the development of governmental policy. *Policy* connotes a series of governmental actions or decisions taken yesterday, today, or tomorrow which may in some way affect the status of a group. Groups, thus, demonstrate *political activity* toward government in order to influence its decision-making. Further, group activities may be partially perceived at one time and not at another. Studies have shown that the greater activity demonstrated by a group, the more discernible its actions will be. Other data shows that groups in the political process are likely to be unstable and constantly shifting. Different political issues and policies bring forth differing combinations of groups. Some groups will be concerned with a single issue while others will be concerned with a broad range of issues. Some groups appear on the political scene for a short duration and others remain for many years.

The data emphasizes the utility of a theory which utilizes the group concept. Group theorists have shown that politics is a continuous series of events closely related to human activity. All of the observable and partially observable activities of people have some connections within the political environment. Group theory assumes that it is the operation of men in continuous contact that gives politics its form and content. By using the most modern research techniques and by studying the scope and intensity of groups in their political roles, group theorists infer that political reality may become observable. An important characteristic of this theory is inclusion rather than exclusion. By providing guidelines for various approaches to the study of government and groups around it, group theory serves as a methodological tool of import for the social scientist.

The Group Basis of Politics: Notes for a Theory*

EARL LATHAM

Earl Latham *is a leading exponent of the group approach to politics. His following article treats the role of groups in politics generally. He describes certain organized groups in our modern society and their various attempts to control the environment in which they operate. He also mentions the continuing conflicts and competition among organized groups as they operate before the organs of government. Professor Latham does not develop here an explicit theory nor a particular methodology of groups in politics.*

The chief social values cherished by individuals in modern society are realized through groups.[1] These groupings may be simple in structure, unicellular, so to speak, like a juvenile gang. Or they may be intricate meshes of associated, federated, combined, consolidated, merged, or amalgamated units and subunits of organization, fitted together to perform the divided and assigned parts of a common purpose to which the components are dedicated. They may operate out of the direct public gaze like religious organizations, which tend

---

[1] "The whole structure of modern society is associational . . . ," according to William Yandell Elliott in *The Pragmatic Revolt in Politics* (New York, 1928), p. 434. The view expressed by Elliott is also asserted by John Dewey in *The Public and Its Problems* (Chicago, 1946). Dewey, however, denies the usefulness of the concept of "society," as a basis for generalizations on the ground that it is devoid of meaning. To pose problems of relationship between the individual and "society" is as meaningless, he feels, as "to make a problem out of the relation of the letters of an alphabet to the alphabet" (p. 69).

* Earl Latham, "The Group Basis of Politics: Notes for a Theory," *American Political Science Review*, XLVI (June, 1952), 376-97.

to have a low degree of visibility. Or they may, like Congress and
many other official groups, occupy the front pages for weeks at a
time. National organizations are usually conspicuous; indeed, so much
is this so at times that they tend to divert the eye from the great
number of groups which stand at the elbow of the citizen of every
small town. Everywhere groups abound, and they may be examined
at close range and from afar.[2]

I. The Group Idea in Social Science

The literature of many disciplines agrees, as it does sometimes in
little else, on the central importance of groups to an understanding
of men in their relations with each other. The science of sociology,
for example, devotes itself to the study of groups and groupings in
society, the forms of group structure and behavior, the role of the
individual in the group and his relation to it, the development of
functional norms of behavior, the tendency of informal groups to sift
themselves into a leadership and the led, the relation of subgroups
to a central body, and so on.[3]

[2] In the small town of Amherst, Massachusetts, there are, not counting
student organizations and official groups in the town government, "well more
than one hundred Clubs, Lodges, Leagues, Guilds, Tribes, Granges, Circles,
Unions, Chapters, Councils, Societies, Associations, Auxiliaries, Brotherhoods,
and Fellowships. Their specialties or special interests, to name a few, include
cards, cameras, stamps, gardens, churches, teachers, speakers, voters, horses, business, service, golf, nature, eating, fishing, gunning, parents, grandparents, an-
cestors, needlework, temperance, travel, and kindergarten" (William L. Doran,
University of Massachusetts Alumni Bulletin, Vol. 31, No. 4, p. 4, Dec., 1948).
[3] See, for example, Talcott Parsons, *The Structure of Social Action; A
Study in Social Theory with Special Reference to a Group of Recent European Writers* (New York and London, 1937); Max Weber, *The Theory of
Social and Economic Organization*, ed. Talcott Parsons (New York, 1947),
especially the concept of the "corporate group," pp. 145 ff.; Vilfredo Pareto,
The Mind and Society, trans. A. Bongiorno and A. Livingston, 4 vols. (New
York, 1938); Gaetano Mosca, *The Ruling Class* (New York and London,
1939). The concepts of the elite and the mass which are developed by Pareto
and Mosca are concepts of group action. For political applications of sociological methods, see the following, in addition to the works of Pareto and Mosca:
Robert Michels, *Political Parties: A Sociological Study of the Oligarchic Tendencies of Modern Democracy* (New York, 1925); Robert McIver, *The Modern State* (Oxford, 1926) and *The Web of Government* (New York, 1947);
and Karl Mannheim, *Man and Society in An Age of Reconstruction* (New
York, 1948). Some of these sociological insights into the structure and processes of politics are not new. For example, John Adams foreshadowed the view

But the sociologists are not alone. The instrumentalist philosophy of John Dewey rejects the abstract individual as a fictional character, and asserts that the individual has meaning only in his relations with others.[4] The psychologists, by different routes, come to the same conclusion. The Gestalt school argues that the basic forms of knowing are comprehensive collectivities, general thought forms and patterns, not atomistic particulars. Modern psychoanalytical theory, as represented by Dr. Karen Horney, rejects the earlier Freudian assumption that the singular person can be understood apart from his culture, and asserts, instead, that what were formerly regarded as innate elements of the personality are induced traits originating in the culture, the result of interpersonal, i.e., group or social, influences.[5] The concept of the group has been indispensable to those working in the combined fields of cultural anthropology and psychology.[6] The concept of the group also is basic to certain approaches to jurisprudence,[7] and it has been helpful in bringing to economics a knowledge of the human institutions through which men dig coal, make soap and battleships, create credit, and allocate the resources of production.

---

that society fundamentally divides into elite and mass when he said, "It already appears, that there must be in every society of men, superiors and inferiors, because God has laid in the Constitution and course of nature, the foundations of the distinction" (Charles Francis Adams, *The Life and Works of John Adams,* Boston, 1856, Vol. 4, p. 427).

[4] John Dewey, *Human Nature and Conduct; An Introduction to Social Psychology* (New York, 1922). See also Dewey's *The Public and Its Problems.*

[5] Karen Horney, *The Neurotic Personality of Our Time* (New York, 1937) and *New Ways in Psychoanalysis* (New York, 1939). For example, Sigmund Freud, *The Interpretation of Dreams,* trans. Dr. A. A. Brill (New York, 1950), describes and explains the Oedipus complex without limiting it to any culture (pp. 160-162, 269-270). But what becomes of the Oedipus complex in a society like that of the Marquesas or the Trobriand Islands, where, anthropologists assert, it does not exist? Modern research suggests that this fundamental pattern in human behavior is a culture trait; for a discussion of the point, see Abram Kardiner, *The Individual and His Society* (New York, 1947), pp. 479 ff.

[6] Well known are the following works: Bronislaw Malinowski, *Argonauts of the Western Pacific* (New York, 1922); Ruth Benedict, *Patterns of Culture* (Boston, 1934) and *The Chrysanthemum and the Sword* (Boston, 1946); Kardiner, *The Individual and His Society;* and Ralph Linton, *The Cultural Background of Personality* (New York, 1945).

[7] As in N. S. Timasheff, *An Introduction to the Sociology of Law* (Cambridge, 1939).

Commons, Veblen, Clark, Andrews, and other pioneers in the empirical study of such economic group forms as banks, corporations, granges, unions, cooperatives, railroads, brokerage houses, and exchanges did much to rectify the notion that some objective law, heedless of men, somehow filled each purse to the exact limit justified by the contribution of its owner to the total of the goods and services of society. The economic theory of a century ago fixed the nature of the economic universe by definition and tended to derive its characteristics by deduction—an economic world inhabited by a multiplicity of individuals in isolation, where combination was a pathological deviation. Such a *defined* (not observed) universe could not fail to work—in the realm of discourse. However, so far have we come from this view that a whole new vocabulary has been invented to explain the operations of an economic community formed of aggregations, clusters, blocs, and combinations of people and things—not individuals in isolation. Few modern writers on economics would be able to discuss their subject matter without reference to "oligopoly," "imperfect competition," "monopolistic competition," and other group phenomena in the economic community.

II. *The Group Idea in Political Theory*

The Utilitarians made the same assumptions about the nature of the political community that they made about the nature of the economic community. While the liberal philosophy of a John Stuart Mill rejected doctrines of natural law and right that were so familiar to the eighteenth century, it retained the feeling that the chief political problems were those that involved the singular individual on the one hand and the "state" on the other. All other and intermediate associations and groupings were dissolved, blanked, and obscured—a kind of sunken hinterland between two dominating mountainous battlements. This exaggerated individualism not only abstracted man from his social environment; it made him more sentient, more responsive to the gentle but compelling dictates of reason, more enlightened about his affairs than the facts justified. The political community seemed to possess characteristics of an Oxford debating society, policy emerging from endless debate, with reason presiding in the speaker's chair.[8]

But Utilitarian theories did not entirely dominate the field of political speculation, even in England. On the Continent and to a lesser degree in England, considerable attention was given to the works of the philosophical idealists—the school of Hegel, Fichte, and Treitschke on the Continent, and of T. H. Green, Bradley, and Bosanquet later in England. The Utilitarians virtually abolished the state, by deduction, and the philosophic idealists virtually abolished the individual, also by deduction.[9] The first imagined the political community to be a loose coëxistence of singular individuals, like marbles on a plate, held loosely together within the circumference of a common restraint but otherwise complete, unengaged, private, and unique. The second rather imagined the political community to resemble beads on a string, of which the separate parts by themselves were incomplete and without meaning, and which existed only to fulfill the pattern of the necklace.

The principal attack, in England at least, upon the political speculations of the philosophic idealists was made by a group of writers professing pluralist doctrines. Figgis, Maitland, G. D. H. Cole, and Laski showed that many of the assumptions of the idealist school were contrary to fact. They showed that the state does not absorb all of the loyalties of the individual in the political community, as had been asserted, but that many lesser associations, such as church, corporation, and trade union, also lay claim to the faith, attachment, devotion, and obedience of the individual, and that these claims are acknowledged by responsive behavior. The state, said the pluralists, is merely one association among a host of associations, both factually and rightfully; and far from absorbing the entire allegiance of the individual, the state must compete with conflicting group loyalties,

[8] This conception is fundamental to John Stuart Mill's famous essay, "On Liberty." For a discussion of the relation between Mill's view and the prevailing doctrine of free speech in the United States Supreme Court, see Earl Latham, "The Theory of the Judicial Doctrine of Freedom of Speech," in the *Journal of Politics*, Vol. 12, pp. 637-651 (Nov., 1950).
[9] For a brief but strong criticism of Hegel, see Bertrand Russell, *Philosophy and Politics* (London, 1947), pp. 16-20.

some of which are invincible. Most people think of themselves first as members of their clubs, lodges, unions, or parishes, and only incidentally as members of the state. And since the state is merely one group among many, it is without superior right to dominate other associations. In its extreme form (in guild socialism, for example), the pluralist doctrine advocated political communities organized syndically by industries, with common affairs administered by common consent, a loose kind of confederation or working alliance.

The pluralists did useful work when they evaporated the misty figment of the state which the idealists had presented as a colossus of unity, a monolith, an absolute, a total system swallowing and assimilating all personal beliefs, attachments, obligations, and relations, endowed with some of the attributes of human personality like will, and having an autonomous and independent life and existence apart from the lives and personalities of the members of the political community. But while this spectral personality was exorcised from the state by the pluralists, they materialized the phantasm in other bodies. The state, they said, did not have a "real" personality, separate and apart from its people; it was not a separate corpus possessing such human attributes as personality and will. What was denied to the state, however, was claimed for other associations, such as churches and trade unions. One would have thought that the arguments that caused the rejection of the real personality of the state should also have caused the rejection of the real personalities of other group associations. Or conversely, if the nonstate associations had real personalities, it was difficult to see why the state should be denied one, since it was also an association. Actually the effort, by words, to make the state disappear did not succeed, because all of the pluralist writers found it necessary to invent a normative, rule-making apparatus to represent the community interests of the constituent group associations, that is, to perform the functions of the state. What they sought to achieve was a political community based upon a federation of constituent groups to replace the consolidated lump that the idealists had been describing, authoritarian and unstriated; and in this endeavor the important insights of the pluralists were at least two. First, they pointed out the undeniable fact of the group basis of society, in both its political and its economic communities. Second, they demonstrated a few of the virtually infinite number of accommodations between the common and the universal on the one hand and the diverse and the particular on the other. These accommodations are implicit in the principle of federalism—a master principle that makes it possible to produce unities out of multiplicities of dissimilar parts, including unities as local as the organizations in the Community Fund and as universal as the United Nations.

The English pluralists did two things at the same time: they made an observation and expressed a hope. They described the group basis of society and then either erected Utopia upon this foundation or employed the insight to rationalize prejudged social and economic reforms. They intermingled wish and fact, and may indeed have been led to the second by the intensity of the first. Some support for this view is supplied by the evidence that writers like Laski, once pluralists, abandoned the doctrine and worked with more authoritarian modes of social reform, ignoring the fact when it seemed no longer to suit the hope. Perhaps for such pluralists the adjective "philosophic" may be employed, as a phrase which suggests the characteristics of system, perception, metaphysics, and value judgment which are found in their writings. The philosophic pluralists accepted the group basis of society, but failed to investigate its forms, mutations, and permutations in a scientific spirit. It has remained for others to carry forward scientific analyses of group behavior, including a number of writers on politics. The word "pluralists" may properly be applied to these investigators since they deal with the plurality of observed group forms, but they are concerned less with prejudged programs of social and economic reform than with the accurate investigation and description of the many phenomena connected with the activities of groups in society. The adjective "analytical" may be added to refer to that species of pluralist who concerns himself with the structure and processes of group forms as they in fact occur. And although analytical pluralism has characterized principal works of sociology, the term is here reserved for political writers, to distinguish them from their philosophic predecessors.

In sum the doctrine of the philosophical pluralists was systematic (although imperfectly so), conceptual, deductive, and normative. That of the many writers here called analytical pluralists was, and is, hypothetical, experimental, empirical, and descriptive. The intellectual roots of analytical pluralism are deep in the history of American thought. In a line through Peirce, James, and Dewey, the psychology has tended to be behavioristic, the philosophy pragmatic, and the metaphysics realistic rather than idealistic. This combination of intellectual elements has turned social inquiry towards process and away from static conceptualism, towards relations rather than structures, and towards consequences instead of causes. Process, relations, and consequences are not, however, the antonyms of concepts, structures, and causes. The distinctions blur, shade, and fuse. It might be more nearly correct to say, therefore, that the analytical pluralists have tended to emphasize the former while not ignoring, nor neglecting the latter. Although the modern approach has much in common with the philosophy of science, fragments of pluralistic politics are to be found in the classics of American political philosophy, notably in Madison and Calhoun.

It is since Alfred Bentley in 1908 that American writers in politics have increasingly accepted the view that the group is the basic political form,[10] although most of the literature follows Pendleton Herring's pioneer work in 1928. Studies have been made of the significance of the group in the enactment of legislation, in the conduct of party activity, in the formulation and execution of public policy, in the process of public administration, and in the protection of civil liberties.[11] The recognition of the importance of groups to a

[10] See Arthur Bentley, *The Process of Government* (Chicago, 1908); Pendleton Herring, *Group Representation Before Congress* (Baltimore, 1929), *Public Administration and the Public Interest* (New York and London, 1936), and *The Politics of Democracy* (New York, 1940); E. E. Schattschneider, *Politics, Pressures, and the Tariff* (New York, 1935) and *Party Government* (New York, 1942); William Bennett Munro, *The Invisible Government* (New York, 1928); Peter Odegard, *Pressure Politics* (New York, 1928); and David Truman, *The Governmental Process* (New York, 1951).

[11] Enactment of legislation: Stephen K. Bailey, *Congress Makes a Law* (New York, 1950); Roland Young, *This is Congress* (New York, 1943). Party activity: Peter Odegard and E. A. Helms, *American Politics* (New York, 1938); E. E. Schattschneider, *Party Government;* V. O. Key, *Politics, Parties and Pressure Groups* (New York, 1946). Formulation of policy: Stuart

study and an understanding of politics has drawn the attention of political scientists to the considerable amount of work done in the related social science fields on the nature of group organization, and, increasingly, materials developed in these allied fields have been used in political writing and in the classroom. For example, closely relevant to politics are the studies of the structure and process of groups as simple, amorphous, and uncontrived as the street-corner gang, as remote as South Pacific islanders, and as near as Middletown.[12] Such studies throw much light upon the contrast between the objective and subjective relationships among people in groups, the difference between the formal and the informal organization which this reflects, the imposed rule and the developed custom, the external and visible structure on the one hand and the internal and invisible network of unconscious, nonlogical personal relationships on the other, the distribution of authority and the distribution of power, the nature of leadership and the relations of leaders and followers, the importance of prestige and status anxieties, and the methods employed to develop and maintain security systems for the protection of the members of the group.[13]

Chase, *Democracy Under Pressure* (New York, 1945); Wesley McCune, *The Farm Bloc* (New York, 1943). Public Administration: Avery Leiserson, *Administrative Regulation* (Chicago, 1942); Gabriel Almond, *The American People and Foreign Policy* (New York, 1950); Robert Dahl, *Congress and the Foreign Policy* (New York, 1950); Pendleton Herring, *Public Administration and the Public Interest*. Civil liberties: David Riesman, "Civil Liberties in a Period of Transition," *Public Policy*, Vol. 3 (Cambridge, 1942), pp. 33 ff.; "Private Attorneys-General: Group Action in the Fight for Civil Liberties," *Yale Law Journal*, Vol. 58, pp. 574 ff. (1949).

[12] These studies are illustrative: William Whyte, *Street Corner Society* (Chicago, 1943); W. Lloyd Warner and Paul S. Lunt, *The Social Life of a Modern Community* (New Haven, 1941); W. Lloyd Warner and J. O. Low, *The Strike, A Social Analysis* (New Haven, 1947); W. Lloyd Warner and Leo Srole, *The Social Systems of American Ethnic Groups* (New Haven, 1945); W. Lloyd Warner, *The Status System of a Modern Community* (New Haven, 1942); Bronislaw Malinowski, *Argonauts of the Western Pacific*; Robert S. and Helen M. Lynd, *Middletown in Transition* (New York, 1937); W. Lloyd Warner, *Democracy in Jonesville* (New York, 1949).

[13] Studies dealing with this material are: Chester I. Barnard, *Functions of the Executive* (Cambridge, 1947); F. J. Roethlisberger and W. J. Dickson, *Management and the Worker* (Cambridge, 1939); F. J. Roethlisberger, *Management and Morale* (Cambridge, 1942); Elton Mayo, *The Social Problems of an Industrial Civilization* (Boston, 1945); Elton Mayo, *The Human Problems of an Industrial Civilization* (New York, 1933); T. North Whitehead,

III. *Organized Groups as Structures of Power*

The conclusion emerges from an inspection of the literature dealing with the structure and the process of groups that, insofar as they are organized groups, they are structures of power. They are structures of power because they concentrate human wit, energy, and muscle for the achievement of received purposes. They are of the same genus, although a different species, as the state. And so we come by still another route to the insight which the philosophical pluralists demonstrated, that the state as an association (or group) is not different from other associations, like churches and trade unions. That which puts both state and nonstate associations in the same category of forms is the common factor of power. Both are associations of people for the achievement of ends common to the members, and the means of achievement is the application of the power of the association to the obstacles and hindrances which block the goal. It is true that the state and other group forms represent power in different packages, that organized groups may be regarded as systems of private government while the organs of the state represent a system of public government. However, the ubiquity of power in human relations, with its manifestations in other group forms than the state, is the reason for believing that the subject matter of politics is power, contrary to the view that its subject matter is the state, which is only one of the engines through which power is exercised.[14] Private government is not only a legitimate but a much neglected subject of inquiry by political science.

Leadership in a Free Society (Cambridge, 1936); Peter Drucker, *The Concept of the Corporation* (New York, 1946); A. A. Berle and Gardiner Means, *The Modern Corporation and Private Property* (New York, 1932); Herbert Simon, *Administrative Behavior* (New York, 1947); Herbert Simon, Donald Smithburg, and Victor Thompson, *Public Administration* (New York, 1950); Sebastion de Grazia, *The Political Community* (Chicago, 1948).

[14] For a study of the political structure and process of an institution of private government, see Oliver Garceau, *The Political Life of the American Medical Association* (Cambridge, 1941), and A. R. Danielian, *The A.T. and T.* (New York, 1939). For general works on the subject of power as the focus of politics, see Bertrand Russell, *Power* (New York, 1938), and Charles Merriam, *Political Power* (New York, 1934). The distinction between private and public government is discussed in Charles Merriam, *Public and Private Government* (New Haven, 1944).

The course of the discussion to this point may be summarized as a doctrine of the politics of plural forms. To use the phrase of John Dewey, the "doctrine of plural forms is a statement of fact: that there exists a plurality of social groupings, good, bad, and indifferent."[15] These groupings have no "real" personality; there is no derivative entity in group organization which is not people, but somehow possesses human attributes. For social groupings *are* people in connected relationships; the connected relationships do not exist apart from the people. To recognize the group basis of society and, by inclusion, the group basis of the political and other communities, is not to lose sight of the individual. Far from it—the individual is the center without which the circumference of the group could not form.

As we have seen, groups exist for the individuals to whom they belong; by his membership in them the individual fulfills personal values and felt needs. To view the individual as the centerpiece of all group forms is to avoid the error of regarding society as a congeries of discrete and disconnected human particles. Recognition of the place and role of the individual in group associations also avoids the error of supposing that political processes move by a blind voluntarism in a Schopenhaueresque world. To repeat the observation with which this paper began, the whole structure of society is associational; neither disjected nor congealed, it is not a multiplicity of discontinuous persons, nor yet a solid fusion of dissolved components.

To say that the structure of the political community is associational is not to elevate other groups above the state, nor really to put them in a relationship of parity, as the philosophical pluralists did. In civil politics, some association does in fact represent the consensus by which the various groups exist in mutual relations. This is the state.[16]

---

[15] *The Public and Its Problems*, p. 73.

[16] Although Bentley refers to the "idea of the state" as one of "the intellectual amusements of the past," he does not reject it completely but indicates that it may have some place in a complete restatement of theorectical political science. In the *Process of Government*, he was not trying to make such a comprehensive restatement but trying to describe political activity, that is, political processes. (See p. 263.) In his later works, the subject is not referred to again. Dewey, on the other hand, is clear that state and government are not the same, that there is no archetypal state, that there could be no state without a government, that the state did not create the government, that the state is a "public," articulated and operating through representative officers. (See *The*

It establishes the norms of permissible behavior in group relations, and it enforces these norms. The fact that men have other group loyalties than the one they bear to the state does not in itself prescribe limits to the activity of the state. This activity is not confined to police functions at the margins where the intersecting and overlapping groups touch each other, because the role of the state is not limited to that of referee in the group conflict. Established as custodian of the consensus, the state helps to formulate and to promote normative goals, as well as to police the agreed rules. In the exercise of its normative functions, it may even require the abolition of groups or a radical revision of their internal structure.

Organized groups, then, are structures of power; the forms of private government differ from the forms of public government principally in that public governments possess the characteristic of officiality, which will be more fully discussed below.[17] Through usage,

---

Public and Its Government, p. 67.) For Dewey, the state is the organization of singular individuals and their relations to the officials and functionaries established to protect the perceived consequences of conjoint behaviors. The perception of such consequences creates the "public," which is the constituent power of the state. The state is not a structure but a relationship. It is an association.

[17] It is useful to distinguish groups in three senses or phases of development: incipient, conscious, and organized. The indispensable ingredient of "groupness" is consciousness of common interest and active assistance, mutually sustained, to advance and promote this interest. Where the interest exists but is not recognized by the members of the putative association, the group may be said to be incipient. Thus, all dwellers in the Caribbean may actually possess certain interests in common—economic resources, strategic position, native populations in a colonial status, exposure to the hazards of weather, and so on—which may produce a consciousness of community, as similar predisposing factors produced the Indonesian Republic. A conscious group is one in which the community sense exists but which has not become organized. An organized group is a conscious group which has established an objective and formal apparatus to promote the common interest. Habitual cooperation of the members of a group is possible without any elaborate apparatus. Mannheim, in *Man and Society in an Age of Reconstruction,* pp. 51 ff., distinguishes between substantial and functional rationality. The first is conscious, contrived, directed action which makes use of deliberate means to produce known ends, efficiently sought. Functional rationality may be likened to what is here called habitual cooperation. Wherever the objective and formal apparatus of the organized group appears in its mature manifestations, it exhibits a very similar general form and pattern. Max Weber, in *Essays in Sociology,* trans. H. H. Gerth and C. Wright Mills (New York, 1946), pp. 196 ff., discusses the phenomenon of bureaucracy, which is not limited to the institutions and behavior of public government but is universal among organized group struc-

the word "government" has come to be associated almost exclusively with the formal official apparatus of presidents, kings, duces, fuehrers, commissars, rajahs, rasses, sachems, sagamores, legislators, councillors, commissioners, mayors, governors, ministers plenipotentiary, ambassadors, judges, and other public officeholders. But who has not heard of "office politics," "faculty politics," "union politics," and so on? These phrases are more than metaphor. They bespeak the general understanding that the phenomena of power appear in unofficial groups as well as in the formal structures of official agencies of the public government. We may therefore add to the subjects which are proper to political inquiry, the activities of corporation managers, trade union leaders, bishops, colonels, trade association executives, boards of directors, trustees of colleges, and other such functionaries. The vocabulary of power in public governments is a key to the understanding of the structure and processes of systems of private government also. It is in the literature of administration, perhaps, that the most notable advance has been made in recognizing the single identity of the problem of power in its public and private manifestations, one test of which is the extent to which the public bureaucracy and the private have exchanged knowledge about the ways in which the management of organizations can most efficiently and effectively be carried on.[18] But this knowledge is not modern. John Wise, the liberal Ipswich theologian of the late seventeenth century, wrote tracts on the *government* of the Congregationalist churches in New England, which he wanted to keep democratic, as opposed to certain bureaucratic tendencies that appeared in his day.[19] He viewed the church as an ecclesiastical polity and discussed its

---

tures. The three principal characteristics of bureaucracy are a fixed distribution of functions, a fixed distribution of authority, and a predictable procedure. By these terms, it is clear that private organizations have their bureaucracies as well as Washington and Whitehall.

[18] To name only a few of these writers, there are James Mooney and Alan Reiley, *Principles of Organization* (New York, 1939); Henri Fayol, *Industrial and General Administration* (London, 1930); Luther Gulick and Lyndall Urwick, *Papers on the Science of Administration* (New York, 1937); Lyndall Urwick, *The Elements of Administration* (London, 1943); Mary Niles, *Middle Management* (New York, 1941).

[19] See *A Vindication of the Government of New England Churches* (Boston: Congregational Board of Publication, 1860.)

organization in political terms which were virtually interchangeable with the vocabulary employed for similar speculation about forms of public government.[20]

IV. *The Dynamics of Plural Forms*

So far, we have been concerned with the nature of the structure of society and its principal communities, and with the composition and classification of the group forms which are basic to both. They have been held still, so to speak, while they were being viewed. But they do not in fact hold still; they are in a state of constant motion, and it is through this motion and its interactions that these groups generate the rules by which public policy is formulated and the community is to be governed. It is necessary now to consider the impulses which animate the group motion and produce these penetrating and far-reaching results.

To consider further a point which has been made, groups organize for the self-expression and security of the members which comprise them. Even when the group is a benevolent, philanthropic association devoted to the improvement of the material and spiritual fortunes of people outside its membership—a temperance or a missionary organiza-

---

[20] The problem dealt with by John Wise involved a few thousands. The same kind of problem today involves millions. For example, the Federal Council of Churches of Christ in America contains twenty-seven different denominations and claims a membership of more than 29,000,000 people, a figure which the total population of the United States did not reach until just before the Civil War. The form of organization is a loose confederation of the following constituent bodies: National Baptist Convention, Northern Baptist Convention, Church of the Brethren, General Council of Congregational Christian Churches, Czech-Moravian Brethren, International Convention of Disciples of Christ, Evangelical and Reformed Church, Evangelical United Brethren Church, Five Years Meeting of the Friends of America, Religious Society of Friends of Philadelphia and Vicinity, the Methodist Church, African Methodist Episcopal Church, African Methodist Episcopal Zion Church, Colored Methodist Episcopal Church in America, Moravian Church, Presbyterian Church in the U.S.A., Presbyterian Church in the U.S., Protestant Episcopal Church, Reformed Church in America, Romanian Orthodox Church of America, Russian Orthodox Church of North America, Seventh Day Baptist General Conference, Syria Antiochian Orthodox Church of North America, Ukrainian Orthodox Church of America, United Church of Canada, United Lutheran Church (Consultive), United Presbyterian Church. It is estimated that there are also seven hundred local and state councils of churches in America, designed to advance interchurch cooperation locally.

tion, for example—the work towards this goal, the activity of the organization, is a means through which the members express themselves. Satisfaction in the fulfilment of the received purposes of the group is an important element in keeping groups intact, as Barnard has shown.[21] Indeed, if these satisfactions are not fulfilled, the group suffers loss of morale, energy, and dedication. It is for this reason that military organizations and the civil authorities to which they are responsible seek to inculcate in the soldier some sense of the general purposes for which force by arms is being employed, in an attempt to identify the soldier's personal purpose with that of the community he serves. The soldier then can fulfill his own purposes in combat, as well as those of various groups in the country whose uniform he bears.

At the same time, security is an object of every group organization if security is understood only in its elemental sense of the survival of the group itself in order to carry forward its mission. At the very least, the interest of security means the maintenance of the existence of the group. In different groups one or the other of these impulses—self-expression or security—will predominate.

Self-expression and security are sought by the group members through control of the physical and social environment which surrounds each group and in the midst of which it dwells. It is an elemental fact that environments are potentially dangerous to every group, even as homes are potentially dangerous to the members of the household, as the statistics of accidents in the home will attest. The military battalion runs the risk of being shot up. The church, new or old, runs the risk of losing its members to other and competing claims of interest and devotion. The businessman runs the risk of losing his profit or his customer to his rival. The philanthropic organization devoted to good works often regards other agencies in the same field with a venomous eye. Councils of social agencies in large cities are sometimes notorious for the rancor with which the struggle for prestige and recognition (i.e., self-expression and security) is conducted among them. Every group, large and small, must come to terms with its environment if it is to endure and to prosper.

There are three modes by which this is done. First, the environ-

[21] In *Functions of the Executive*.

ment may be made safe and predictable by putting restraints upon it. Jurisdictional fights between unions may be explained in this way. Jurisdictional fights are battles in which each claimant union seeks to make an environment for itself in the area of dispute, but to exclude its rival from this environment. On the employer side, the Mohawk Valley Formula was a pattern of actions in a planned sequence by which employers, if they followed it, could break union movements. The objective of this formula was to discredit each union and its leadership and to enlist the support of the townspeople on the side of the plant; it thus was a concerted plan to make an environment unfavorable to the success of unions. One overcomes the hostility in the environment most directly by destroying the influence which creates the hostility.

Second, the environment may be made safe and predictable by neutralizing it. In the propaganda war of giant world powers, the effort is ceaseless to neutralize the effects of propaganda with counter-propaganda so as to render the international environment favorable, or at least not hostile—that is, neutral. The Atlantic and Pacific Tea Company similarly bought a great deal of advertising space in newspapers all over the country to counteract the expectedly unfavorable impressions created by a Department of Justice action against it under the anti-trust laws. The object, among other purposes, was to make the customer-inhabited environment of the business enterprise favorable if possible, neutral at the least, concerning the merits of the charges against it.

Third, the environment may be made safe and predictable, and therefore secure, by conciliating it and making it friendly. Even where there is no manifest hostile influence, a credit of good will may be accumulated by deeds and words which reflect favorably upon the doer. It is true that concessions to a potential hostile force may work sometimes, and again they may not. In the struggle of free nations with the dictatorships, appeasement did not succeed in producing that conciliation which was hoped for it. Nonetheless, politicians are constantly at work making friends and increasing votes by performing favors of one kind or another. Friendliness towards soap is generated on the radio by endless broadcasts of simple tales of never-ending strife and frustration. And during the Second World War advertising by business enterprises was a means of cultivating and keeping good will for the products advertised, even though there was no market for them because of the wartime restrictions on production.

All of these are methods by which the environment in which groups dwell is made safe and predictable to them, and therefore secure. And because the relations of people are myriad and shifting, subject to cycles of deterioration and decay, because the environment itself changes with each passing hour, there is a ceaseless struggle on the part of groups to dominate, neutralize, or conciliate that part of their environment that presses in upon them most closely. In this struggle, there is an observable balance of influence in favor of organized groups in their dealings with the unorganized, and in favor of the best and most efficiently organized in their dealings with the less efficiently organized. Strong nations tend to take advantage of the weak, and imperial powers to take advantage of their colonies. Or, to put it another way, organization represents concentrated power, and concentrated power can exercise a dominating influence when it encounters power which is diffuse and not concentrated, and therefore weaker.

The classic struggle of farmers against business enterprise is a case in point, the latter at first being more efficiently organized, and able (before the farmer became "class conscious") to gain advantages which the farmers thought exorbitant, under conditions which the farmers found offensive. But organization begets counterorganization. The farmer organizes in the American Farm Bureau Federation or the National Grange, and uses his influence with the legislatures to write rules to his advantage. In some states of the Middle West, for example, legislation even prescribes the terms of contracts for the sale of farm equipment. But the organized farmer pays little attention to the tenant and the sharecropper, and they in turn experience an impulse to organize for their own advantage. The history of the development of farmers' organizations is instructive; the whole program of farm subsidies which has evolved in the last twenty years may be seen as an effort on the part of the farmer (organized for the purpose) to make himself independent of the vicissitudes of the business economy, that is, to take himself out of the environment which he can control only imperfectly, and to insulate himself against economic adversity.

In the constant struggle of groups to come to terms with their environments, one other phenomenon of group politics may be noted. Simple groups tend to become more complex. And the more complex they become, the greater is the tendency to centralize their control. The structure of the business community in 1950 is different from that of 1860 precisely in that relatively simple forms of business organization have become complex—have gone through federations, combinations, reorganizations, mergers, amalgamations, and consolidations in a growing tendency to rationalize the complexity and to integrate the elements in comprehensive structures. Monopolies, combinations, cartels, giant integrated enterprises are characteristic of a mature phase of the evolution of group forms. Furthermore, the history of federal administration amply shows that the tendency of simple forms of organization to become complex by combination and to develop centralized bureaucracies to cope with this complexity is to be observed among official groups as well as among the groups, like the CIO and the American Legion, which dwell outside the domain of public government.

What has been said about farmers' organizations and business enterprises supports the conclusion that the operations of the economic system lend themselves to political interpretation, that is, to analysis in terms of the struggle of economic groups to exercise power. A recent book by Kenneth Galbraith uses political analysis to describe and explain the workings of an economy characterized no longer (if ever) by a multiplicity of small sellers without decisive market power, but by the existence of a few big firms in various industries, surrounded by a fringe of small ones.[22] Professor Galbraith does not think that the competitive model of previous economic theory is adequate to explain present-day economic activities, and for "competition" would substitute the concept of "countervailing power." Coun-

[22] Kenneth Galbraith, *American Capitalism, The Concept of Countervailing Power* (Boston, 1952).

tervailing power is the development by disadvantaged sectors of the economy of resistant strength to check and balance the concentrations of private market-power represented by oligopolistic industry; and one of the functions of government is to encourage private associations to build up "countervailing power." This thesis, of course, challenges much economic thought regarded as orthodox.

The struggle of groups to survive in their environments and to carry forward the aims and interests of their members, if entirely uninhibited, would produce violence and war. Social disapproval of most of the forms of direct action, however, reduces this struggle to an effort to write the rules by which groups live with each other and according to which they compete for existence and advantage. Thus, in the development of mature institutions of collective bargaining from the raw material of unorganized workers, the time comes when violence, disorder, and force are put to one side as the normal aspect of labor relations and the conduct of negotiations occupies the energies of the leaders. In the relations of nations to each other, there has been a persistent effort to substitute diplomacy and the rule of law for war as the arbiter of the differences among national groups. As groups come to put away gross forms of coercion in their dealings with each other, by equal degree the area widens within which the behavior of each is subject to codification by rules. The struggle for advantage, for benefits to the group, for the self-expression and security of its members, tends then to concentrate upon the writing of the rules. Among the forms which the rules may take are statutes, administrative orders and decrees, rules and interpretations, and court judgments.

V. *The Concept of Officiality*

We come then to the apparatus of the state which, through its manifold offices—legislatures, councils, agencies, departments, courts and other forums—maintains a system of instrumentalities for the writing and enforcement of the formal rules by which the society is governed. All of these instrumentalities are themselves groups, and they possess a sense of group belonging and identification which is very strong. In what respect, then, are these groups different from the more numerous groups outside the structure of public government? In a political sense they are not different at all, but exhibit the internal social and political characteristics of group forms which are separate from the state apparatus. But there *are* differences in behavior which may be observed. The Bureau of Internal Revenue collects taxes, that is, it take a portion of the substance of individuals and corporations—but individuals and corporations do not take a portion of the substance of the Bureau of Internal Revenue. The policeman on the corner is permitted to blow a whistle at an automobile driver and stop his travel, but the driver of the automobile is not permitted to blow a whistle at the policeman to prevent the latter from walking up and giving him a tag. Why is there this unilateral relationship between some groups and others? How does it happen that a man with a badge may give orders to men without badges, and that the reverse relationship does not prevail? The answer, of course, is that the law permits this: it establishes the difference between the badge-wearer and the others. But this answer does not go far enough. The Eighteenth Amendment was also "law" in the sense that it was on the books. For law to have force, there must be popular consent and understanding to support the law. In the example of the policeman, there is a social understanding that approves the unilateral relation between men with badges and men with boutonnieres. It is a part of the political consensus—the understood and agreed conditions of life in a civil society—that certain groups will be permitted to act like badge-wearers. The groups so privileged collectively make up the instrumentalities of the state, and such groups are distinguished from others only in their possession of the characteristic of officiality. The designation "official" is the sign which manifests that the bearer is authorized by the social understanding to exercise against all groups and individuals certain powers which they may not exercise against him. The concept of officiality, then, is the sum of the technical differences which are rooted in the social understanding as to who does what to whom; and the difference between the public and private groups is the "officiality" of the former.

What is the function in the total group struggle of the complex of official groups? What role do these groups play in the restless flux of effort on the part of groups to dominate, neutralize, or conciliate the environment in which they seek to survive? Addressing ourselves to these questions, we find that the principal function of official groups is to provide various levels of compromise in the writing of the rules, all within the body of agreed principles that forms the consensus upon which the political community rests, and that each of the three principal branches of government has a special role in performing this function.

The legislature referees the group struggle, ratifies the victories of the successful coalitions, and records the terms of the surrenders, compromises, and conquests in the form of statutes. Every statute tends to represent compromise because the very process of accommodating conflicts of group interest is one of deliberation and consent. The legislative vote on any issue thus tends to represent the composition of strength, i.e., the balance of power among the contending groups at the moment of voting. What may be called public policy is actually the equilibrium reached in the group struggle at any given moment, and it represents a balance which the contending factions of groups constantly strive to weight in their favor.[23] In this process,

[23] John Fischer, "Unwritten Rules of American Politics," *Harpers Magazine,* Vol. 197, pp. 27–36 (Nov., 1948), expresses the thesis that Calhoun, who devised the doctrine of the concurrent majority, provides the key to an understanding of American politics today. Fischer asserts that the legislative system, especially as it functions in Congress through committees, is a modern-day institutionalization of Calhoun's concurrent majority, in which no important interest is forced to accept legislation unfavorable to it, at least in the particulars in which its interest is immediately invested. Economic interests and others also, through the groups in which they are organized, according to Fischer then exercise a minority veto on legislation which concerns them— like the minority veto that Calhoun sought to establish for the protection of the interests of the South.

This view, however, gives too much credit to Calhoun. Far from having the key to the mysteries of American politics, Calhoun was outside the main-stream of American political thought and tendency in his own time. He was closer to Andre Vishinsky than to any American politico of our day. In fact, Calhoun could have written Vishinsky's speech of November 24, 1948, to the United Nations General Assembly's Ad Hoc Political Committee in which he said, "The veto is a powerful political tool . . . . Perhaps we use it more, but that is because we are in the minority and the veto balances power. If we were in the majority we could make such grandiloquent gestures as offer-it is clear that blocks of groups can be defeated. In fact, they can be routed. Defeated groups do not possess a veto on the proposals and acts that affect them. But what they do possess is the right to make new combinations of strength if they are able to do so—combinations that will support a new effort to rewrite the rules in their favor. This process of regrouping is fully in accord with the American culture pattern, which rates high in the characteristics of optimism, risk, experimentalism, change, aggressiveness, acquisitiveness, and colossal faith in man's ability to subdue and bend nature to his desire. The entire process is dynamic, not static; fluid, not fixed. Today's losers may be tomorrow's winners.

In these adjustments of group interest, the legislature does not play the part of inert cash register, ringing up the additions and withdrawals of strength; it is not a mindless balance pointing and marking the weight and distribution of power among the contending groups. Legislatures are groups also and show a sense of identity and consciousness of kind that unofficial groups must regard if they are to represent their members effectively. In fact, each of the two houses of the Congress has a conscious identity of special "house" interest, as well as a joint interest against the executive establishment. More will be said of the struggle of official groups among themselves below. At this point it may be noted that the dignity of the Congressman is an expression of his official group interest, and that it cannot be invaded lightly. Legislators have to be approached with a certain

---

ing to waive the veto on this or that" (*New York Times,* Nov. 25, 1948).

In the functions which the American legislature performs, it is clear that no minority exercises a *veto* on legislation that affects it. Certainly no veto power is recognized in law and none is exercised in practice. The assumption that there is a minority veto, as Fischer asserts, must show that minorities can always exercise it, as they do in the United Nations Security Council, and that no minority is without it. So far as the first is concerned, what veto did business men interpose against the enactment of the Wagner Act of 1935? How successful have the bankers been in applying a veto to the currency reforms of the last decade? How successful were the labor unions in opposing the enactment of the restrictive features of the Taft-Hartley Act? Where were the vetoes in these and many other instances that might be cited? The answer is that they did not exist. In addition, the hypothesis of a minority veto fails to account for the failure of substantial minorities to get a hearing, let alone exercise a veto. Among these are Negroes, small business men, share-croppers, Oakies, and so on.

amount of deference and tact; they may be pressured, but some forms of pressure will be regarded as too gross. The Congressman, like men everywhere, comes to his position bearing in his head a cargo of ideas, principles, prejudices, programs, precepts, beliefs, slogans, and preachments. These represent his adjustment to the dominant group combination among his constituents. If he mistakes the pattern of his support or acts too independently of its desire, he loses his seat, as some Congressmen have, after one full term.

The function of the bureaucrat in the group struggle is somewhat different from that of the legislator. Administrative agencies of the regulatory kind are established to carry out the terms of the treaties that the legislators have negotiated and ratified. They are like armies of occupation left in the field to police the rule won by the victorious coalition. Thus the Transportation Act of 1920 substantially augmented the role of the Interstate Commerce Commission by vesting it with authorities acceptable to labor unions, investors, weak roads, and shippers. The Robinson-Patman Act of 1936 similarly gave to the Federal Trade Commission the authority to control the price practices of one classification of business groups in favor of another, by limiting the power of the chain stores in favor of independent merchants. The defeated coalition of groups, however, does not cease striving to wring interpretations favorable to it from the treaties that verbalize its defeats. Expensive legal talent is employed to squeeze every advantage which wit and verbal magic can twist from the cold prose of official papers; and the regulatory agencies are constantly besought and importuned to interpret their authorities in favor of the very groups for the regulation of which they were originally granted. This campaign against unfavorable rules which losing coalitions of groups address to the bureaucrats appointed to administer them is, of course, in addition to their constant effort to rewrite the rules in their favor through compliant legislators. Where the balance of power is precarious, the law will remain unsettled until the balance is made stable. This is especially true in the enforcement of the labor relations and anti-trust laws.

The function of the judge is not unlike that of the legislator and the bureaucrat, as the function of the bureaucrat is not unlike that of the legislator and the judge. The judiciary, like the civilian bureaucracy, is one of the instrumentalities for the administration of agreed rules. But the responsibility rests with the judge, more than with either the legislator or the bureaucrat, to develop a more or less homogeneous and objective pattern of rules from the many strands supplied by the statutes, administrative decress, and causes of private clients.[24] The judiciary is a superior agency to the bureaucracy in performing this important and fateful task, and it is in this superiority that its distinguishing characteristic lies. All other distinctions (procedural mainly) between the judges and the bureaucrats are derived and secondary, not innate.

VI. *The Group Struggle of Officialdom*

In the small universe of official groups—small at least by comparison with the infinite group configuration outside the official domain—the same phenomena of struggle for self-expression and security take place that may be witnessed in the various nonstate communities of the society. In fact, some interesting variants are thrust into the entire political process by the existence of the official groups in what is often a state of rivalry. The Founding Fathers made sure that rivalries would occur by separating the powers of the government. It was their intention to prevent the public powers from being brought to focus in the same public authority and to endow each separated public authority with the capacity to fend off attempts by the others to invade its domain. The object of this, as Mr. Justice Brandeis said in an important case in which the rivalry of official

---

[24] Much ingenuity and resourcefulness go into the production of an objective and homogeneous pattern of law. Benjamin Cardozo, in *The Nature of the Judicial Process* (New Haven, 1925), confessed that the function of the judge is creative and original in those many interstices of the law left vacant by the statutes and administrative decrees. James M. Landis, in *The Administrative Process* (New Haven, 1938), presented a case for judicial self-restraint in the relations between the courts and the bureaucrats. In fact, the judiciary and the regulatory agencies of the quasi-judicial kind may be regarded as rival bureaucracies, with overlapping jurisdictions. The judges have been jealous for a half-century of the threat represented by the bureaucracy to their historic monopoly to say what the law is; and until recent years at least, they protected their security against this threat in their environment by dominating the danger, and nullifying it on appeal.

groups was at issue, was "not to promote efficiency but to preclude the exercise of arbitrary power. The purpose was not to avoid friction, but *by means of the inevitable friction incident to the distribution of government powers among three departments,* to save the people from autocracy."[25]

The Congress is traditionally suspicious of the President, and historically has sought to dominate the executive establishment. The chief executive of any business enterprise is permitted to manage such staff facilities as personnel and budget, but Congress prefers to exercise these powers of the President itself. Thus when Congress set up the Tennessee Valley Authority, it reserved to itself the authority, by concurrent resolution (not subject to the veto), to remove the members of the board of directors.[26] In the Lend-Lease Act of 1941 and the Emergency Price Stabilization Act of 1942, to name only two, Congress wrote language into the statutes reserving to itself the authority to withdraw from the President the powers conveyed by those acts of legislation. And time and again Congress has sought to force from the President's subordinates the surrender of information deemed by him to be confidential.[27]

One of the prime deterrents to the development in the United

[25] Italics supplied. The case is *Myers v. United States,* 272 U.S. 52 (1926), which involved an attempt by Congress to exercise the power which presidents supposed they possessed to remove officials at will. The jealousy which Congress had displayed towards the Chief Executive is both extensive and historic. The Budget and Accounting Act of 1921 was vetoed by Wilson when it first passed Congress because Congress had reserved to itself the authority to dismiss the Comptroller-General and Wilson believed this to be unconstitutional (*Congressional Record,* 66th Cong., 2d sess., Vol. 59, pp. 8609–8610, June 4, 1920). Wilson's veto was anticipated by the observation he made in his book, *Congressional Government* (New York, 1925, 1st ed., 1885): "It is not often easy to see the true constitutional bearing of strictly legislative action; but it is patent even to the least observant that in the matter of appointments to office, for instance, senators have often outrun their legal rights to give or withhold their assent to appointments, by insisting upon being first consulted concerning nominations as well, and have thus made their constitutional assent dependent upon an unconstitutional control of nominations" (pp. 48–49).

[26] See *Morgan v. Tennessee Valley Authority,* 115 F (2d) 990 (1940), certiorari denied, 312 U.S. 701 (1941), where the court held that the authority of the President to remove such directors for any cause he chose was not limited by this congressional reservation of power.

[27] See the discussion of this problem in the *New York Times,* Sept. 3, 1948, p. 5.

States of an adequate federal civil service is the manifest hostility, relentless and unceasing, which Congressmen pour out upon officials of the executive establishment. One former official of the federal government said that it was "like being nibbled to death by ducks"; and former Secretary of the Interior Krug, when asked, at the start of the Korean War in July, 1950, whether he would return to Washington to mobilize industry as he had in the Second World War, replied that he would seek a painless death by joining the military forces this time.

It has been pointed out that overlapping but different combinations of economic groups are marshalled behind the President and Congress in this historic duel.[28] The rivalry between the Congress and the executive establishment would be natural and expected because of the inherent group interest of the functionaries, but the struggle is exacerbated by the support that each of the contestants is given by alliances and coalitions of groups whose interests are at stake in the outcome. Furthermore, the leverage in this contest is with the Congress. As Woodrow Wilson said, "The legislature is the aggressive spirit. It is the motive power of the government. . . .[29] Even when, as in the national elections of 1948, the Congress and its own particular and unique behavior are made an issue and a new Congress is returned, the new congress may behave much as the old one did. The presidential power to campaign for a mandate from the people does not necessarily mean, when he gets one, that Congress will enact it.

The rivalry between the judiciary and the executive has sometimes emerged in spectacular form, as in the duel between Jefferson and Marshall and in the unsuccessful Court Plan which Roosevelt

---

[28] See Wilfred Binkley, *The Powers of the President* (New York, 1937). Binkley's thesis is that the conservative groups have tended to support Congress and the popular and less conservative groups have tended to support the President. The Whigs and the Republicans in the main have preferred a strong Congress and a weak President, while the Democrats, in the New Freedom, New Deal, and Fair Deal versions, at least, have preferred a strong President and a weak, that is, subordinate but not docile, Congress. The alternation of strong and weak presidents, and contrariwise, strong presidents and strong Congresses, is the result of the shifts in the balance of power among the multifarious groups that constitute the society.

[29] *Congressional Government*, p. 36.

submitted to Congress in 1937; but the enduring struggle has really taken place below the surface of public events and out of the public gaze, in the silent duel waged by the judiciary against the regulatory agencies. The chief characteristic of the regulatory agency of the quasi-judicial kind is that it combines in one instrumentality the legislative, the executive and the judicial powers. It is a device invented by necessity for bringing to a focus the public powers (otherwise separated in the Constitution) for the regulation of conditions which any single one of the three traditional powers had been found inadequate to regulate.

The judges have looked at the work of these agencies with split vision and have persisted in separating the powers that necessity and the legislatures had put together. Many anomalies have resulted. At first the courts regarded rate-making as legislative in nature and not for the judges. Said the Supreme Court in the celebrated case of *Munn v. Illinois* in 1876, "For protection against abuses by legislatures the people must resort to the polls, not to the courts. . . ."[30] Eventually, however, the judges came to regard the reasonableness of rates not as a question to be decided at the polls but one to be decided in the courtrooms, that is, a judicial question; but up to the present time the rate-making process of quasi-judicial agencies is still called legislative in nature.[31] The entire logomachy of words and definitions contained in the law of jurisdictional facts and evidentiary facts has developed from the concern of the judges to keep within their hands the determination of the kinds of question that historically have been decided by judges. This is understandable, perhaps; but the judges, having the last word on questions of jurisdiction, have tended to decide the close votes in their favor, as well as many that should not have been in their favor at all, and have thus moved some of the legal profession to urge that the judges retain authority in the matter in which they are expert—to wit, the law—and yield to the administrative bodies the authority to decide matters in which they are expert, such as questions of valuation.

[30] 94 U.S. 113.
[31] See *Federal Power Commission v. Hope Natural Gas Company*, 320 U.S. 591, 64 S.Ct. 281, 88 L.Ed. 333 (1944).

Except where the simulacra of the judicial process were on display, the judges have tolerated a great range of unreviewed discretion in executive agencies. Thus due process is not necessarily judicial process.[32] But where the executive process appeared to rival the judicial, the judges have been stern and adamant. The Administrative Procedure Act of 1946 perpetuates the internal separation of powers within the executive agencies and thus institutionalizes and sanctifies by legislative enactment the rule that the judges had enforced by themselves.

It might be mentioned that even within the structure of official agencies in a single branch of the federal government, competition of group interests takes place. Mention has been made of the consciousness of a separate group interest in each of the two houses of Congress. Competition among the official groups in the executive establishment is both long-standing and notorious. The extended contest over unification of the military services, and the resistance of the Navy in 1949 to the curtailments enforced against it in favor of the Army and the Air Force by the Secretary of Defense, is a case in point. Many others will come to mind, as will instances which show that the states are not immune from the effects of rivalry among official groups. State departments of health, for example, are often in conflict with state departments of industry over matters that fall within the jurisdictions of both, such as the prevention and control of diseases induced by industrial occupations.

To carry analysis still a step further, we note that the subgroups of single official groups may be in competition with each other. Accordingly, committees in both the Senate and the House of Representatives frequently contest for jurisdiction over bills, parts of which fall within the competence of more than one group. In the Senate struggle in 1948-1950 over the repeal of the discriminatory tax on oleomargarine, for example, it became a matter of vital importance whether the Senate Committee on Agriculture got hold of the repealer or the Senate Committee on Finance, for the first was dominated by the farm groups opposed to repeal while the second

[32] *Murray's Lessee v. Hoboken Land and Improvement Company,* 12 Howard 272 (1856).

was not. The Legislative Reorganization Act of 1946 split jurisdiction on anti-trust matters between the Senate Judiciary Committee and the Senate Committee on Interstate and Foreign Commerce, with amendments to the Clayton Act under the jurisdiction of the Judiciary Committee and amendments to the Federal Trade Commission Act under the jurisdiction of the Committee on Interstate and Foreign Commerce. The vital position which such committees hold in the legislative processes of Congress intensifies the effort of partisans in the group struggle to get their favored view before them.

There is also group tension and conflict within the structure of bureaus and divisions of single agencies and departments in the family of official executive groups. Thus within the Department of Agriculture there was once a right-left axis along which some of the bureaus tended to line. In the middle period of the New Deal, the Farm Security Administration, speaking for the small farmer, the tenant, and the sharecropper and advocating a generous lending policy, was in strife with the Farm Credit Administration, the Soil Conservation Service, and the Agricultural Adjustment Administration over the question of conversion to a defense policy, part of which involved the proposed establishment of an integrated and unified set of field services for the Department of Agriculture. In this contest, the Farm Credit Administration won over the Farm Security Administration. Within the War Department the Corps of Engineers is so powerfully entrenched, with civilian support among Congressmen interested in river and harbor improvements, and behind them business groups in the "improved" localities, that it was able to defy the command of the Commander-in-Chief in wartime in a dispute between the Corps and the Bureau of Reclamation over the building of dams in the Central Valley of California.[33]

The struggle of subgroups within a department is to be found even in lower levels of administration. Divisions within bureaus may be, and often are, in contest with each other. Management improvement

[33] Commission on Organization of the Executive Branch of the Federal Government, *Task Force Report on Organization and Policy in the Field of Natural Resources* (Washington, 1949), Appendix 7, "The Kings River Project in the Basin of the Great Central Valley—A Case Study," pp. 149–182.

divisions or units of organization may and do run as rivals to finance and accounting divisions, and the personnel division or office is often the butt of bitter humors by all the others.

Attendant upon group spirit are feelings of belonging and not belonging, an acceptance of those within the group and a hostility to those outside, the fastidious sense of jurisdiction engendered by these feelings, the desire for status and prestige, the wish to be admired and to feel of account—and all of these characteristics of the behavior of people in groups are to be found where people are or have been in groups: in public government and in private enterprise, in school, college, and fraternity, in the Bank Wiring Room of the Western Electric Plant in Hawthorne, Illinois, and in the Acropolis in an earlier and more classic time. The group struggle, then, is apparent in the universe of unofficial groups and in that of official groups. Furthermore, these are not separate universes. They are one. Official groups are simply inhabitants of one pluralistic world which is an aggregation, a collection, an assemblage, a throng, a moving multitude of human clusters, a consociation of groups, a plurality of collectivities, an intersecting series of social organisms, adhering, interpenetrating, overlapping—a single universe of groups which combine, break, federate, and form constellations and coalitions of power in a flux of restless alterations.

VII. *Conclusion*

To some, this view of the political process may seem formless, inchoate, ambiguous, and disordered. It may be felt that little is gained in making the interaction of groups the central fact of politics without further definition and characterization of the groups that interact. But the state of the discipline is such that one is scarcely justified in being more precise. It is suggested here only that a framework exists within which political processes may be more specifically and accurately described. Galbraith's concept of the "countervailing power" is an example of the application to economic phenomena of the method advocated here. If American history could be reconsidered and rewritten in terms of the dynamics of group struggle, history would indeed provide that insight of the past leading to an understanding of the present which it frequently claims to provide, but seldom does. What is called "political history" is at present usually the life and hard times of the official functionaries of public government, when it is not the chronicles of the wars we have fought.

Some may miss in the concept under discussion the *mystique* of the law, with its authoritarian constructs, its assumption that there *must* be a supreme power, life father in the household or the Absolute, some authority which arranges disorder and judges our transgressions and supplies us in an infinite universe with a finite demesne of which we can see the walls, and feel secure. A political process which is circular, as Einsteinian space is thought to be, which bends back upon itself, in which the directions of North and South are meaningless, is an unhandy place in which to try to locate finality. However, we deceive ourselves to clothe men in gowns and call them supreme, or sovereign, or all-powerful. We sometimes deceive ourselves when we call them "Excellency," or "honorable." The celebrated finality of Supreme Court decisions, which was part of the folklore of the law before 1937, is seen in 1952 to be chimerical. Yet since 1937 the justices have only more obviously performed the function that they performed before 1937, namely, that of serving as one more level of official compromise in the never-ending march and countermarch, thrust and parry, among economic groups, enforcement agencies, legislators, and executive functionaries. The differences between the official and the unofficial groups are acknowledged, and they have been characterized; but it is the underlying similarity that strikes the eye. Both groups are points of power and compromise in a continuum of interactions.

Just as the political process described in the preceding pages may seem to some to lack the Euclidian perfection of the juristic view of the political world, others may feel that it lacks the quality of ethical sanction, that "values" are omitted, that purposive and normative elements in human conduct are neglected and ignored. But this is not so. Groups exist to fulfill the desires of those who comprise them, to achieve their choices, attain their goals—and to propagate ethical principle according to the lights of their members. If there is a multiplicity of such groups, so is there a multiplicity of ethical systems.

Finally, it may be asked, "Whatever became of the individual?" He was introduced briefly as the beneficiary of group forms and then whisked off the page. Are not individuals as well as groups important in the political process? What of a Roosevelt? What of a Ghandi? Were these not individuals, and were they not influential as political actors, and not memorable merely as the passive recipients of the fullness of group life? To this it may be said that individuals are, of course, important as political actors, when they move others to responsive behavior, or represent them, or acquire their support or tolerance. That is to say, they are significant politically in the group relations they establish and organize, or modify, or destroy.

And if it be said that these notes for a theory tell us nothing new, that we knew all of this before, the answer must indeed be the humble one suggested by the author of the *Anatomy of Melancholy*: "We can say nothing but what hath been said. Our poets steal from Homer."

"The Group Basis of Politics": Notes on Analysis and Development*

ROBERT T. GOLEMBIEWSKI

The resurrection of Arthur Bentley and his thought by David Truman created controversy among contemporary political analysts. Both Bentley's methodology and political insights came to be widely criticized. Group theory was judged antidemocratic because it played down the overriding importance of the individual. Further, group theory, according to its detractors, does not provide sufficient and accurate accounting of the roles played by political institutions and the cultural environment. In this article, Professor Robert Golembiewski offers a defense of the usefulness of Bentleyan thought. Further, he cautions that certain political writers have become so preoccupied in their attempts to tear down certain aspects of group theory that they are missing some of its positive contributions.

Academics who make scholarly book on trends in the literature must heed "the group theory of politics." For there is much evidence that the approach is being de-emphasized for a third time. Arthur Bentley's *The Process of Government* is, of course, the most prominent of the contributions apparently headed for disciplinary oblivion.[1]

[1] The history of the first two discovery-reaction sequences is reviewed in the Introduction to Arthur F. Bentley, *The Process of Government* (Bloom-

* Robert T. Golembiewski, " 'The Group Basis of Politics': Notes on Analysis and Development," *American Political Science Review*, LIV (December, 1960), 38–51.

This paper attempts to blunt the recent criticism by directing students to the unfinished (and largely untouched) business of exploiting "the group approach." The prime vehicle for this effort will be Bentley's *The Process of Government* rather than the corpus of his work or that of his interpreters.

A three-fold rationale supports this analytical visit to the tap-root of "the group approach." Primarily, critics have avoided the issues posed by Bentley. Moreover, pleas for abandonment of his approach often reflect an important misconception. Consider Rothman's conclusion that "there is certainly room for studies of the kind which rely upon the mature judgment of their authors, rather than being bound by conceptual schemes which appear to be simple keys to reality, but which only serve to blind students to the obvious facts of politics." [2] No one, of course, should be bound by inadequate conceptual schemes in the long run. But all empirical work must be based upon more or less adequate conceptual schemes in the short run. This implies the perfection of methodology, for which mature judgment is a necessity but not a substitute. Finally, the desire to disengage research from "the group approach" waxes strong just as significant advances seem likely to accrue from modest analytical innovations.

I

Four underlying elements constitute the vitals of Bentley's *The Process of Government*. Their combinatory effects tend to be neg-

---

ington, 1949), esp. pp. xvii–xviii. The volume was published a half century ago (Chicago, 1908) and reprinted some years later (Bloomington, 1935). All quotations below from Bentley are from the 1949 reissue.

The recent critical literature is large. Selected references cited below are: Peter H. Odegard, "A Group Basis of Politics: A New Name for an Old Myth," *Western Political Quarterly*, Vol. 11 (September, 1958) pp. 689–702; Bernard Crick, *The American Science of Politics* (Berkeley, 1959), pp. 118–30; Joseph La Palombara, "The Utility and Limitations of Interest Group Theory in Non-American Field Situations," *Journal of Politics*, Vol. 22 (February, 1960), pp. 29–49; and Stanley Rothman, "Systematic Political Theory: Observations on the Group Approach," this *Review*, Vol. 54 (March, 1960), pp. 15–33.

[2] Rothman, *op. cit.*, p. 33.

lected. But they outline Bentley's purposes as well as spotlight the methodological apparatus necessary to exploit his insights. These elements include, in order: one of strategy, two of tactics, and one of the stuff of Bentley's approach.

Bentley spelled out the strategy of his argument bluntly:[3]

> If a statement of social facts . . . lends itself better to measurement . . . that characteristic entitles it to attention. Providing the statement does not otherwise distort the social facts, the capability of measurement will be decisive in its favor. The statement that takes us farthest along the road toward quantitative estimates will inevitably be the best statement.

His approach thus called for a reorientation around "political analysis" rather than the traditional emphasis upon "political philosophy." [4]

This reorientation has raised serious questions. To illustrate, Odegard pithily wondered if "the group theory" does not "in effect defend the principle that Might is Right?" [5] He reflected the judgment of many scholars. Their concern is that political analysis will define its values in terms of its findings if the problem of values is not handled explicitly. This concern is felt sharply even by those who have a strong commitment to the approach for which Bentley argued.[6]

Such questions, however, are largely beside the point of disciplinary necessity or Bentley's intentions. Practically, the growing and successful poaching by students of other disciplines establishes the necessity of Bentley's general approach most decisively. More basically, the three following elements of Bentley's contribution preclude such questions.

The second major element of Bentley's work is his search for a "theory" applicable to the "material of the governmental process."

---

[3] *Op. cit.,* p. 20.
[4] Ernest Barker, *The Study of Political Science and Its Relation to Cognate Studies* (Cambridge, England, 1928), p. 42.
[5] Odegard, *op. cit.,* p. 701.
[6] Oliver Garceau, for example, stressed the conflict of the study of behavioral uniformities and the "liberal, democratic faith" in man's capacities as an individual; see his "Research in the Political Process," this *Review,* Vol. 45 (March, 1951), p. 69.

Bentley was interested, without exception, in "empirical theory." His meaning is modern. That is, briefly, theory for Bentley was a set of descriptive statements about the empirical world; and a theory was to be considered valid only as long as it was consistent with observations of relevant phenomena. A "bad" empirical theory, then, serves only the temporary (if vital) function of focussing research attention. A "mistaken" theory may of course distract that attention toward irrelevancies. But a "good" empirical theory serves this quartet of purposes: it is

> (1) *aggregative,* since theory indicates the set of relations which are regarded as existing in some empirical universe;
> (2) *suggestive,* since theory implies possible empirical relations other than those specifically provided for;
> (3) *predictive,* since theory permits the prediction of relations in some empirical universe; and
> (4) *corrective,* since theory permits continuous internal retesting by the comparison of empirical observations with derivations from the properties of the theory.

The general difficulty with this second element of Bentley's work stems, in large part, from a failure to distinguish purely empirical theory from "goal-based, empirical theory." The latter is the theoretical statement of the empirical conditions necessary to achieve a particular set of values. Bentley is not at all interested in such theory, with substantial reason. For much progress can be made in empirical theory before any agreement on goal bases is reached. Moreover, empirical theory has a logical precedence: the *description* of the effects of groups with specific properties upon member behavior under specified conditions must precede the *prescription* of the conditions necessary to achieve a particular value-set, *e.g.,* high productivity in industrial work units.

Critic and acclaimer alike tend to overlook Bentley's clear distinction. Thus both usually speak of *"the* group theory." Moreover, many "group theorists" work both sides of the street of empirical theory, simultaneously and often unconsciously. For their work often assumes that the normative "ought" is defined by the empirical "is." This contributes to the confusion of the two types of empirical theory. With similar effect, the critic (usually implicitly) approaches "the group theory" as if it were goal-based, empirical theory. Thus Odegard complained that:[7]

> If politics is a process for the *peaceful allocation of values* in society, political scientists must take account of the values no less than the process of allocation. . . . A theory of politics which excludes where it does not frankly reject a concern for values, which denies that reason has a significant role to play in the process of government, and which devalues the individual by its exaltation of the group is, I suggest, inadequate.

Bentley, in addition, left no doubt as to his position on a third theory-type, "utopian theory." This is a type developed logically from an arbitrary set of goals, definitions, and axioms. As Bentley strikingly noted, the scholar utilizing the utopian approach settles "his whole study in advance by a whole mass of assumptions. . . . Such a study is merely a systematization and dignifying of [the student's] outlook on the world."[8] Utopian theory has its uses, of course. Even though there is no "space" corresponding to that of plane geometry, for example, its assumed properties correspond closely enough to empirical dimensions for some practical purposes. But reliance on utopian theory involves potentially high risks of confusion; and especially in social study (as Bentley understood). This potential was all the greater because empirical and utopian theory often were equated: much purportedly empirical theory reflects utopian assumptions consistent with the predilections of the formulator rather than with empirical reality.

Despite Bentley's strictures, however, convenience has encouraged the equation of utopian and the two empirical theory-types. Paradoxically, the existing "group theory of politics" is essentially a utopian theory.

The third element which characterizes Bentley's work is a tactic

[7] Odegard, *op. cit.,* p. 701.
[8] *Op. cit.,* p. 195.

derived from his theoretical emphasis. This book is in part a conscious polemic. Thus he called attention to "certain exaggerations, or at least certain shades of overemphasis," and he warned that "if my line of criticism should be applied literally . . . there would be an exaggeration in its statement." [9] The tactic had negative effects. For it tended to obscure his basic issues in a sometimes vigorous counter-polemic. But the shock effect was intended. Its purpose was to pry students loose from their utopian theorizing, or at least to force them to recognize their method and its limitations. The goal was the encouragement of empirical theory. So his early chapters inveigh against utopian theorizing *via* a wide-ranging critique of the work of many leading scholars. Similarly, he time and again referred to *The Process of Government* as "an anticipation of results" deriving from his empirical reorientation rather than as itself a useful empirical theory.[10] This emphasis, too, tends to escape critic and supporter alike.

"Activity," the "stuff" of his approach, is the fourth related element in Bentley's contribution. He desired to direct scholars from the fluff of utopian work toward the "hard stuff" of empirical reality. Hence his strong stand against utopian theory, the product of "pure reasoning" as a method. He regarded the "feelings" and "ideas" derived from utopian theory—and proffered as causes of behavior—as "soft," that is, intangible, unmeasurable, and thus uncommunicable. In contrast, he conceived "activity" as "hard," that is, objective, measurable, and communicable, and so capable of supporting his empirical ambitions. He stated his position emphatically.[11]

> The 'ideas' and 'feelings' serve to give the individual man his orientation in the social activity in which he is involved; they serve, so to speak, to define him as an individual. There is no idea which is not a reflection of social activity. . . . He knows what he feels, and indeed even that he feels, only in terms of other men's lives.

[9] *Ibid.*, p. 443.
[10] *Ibid.*, p. 484.
[11] *Ibid.*, p. 177.

But Bentley is not as simplistic as some imply. Principally, his position tends to be misunderstood. What he proposed is reasonable enough: the specification of empirical referents for purported empirical propositions. His approach was *via* method, although the products of a method (*e.g.*, "feelings") seem at first glance to have been his target. That is, Bentley set himself against utopian theorizing: *e.g.*, an "idea" (*Das Volk*) is attributed to an assumed subject (a "race") and then is used to explain the subject's behavior. Bentley, in contrast, was convinced that many "ideas" and "feelings"—especially those relevant to politics—were products of groups whose properties could be specified. Such groups provided empirical referents to restrict the preoccupation with free-floating "ideas." So he continually directed (or more accurately, over-directed) attention to the "activity" of an "idea" to prevent its mere assumption.

Consistently, Bentley admitted "ideas" or "feelings" *if* they were isolated empirically. For example, he noted that the "habit background," or sub-culture of a specific group, may "usefully be taken into reckoning as summing up a lot of conditions under which the groups operate." But he cautioned that such reliance might inhibit investigation and encourage utopian theorizing. Consequently, he urged that the empirical properties of any "habit background" be established with care and constantly checked for change.[12]

Critics stress, about equally, Bentley's neglect of "ideas" or his illegitimate use of them.[13] The former critics reveal careless reading; the latter overlook Bentley's primary concern with method rather than with its products. Thus Bentley would not have criticized "ideas" or "feelings" had they been the empirical products of satisfactory polling techniques rather than variably acute, but typically conflicting, utopian speculations of scholars of his day.

Two other factors also encourage an unjustly simplistic characterization of him. First, one senses a good deal of tongue-in-cheek in Bentley's analysis of the "stuff" of his approach. Indeed, he warns against too literal an interpretation of his analysis. This warning

---

[12] *Ibid.*, pp. 218–19.
[13] Crick, *op. cit.*, for example, stresses the former position; and Odegard, *op. cit.*, pp. 694–95, stresses the latter.

seems to apply, for example, to his tortured treatment of "activity," which strongly suggests an attempt to bamboozle his readers with an extravagant example of the method he reproached them for using.[14] But exactness does not trouble him. "If any of these things lead us to interesting paths," he wrote, "we shall be prepared to follow them heedless of definitions. Who likes may snip verbal definitions in his old age, when his world has gone crackly and dry." [15] Second, he tends to be judged by his self-admitted "overemphases" (e.g., the sharp thrust above). This distracts attention away from the balance of his argument, which is more delicate.

II

Nothing is gained by setting too optimistic boundaries for Bentley's accomplishments. But this is normally done. *The Process of Government,* its acclaimers imply, is a monumental end-point in the study of politics. Bentley's critics, in turn, assume that the work ought to be judged as a "general theory." Both positions are grossly exaggerated. Arguments based upon them are thus unrewarding, being polemics on the one side and cheap victories on the other.

The Process of Government, as Bentley saw it, was a far more limited work and yet more far-reaching. It was limited in that he knew he had sketched, at best, the rough outlines of an empirical theory, and that based upon fragmentary and inadequate empirical research. Only the method he proposed to apply to his skeletal theory differentiated him from the utopian theorists against whom he railed. But this was an important "only." As he noted in explaining his use of historical illustrations:[16]

---

[14] Bentley distinguished: "activity"; "tendencies toward activity"; and "tendencies which have no clearly evident action following after them" because they are "suppressed, blocked, postponed, or inhibited." The latter two types are necessary, *e.g.*, to explain the emergence of new groups. But the necessity had its price. Thus "tendencies to activity" were proffered as a "stage of activity" and the same as, although different from "activity." "Suppressed tendencies," as Bentley acknowledged, defied even such audacity. *The Process of Government,* pp. 186–89.

[15] *Ibid.,* p. 199. On the apparent pointlessness of his ire, see the discussion of definition below.

[16] *Ibid.,* pp. 330–31n.

> I wish . . . to say frankly that I am writing without detailed
> verification [which] is, of course, an absolutely essential pre-
> requisite [for empirical theory]. Here, however, I . . . use
> such rough knowledge of history as we have to throw light
> on the group method of interpretation. The group method is
> for its part only of value so far as it can be used in specific
> interpretations . . . If there is any of the material of the
> governmental process which is not capable of statement by
> the method I propose, then I am open to serious criticism . . .

But he also made far-reaching claims for his effort: he believed the
"group" was a useful focus for empirical theory; and he believed he
had presented useful methodological directions for the required
empirical effort. Thus he described the book as a "method" or a
"tool" rather than a "system" or a "theory." He did not consider that
his methodological suggestions were complete; rather, his efforts
constituted "more of an anticipation of results than a statement of
method." But he did hold that *his basic methodology was valid.*[17]
Realistically, then, an estimate and an explanation of the degree of
his fulfillment of his analytical ambitions must tap both the adequacy
of his focus for theory and the long-run utility of his methodological
suggestions in permitting the development of an empirical theory
around this focus.

Bentley straightforwardly asserted his claim for the greater adequacy of the "group" as a focus for empirical theory. The other possible foci were: "ideas" or "feelings" and similar utopian products;
and a mechanistic and rational theory which Bentley called *the* theory
of politics. These two foci for theory are descriptively inadequate,
Bentley maintained, "even in the most deliberative acts of heads of
governments." The "group" focus permits the required empirical
description "much more fully": it "points solidly to the social content,
always in individuals [as in the traditional theoretical foci], *but never
to be stated adequately in terms of individuals* [unlike the traditional
foci]." [18]

This claim forces no denial out-of-hand. Indeed, it understates

[17] *Ibid.,* p. 482.
[18] *Ibid.,* pp. 197, 447. (my emphases)

Bentley's contribution. For his core theoretical insights were far ahead of his time and constitute an important part of the century-long theoretical and methodological change which supports the modern study of social organization.

Bentley must share credit with many others for certain elements of his contribution to that study. Indeed, he acknowledged a long list of indebtednesses in his Chapter XXII for directing him toward the "group" as a theoretical focus. It was a focus that opened significant research avenues. Thus it permitted the successful treatment of the previously awkward problem of the "inconsistency of behavior"—that is, the common observation that any individual performs apparently contradictory behaviors. Earlier theories emphasized the individual and some macroscopic social "unit" in explaining behavior. Such theories could explain apparent behavioral inconsistency only with some tortured utopian sleight-of-hand, unless students were willing to support the proposition that the empirical study of behavior was pointless.[19] Bentley, in contrast, preserved the notion of the consistency of behavior by shifting the explanatory focus (in many cases) to the changes in the "reference groups" or "membership groups" influencing an individual's behavior. This explanatory focus has been validated many times.[20] Many social units, in effect, could do the explanatory job that often eluded the two research units of the individual and the macroscopic "society."

But Bentley surpassed early students of social organization as well. The seminal nature of his work is illustrated strikingly by his accurate perceptions of the directions which fruitful research would take. Consider his treatment of the problem of definition. He is often chided for his neglect of a convincing definition of "group" or of "interest." This neglect was intended and, primarily, reflects his opposition to utopian theory, whose starting point is definition. The

---

[19] For ample evidence of the state of the literature, see Gordon W. Allport, "The Historical Background of Modern Social Psychology," in Gardner Lindzey, ed., *Handbook of Social Psychology* (Cambridge, Mass., 1954), Vol. I, pp. 3–56.

[20] For one of the early experiments, see Leon Festinger, "The Role of Group Belongingness in a Voting Situation," *Human Relations*, Vol. 1 (1947), pp. 154–80.

neglect also reflects an important awareness. For he realized that early social analysis involved more voluminous description than tidy definition. To put words in his mouth: "If I could define 'group' adequately," he would say, "there would be no point to writing *The Process of Government.*" Early definitions, indeed, would be likely to impede the development of the dimensions which would eventually permit precise designations.

More specifically, his core concepts also have proved useful foci for research in social organization. "Activity," for example, has been particularly prominent, although Bentley does not always provide the inspiration for its use. At one extreme, the concept has been utilized in efforts to reorient entire disciplinary areas, as in John R. Commons' "collective economics," which is meant to supplant traditional economic theory and the individualistic assumptions upon which much of it is based.[21] At the other extreme, "activity" has been the basis for sophisticated observer systems designed to permit the description of behavioral sequences in great detail.[22] A substantial empirical literature has been built upon such systems.

Bentley's preliminary development of the "group" focus also anticipated two other major, longer-run directions of research in social organization. First, he suggested a primitive but fruitful typology of "groups," which he argued was necessary to permit the development of an empirical theory having high predictability. This typology included several varieties of "political groups" as well as racial and sectional groups. But he also isolated "underlying groups." They were underlying in several senses: in them the individual developed his need for group affiliation and assimilated a style of group participation, which varied between "cultures" and was reflected in varying participation in political groups; and these groups were relatively permanent, intense affiliations, of which political groups were but transitory and skin-surface reflections.[23] This typology thus previewed

---

[21] *The Economics of Collective Action* (New York, 1950).

[22] Robert F. Bales, *Interaction Process Analysis* (Cambridge, Mass., 1951).

[23] *The Process of Government*, pp. 434–36. The "underlying group" is patently similar to the "primary group" concept developed at about the same time by Charles H. Cooley in his *Social Organization: A Study of the Larger Social Mind* (New York, 1909). Cooley's seminal role in the development of the modern study of social organization is often stressed.

the emphasis of the research of a half-century later. For it sketched the clear outline and importance of the research unit—the small group —which has proved so useful in the early controlled studies of social organization. This feature of the typology also requires underscoring because of its general neglect: the group focus is not monolithic, and certainly not restricted to "pressure groups."

Second, Bentley also stressed the isolation of the important "some-things" to describe groups and to validate the "group" as a focus for theory. This modern emphasis distinguishes him from many of his contemporary "group theorists." For example, even the purported empirical theory of the extraordinarily influential LeBon was built upon an undifferentiated "crowd" concept and was self-fulfilling rather than self-correcting.[24] In contrast, Bentley explained his search for group dimensions in this way.[25]

> . . . I am not so much attempting to get results as to indicate methods, and . . . I do not regard the extent of my study of the widely scattered facts of government as great enough to warrant me in being dogmatic about the exact *number or varieties* or even the *typical relationships of groupings.*

His many suggestions of possible differentiating dimensions covered the broad spectrum from the personality characteristics of members to the specific "habit background," or subculture, within which a group was situated.[26]

The scope of the description Bentley proposed can be suggested generally. It was nothing less than the isolation of the relevant dimensions of reality, and hardly the simplistic classification of "farm groups," "labor groups," and so on. "When the groups are adequately stated," he wrote in reflecting his broad empirical ambitions, "every-

---

[24] Allport, *op. cit.,* p. 26, notes that: "Perhaps the most influential book ever written in social psychology is LeBon's *The Crowd* (1895)." LeBon's "crowd" concept, however, was applied indiscriminately to juries, legislatures, electorates, and so on (that is, when they behaved in the inelegant way Le Bon said crowds behaved). Moreover, the "crowd" was a "condition" for Le Bon rather than a conceptual entity whose properties required description.
[25] *The Process of Government,* p. 434. (my emphases)
[26] *Ibid.,* pp. 218–22.

thing is stated. When I say everything, I mean everything. The complete description will be the complete science. . . . There will be no more room for animistic 'causes' . . .".[27]

This position has alienated many scholars. The easy interpretation of this position emphasizes Bentley's tiring monomania. But the interpretation is too facile. Bentley simply proposed to exclude all the "ghosts" of utopian theory from his empirical effort. Incidentally, critics tend to drop his last sentence in this passage.[28] This seems to reflect their failure to distinguish types of theories.

Moreover, the complete description of "the groups" of Bentley's broad typology would cover the immense analytical range from the properties of the groups to the "ideas" and "feelings" which comprise the behavioral rules-of-the-game for the many overlapping groups. The "group" concept, in fact, is a strategic one for precisely this reason. To illustrate specifically with but one type of "group," the *internal analysis* of the small group requires three emphases: the description of microscopic sub-cultures; the charting of small social structures; and the study of processes by which personality elements are developed and elaborated in the group experience. Such internal analysis permits quite discriminative prediction. But more precise prediction requires *relational analysis*. Thus confidence in predictions is increased by the specification of such environmental properties as the technology a group employs or the formal organization in which a group is located.[29] As three eminent students of the small group concluded, in sum, its study "does not 'belong' to any one of the recognized social sciences alone. It is the common property of all." [30]

Interestingly, Bentley's critics sometimes want to have their critical cake and eat it as well. Thus his assertion that "everything is stated" with adequate group description is often parodied. Concurrently, the attempt is made to isolate group study from the very phenomena

[27] *Ibid.*, pp. 208–9.
[28] Rothman, *op. cit.*, p. 15, for example, does so.
[29] See my development of this position in "The Small Group and Public Administration," *Public Administration Review,* Vol. 19 (Summer, 1959), pp. 149–56.
[30] A. Paul Hare, Edgar F. Borgatta and Robert F. Bales, *Small Groups: Studies in Social Interaction* (New York, 1955), pp. v–vi.

whose systematic examination he urged to flesh-out his theoretical skeleton. That is, the undifferentiated "group" concept itself is required to explain "everything." This, in turn, is precisely (and correctly) the position for which Bentley's followers are chastised.[31]

III

Despite the magnitude of the theoretical breakthrough to which Bentley contributed its follow-up in "the group theory" leaves much to be desired. If we ask why, my emphasis in answer is upon a single explanatory factor: Bentley's inadequate methodology which hindered, if it did not preclude, the exploitation of his core theoretical insights. More specifically, this section will demonstrate the lack of methodological development of "the group approach." The two following sections will explain, respectively, why this methodological impasse occurred and how it can be overcome.

That Bentley's methodological ambitions have not been realized is easily demonstrated. First, most of his followers presume that he stressed a subject matter. But he was rather interested primarily in how a subject matter should be exploited, whatever it was;[32] he was deeply involved with the problems of the isolation and transmission

---

[31] Rothman, op. cit., p. 19, for example, scored Truman's use of the "status-role" concepts. He noted that "status-role" and the "group" are on different analytical levels. The latter is an "abstraction from action"; the former, a "type of actor." In addition, the "traditional definition" of the dual concept requires: "(1) its application throughout any social system, and (2) its use as a variable which is at least as important if not more important than group membership for explaining individual attitudes."

The position is curious. For the "group" is an "abstraction from action," as all concepts are. By the same reasoning Rothman would preclude the existence in the same theory of electron and valence, which are in his terminology an "actor" and an "abstraction from action," respectively. In addition, "status-role" is defined only in terms of group membership. Weighing the importance of the concepts and group membership, then, is fatuous. Finally, the concepts are inextricably of "the group approach." They have proved useful, for example, in the study of small groups as well as of the broader "social system." Indeed, Bentley himself emphasized the importance of status and role in specifying the properties of various groups in his typology. The Process of Government, p. 228.

[32] For Bentley's vigorous denial of paternity of the "pressure group" literature, see his "Kennetic Inquiry," Science, Vol. 112 (December 29, 1950), pp. 775–83.

of knowledge about empirical reality.[33] But, although he himself knew better, his lot has been to legitimate a subject matter rather than to inspire methodological innovation. Second, consistently, scholars taking his lead have rewritten the frontispiece of *The Process of Government* to read: "This Book is a Complete Statement of a Comprehensive Theory." Bentley's frontispiece, however, more accurately says: "This Book is an Attempt to Fashion a Tool." Third, the few existing elaborations of his contributions are new versions of the "ghosts" of utopian theory which he sought to banish. There were a few dissenters.[34] In general, however, students rushed upward to dizzying theoretical heights, as in the postulation of "group equilibrium." As Latham articulated the notion:[35] "What may be called public policy is actually the equilibrium reached in the group struggle at any given moment." Without the development of the social counterparts of "entropy" or "blood pressure" and the like, however, such attempts must take place at a mystical level. That is, no testing is possible without such empirical dimensions. Thus the acute scholars who have contributed to such formulations encouraged utopian theorizing by the less gifted in assuming that methodological problems had been solved—rather than merely posed—by Bentley.

IV

That Bentley succeeded only in part in reorienting analytical methods should not provoke wonder. For he did not provide a research medium convenient for early efforts. Nor did he provide methodological directions useful at any stage of empirical study.

His research medium, first, imposed enormous practical difficulties which overwhelmed early researchers. For example, the "laboratory experimentation in society" which he suggested for the "interests" was (and is) a formidable proposition.[36] The history of the application of a natural-science approach to the conceptual breakthrough to

[33] *The Process of Government*, p. 202.
[34] Phillip Monypenny, "Political Science and the Study of Groups: Notes to Guide a Research Project," *West Political Quarterly*, Vol. 7 (June, 1954), 184–85.
[35] Earl Latham, *The Group Basis of Politics* (Ithaca, 1952), p. 36.
[36] *The Process of Government*, p. 482.

which he contributed documents the point. The most startling research advances in the study of social organization have come but recently in small-group analysis, after a half-century search for a manageable research medium. The small group is an important—but hardly exclusive—research medium for the controlled study of behavior. However, the small group has research advantages—especially limited size—which encourage early methodological progress *via* testing and retesting. Moreover, such study provides an object lesson in the methodology necessary to develop an empirical theory for less amenable research units.

Ironically, Bentley did recognize the existence of "underlying groups." But, in a few revealing passages, he chose "political groups" as his first subject for study. He explained:[37]

> It would seem at first sight that the political process could not be studied till the process of the underlying groups had been studied, for political groups are built up out of, or, better said, upon, the other groups. Political groups are highly differentiated groups reflecting, or representing, other groups, which latter can easily, and I believe for most purposes properly, be regarded as more fundamental in society. The political process goes on, so to speak, well up toward the surface of society . . . .
>
> Nevertheless, it is my conviction that political groups, highly differentiated as they are, can well be studied before the other groups. . . .

His conviction seemed to rest upon the importance of such "political groups," rather than upon methodological grounds. Sympathy with his ambitions comes easily. But the complexity of his subject matter encouraged the tangled regrowth of the very utopian theory which provoked his effort.

His methodological suggestions, second, were inappropriate. Consider his analytical goals: some means for the accurate perception of reality; and some means for the clear and consistent reporting of such

[37] *Ibid.*, pp. 209-11.

perceptions. Only thus, he correctly argued, could empirical theory be developed and order be made out of the confusion of utopian theories, each offered as the key to reality but none subjected to the tests which would validate its claim. His solution was the postulation of a "universal base"—"activity"—to measure social phenomena. This did not succeed in measuring social life, he sometimes realized. But he felt it did provide "a foundation upon which a coherent system of measurements can be built up."[38]

However, Bentley fell into a trap which has ensnared other scientific pioneers.[39] Basically, he encouraged a sharp distinction between "things" and "relations between things." "Things" are "hard" and "real." "Relations between things" are abstractions, as one student articulated it, "phases of our experience with which we can deal only by thinking or talking about them. They cannot be heard, seen, or pointed to with any part of our bodies. . . ."[40] In dealing with "activity," Bentley often implied, one is dealing with "things," "hard" reality. All other concepts are "ghosts," non-empirical constructs of the imagination.

The distinction is an important one. But Bentley's conclusion was unfortunate. For there could be no science without "relations between things" such as atomic structure or electrical field. The implied "hard" conception of reality is thus inadequate and misleading. As Horowitz and Perlmutter explained:[41]

> To ask the question of whether [a conceptualized dimension of reality] 'exists' is really to ask 'what are the scientific criteria for reality and existence?' . . . existence is tentative, or relative, at any stage of a science and any concept which has explanatory power, is defined in relation to other concepts, is subject to experimental test, and has not yet been 'disproved,' can be said to have this tentative existence.

[38] *Ibid.,* p. 202.
[39] See, for example, Floyd H. Allport, *Institutional Behavior: Essays toward a Reorienting of Contemporary Social Organization* (Chapel Hill, 1933).
[40] *Ibid.,* p. 15.
[41] Milton W. Horowitz and Howard V. Perlmutter, "The Concept of the Social Group," *Journal of Social Psychology,* Vol. 37 (February, 1953), p. 80.

Thus Bentley's professed aim was the use of natural-science methods in the study of politics, but his separation of "things" and "relations between things" precluded the application of these methods.

Relatedly, Bentley gave ample encouragement to students to succumb to what has been called "The Fallacy of Misplaced Concreteness." This is the common belief that, in the words of one student, "for anything to be real it must have 'simple location' in physical space-time."[42] Bentley's emphases upon "activity" suggest such a "simple location" for behavior. Meaningful empirical description, however, does not require "simple location": many of the useful "somethings" in the empirical sciences, to illustrate, are ratios between several component elements which have no physical space-time locus. Thus any description limited to "simple location" would be incomplete, at best.

Bentley's emphasis in these two particulars is not monolithic. On many occasions, for example, he argued that it was necessary only to catalog as much "activity" as possible to understand political behavior.[43] This again reflects his conception of reality as "hard" and with "simple location." On the other hand, Bentley often displayed great sensitivity to the more subtle character of empirical investigation. Thus his brief analysis of multiple group-memberships, conceived as a large number of planes passing through the individual's life-space, suggests the enormously complicated problem of workably defining a "group," let alone restricting it to a "simple location." [44] And he also cautioned that the analysis of the formal structure and overt activities of a group is inadequate for scientifically useful description.[45]

The grosser aspects of Bentley's argument have prevailed, however. The conception of a "hard" reality with "simple location" patently underlies the generally low-level description in the literature. This triumph of the gross over the subtle must be attributed to his inadequate methodological directions. Tersely, he provided a devas-

[42] Quoted, ibid., p. 80.
[43] The Process of Government, p. 188.
[44] Ibid., pp. 204-5, 207.
[45] Ibid., pp. 210-11.

tating critique of then-existing research. The "ghosts" of "feelings" and "ideas" typified for him the results of a pliable methodology which could be stretched to cover lack of empirical knowledge. He also offered the attractive goal of an empirical theory. But he provided no adequate route from the critique to the goal. His emphasis upon "hard," "simply-located" reality was a procedural *cul-de-sac*.

V

The means to attain Bentley's objectives without forcing reality into a too-restrictive mold, however, are not out of reach. Indeed, the methodological knowledge is available. In addition, some disciplinary work points in the direction of the required innovations.[46] The following brief analysis, then, will try to capitalize on these opportunities for easing the developmental work in the discipline. It will also spotlight Bentley's methodological inadequacies.

The required innovations in method constitute the ground rules of, or the general limits for problem-solving in, empirical research. They underlie the discussion of the two empirical theory-types above, and differentiate them from utopian theory. They police the solution of the two problems of research at the middle-range theoretical level: the isolation of the important "somethings" in any problem area (the problem of *nominal definition,* or conceptualization); and the development of techniques for the consistent measurement of the degree to which these important "somethings" exist at any point in space-time (the problem of *operational definition,* or operationalization).[47]

Nominal definition is vital, for it concerns the isolation of those properties necessary to describe a problem area. Beginning efforts are seldom very precise. Consequently, finer prediction usually requires

---

[46] La Palombara, *op. cit.,* p. 30, has proposed the comparative examination of some middle-range propositions to determine whether or not the "interest group" focus is a useful one in the "construction of a general [empirical?] theory of politics."

[47] In general, see William J. Goode and Paul K. Hatt, *Methods in Social Research* (New York, 1952), esp. pp. 41-53. Bentley's later work also bears on these problems, particularly his *Inquiry into Inquiries: Essays in Social Theory* (Boston, 1954), pp. 113-40.

the substantial modification of early conceptions and the theory to which they led. Early conceptions of "crime," for example, suggested its relations to poverty and slums. Modifications of the concept to include "white collar crimes"—as well as the traditional crimes against property and person—induced marked theoretical changes.

Bentley displayed a definite respect for the problems of nominal definition. Thus he avoided premature definitions which might be permanent as well as procrustean. For example, "activity" was conceived tentatively as broad and highly differentiated.[48] In addition, he began the isolation of the dimensions necessary to describe the chaos of "activity" parsimoniously. Illustratively, he warned against the exclusive use of such measures of "activity" as legislative roll calls. They may be helpful. But the underlying dimensions of the voting process, paramountly, must be isolated. He advised students, then, "to measure the measure, to go far back and examine the quantities that have been in play to produce the given results." [49] Bentley's "habit background" was one of these background dimensions which give different "meanings" to the same "activity" in different "societies." [50]

He discouraged a similar sensitivity to nominal definition in his followers by his emphasis upon reality as "hard" and with "simple location." His contribution need not be denigrated because of such difficulties, however, for the processes of concept formation are ineluctably subtle.[51]

The problems associated with operational definition were beyond Bentley in *The Process of Government* and still elude his followers. It would be anachronistic to argue that the 1908 Bentley ought to have been aware of such problems. For natural scientists still were to

[48] *The Process of Government,* p. 194.
[49] *Ibid.,* p. 202.
[50] He was interested in "certain special activities of men, which can be stated, environment and all. That is our raw material. Our . . . fertile land ready for immediate use . . . is a good illustration. Given no increasing population, no improving transportation, that land would have little meaning. . . . Given a population of *different activities,* it would have a *different meaning." Ibid.,* p. 202. (my emphases)
[51] Generally, consult Carl G. Hempel, *Fundamentals of Concept Formation,* Vol. II, No. 7, of the *International Encyclopedia of Unified Science* (Chicago, 1952).

formulate firm notions about operational definition. But, as a matter of fact, his lack of awareness had a determinant influence on the development of "the group approach." Specifically, the process of developing operational definitions is an important guide in the development of useful nominal definitions. In sum, general directions of *how* to measure (operations) are helpful guides to *what* to measure (conceptualizations). Moreover, operational definition permits the transmissibility of results and consistent retesting which Bentley sought.

The goal of operational definition suggests its utility: the development of valid and reliable measures of phenomena as nominally defined. There are no easy answers to either validity or reliability: operations are mere conventions whose only test is consistent predictive utility. When a specific operation does not permit consistent prediction, there are three analytical possibilities. First, the nominal definition underlying the operation does not in fact identify a uni-dimensional and important (*i.e.*, predictively useful) aspect of reality. Second, the operation does not validly measure the empirical phenomena marked out by the nominal definition. Thus an operation may indiscriminately tap two or more dimensions of reality. Application of this operation would result in mixed results over replicatory studies, since (because of their independent character) two or more dimensions would not always co-vary. Third, the operation does not permit reliable observations of the same phenomena by the same observer at different times or by different observers at the same time. More than one of these possibilities may apply to any specific case of inconsistent prediction.

There is patently much room for developmental work implicit in these complex analytical possibilities. And all of them will be investigated many times in any problem area as its empirical theory moves toward greater comprehensiveness and fineness of prediction. This subtle process of intellectual advance stands in marked contrast to the "hard" concept of reality which Bentley often reflected. Moreover, polemics are not necessary to establish the point.[52]

[52] For an analysis in depth of one concept, see my "Management Science and Behavior: Work-Unit Cohesiveness." (Unpublished Ms.)

VI

The skeleton of this analysis is simple. It has served to isolate a number of important component elements of Bentley's contribution; it has stressed the neglect of these components in the research literature; and it has outlined an avenue for future development.

Not much more can be said without being repetitious. Two points, however, require emphasis. First, political science and the social sciences generally are characterized by fantastic discontinuity—one of the unfortunate consequences (and causes) of the research fads which periodically sweep across them. This is the justification for my attempt here to build upon the work of Bentley and the many valuable empirical studies he induced. These studies constitute what might be called the "natural science" stage of the discipline. It is time to move along to the development of empirical theory, deriving from and improving upon the data and insights of this literature. The experience of other areas of scientific inquiry—suggested in the brief review of nominal and operational definition—certainly gives hope and direction for such an effort.

Second, there can be no methodological revolution. Like Newton, one can see only a little further. This is the sense of Bentley's position that the methodology of establishing reliable statements of the "group facts" must be developed "out of materials which in cruder forms are now available." Thus Bentley himself could go only part of the way toward inducing the theoretical and methodological innovations toward which he aspired. Fortunately, however, only small further innovations in method (if they imply much effort) are required to achieve a major research breakthrough in "the group theory," to push beyond what Bentley cannot be expected to have known and beyond his incomplete break with the restraints of the leading ideas of his time.

The time is ripe, in short, to leap to Bentley's shoulders with newly available knowledge; it is not a time to nip at his heels because he did not do what he did not intend to do.

II
PRESSURE GROUPS
AND SOCIETY

Foreword

American societal and political order is interest based. Significant economic interests of business, labor and agriculture exist within this order. The existence of such interests and the political power they wield are not unique to the American political system. One can say this has also been the pattern for other nations throughout history. Classical writers such as Plato, Aristotle, Cicero and others clearly described the ruling interests in ancient Greek city-state systems and in Rome. Historians have documented how various guilds in the Middle Ages strongly influenced trade and commerce during that period.

The broadly-gauged interests of business, labor and agriculture are characterized by their heterogeneity not only among themselves as far as political aspirations, organization and membership but also within themselves. Subdivisions exist within these three broad interests which likewise produce political and social differentiations. Not all businessmen join nor have their economic interests served by either the National Association of Manufacturers or the Chamber of Commerce. Within agriculture, divergencies exist which allow no one farm organization to represent all the tobacco producers, dairymen, apple growers or livestockmen. The same is true for labor; cleavages exist which have produced numerous and diverse labor organizations.

Group differences, however, extend beyond mere membership and political aspirations. The size, leadership, unity, wealth, public acceptability and political access of pressure groups vary greatly. Labor unions and/or farm organizations will embody these characteristics in varying degrees. The presence or absence of one or more of these may indirectly determine political success.

Size or numbers alone, for example, do not guarantee success. The American Federation of Labor–Congress of Industrial Organizations (AFL-CIO) today numbers approximately 14 million members which makes it some 60 times larger than the American Medical Association (AMA), but it cannot be said that the AFL-CIO is 60 times more powerful than the AMA. What the AMA lacks in numbers it makes up in unity and wealth, which allows it to counterbalance, rather effectively, the larger AFL-CIO. The Congress of Racial Equality (CORE) an organization smaller than many business and labor organizations and also with smaller assets is able to gain economic and social goals for its members through the unrelenting energies of its supporters and their dedication.

In our technological society, groups are becoming increasingly politicized. Their memberships are becoming more involved with politics because of the scope of governmental activities which benefit some groups and hurt others. Also, the centrifugal tendencies of our political arrangements—divisions of power and checks and balances—encourage political activities by interest groups. Because of these tendencies governmental power is interstitial and policy-making is decentralized which tends to make the system responsive to different pressures or functionally-oriented groups. Further, the diffusion, lack of discipline and centralized control within our party system prevents them, in some instances, from effectuating group demands. Certainly on the state level, party systems exist in uneven fashion. In those states where the two parties compete on even terms, they can deal with group demands from an independent base. In other states, where there may be only one party or a factional system, the base is too narrow and interests must work outside in order to assert their claims. On the other hand, at the national level the apparatus of the parties has been largely successful in incorporating group claims into their platforms. For example, the national platforms of both major parties pledge support for civil rights and for continuing medical care for the aged of the country.

Pressure groups, then, are fully cognizant of the power and scope of the national government and its effect on their economic livelihood. Government is constantly bombarded by conflicting group demands. Businessmen want fewer taxes, workers want protective legislation and farmers want governmental subsidies. The multifarious activities and policies of our national government are given form and content by group pressures and their demands. Government is continually responding, both affirmatively and negatively, to these group demands which constantly arise within the economic community.

Businessmen in Politics*

ANDREW HACKER
and
JOEL D. ABERBACH

The mobilization of organized labor into party workers and voters has stimulated a counter-organization within the ranks of business. According to the authors of this essay, Andrew Hacker *and* Joel Aberbach, *numerous large and small corporations began to offer political seminars, classes and workshops for middle-management personnel and others. These were aimed at raising the level of political participation of corporate employees. By and large, these political "re-education" programs did not produce the expected results because political participation (and non-participation) is based upon many factors—some known, some unknown.*

Introduction

The "businessmen in politics" movement began in earnest with the announcement of the results of the 1958 congressional election. There was no doubt that this election was a striking victory for the Democratic Party and a humiliating rout for the Republicans. Whereas the line-up in the Eighty-fifth Congress' House of Representatives consisted of 235 Democrats and 200 Republicans, the margin in the newly-elected House widened to 282 to 153. Moreover the Senate lost, through defeat or retirement, such pro-business lawmakers as

* Andrew Hacker and Joel D. Aberbach, "Businessmen in Politics," *Law and Contemporary Problems,* 27 (Spring, 1962), 266-79, published by the Duke University School of Law, Durham, North Carolina. Copyright, 1962 by Duke University. Reprinted with permission from a symposium, *The Electoral Process, Part I.*

John Bricker, Edward Thye, George Malone, Arthur Watkins, Chapman Revercomb, Alexander Smith, William Knowland, and William Jenner. There were further indications that the new arrivals in both houses of Congress had been supported by trade union funds and the doorbell-ringing campaign of the AFL-CIO's Committee on Political Education (COPE). The next two years would be difficult ones for business, at least so far as the legislative prospect was concerned. Nor was it heartening to know that in five out of six states voters rejected "right to work" law referenda.

In anticipation of and in response to this turn of events, the members of the business community began to sound warnings. An executive of the Gulf Oil Corporation minced no words in calling attention to the "predatory gangsterism and crackpot socialism that are thriving and expanding under labor's congressional benevolence."[1] The president of du Pont, looking over the election returns, complained that "corporations as such are disenfranchised and are without political identity."[2] Less than a month after the Eighty-sixth Congress settled down to business a Ford Motor Company spokesman felt entitled to speak of "labor's domination of the present United States Congress."[3]

The answer, of course, was for businessmen to get into politics and to act as a countervailing force against trade union power and the general trend towards socialistic legislation. The president of the United States Chamber of Commerce exhorted that association's members:[4] "We must roll up our sleeves and get to work at the precinct and ward levels where political decisions are made and officeholders chosen." Another Chamber official chided businessmen for thinking that post-election lobbying would secure their interests. "Too much effort to enact sound legislation takes place too late after

[1] Archie D. Gray, quoted in Washington *Post and Times Herald,* Sept. 23, 1950, p. 26.
[2] Crawford H. Greenewalt, *A Political Role for Businessmen,* address delivered before the North Carolina Citizens Association, March 25, 1959.
[3] Thomas R. Reid, *Political Action: A New Dimension of Responsibility for Management,* speech delivered before the American Management Association General Management Conference, Jan. 26, 1959.
[4] William A. McDonnell, quoted in *Time* magazine, Oct. 6, 1958, p. 82, cols. 1-2.

the legislators are elected," he said.[5] Executives would, of course, prefer to attend to their business concerns and not get involved in extra-curricular activities. However it was becoming clear that the economy overlapped the political arena in important ways, and like it or not management personnel would have to find the time for taking on political responsibilities. A General Electric official admitted that busi-nessmen were being "dragged unwillingly into politics by our ideo-logical competitors and intended executioners."[6] A survey of 2,700 *Harvard Business Review* subscribers revealed that seventy-one per cent of them felt that it was proper for companies to give executives time off to work in political campaigns.[7] From the end of the summer of 1958, gathering momentum after the votes had been counted in November, and continuing throughout 1959 and 1960, politics be-came the great concern of America's corporate community. It seemed that every second speech delivered by a major executive was on this subject. And, in the American business tradition, talk was to be fol-lowed by action.

The rationale of the "businessmen in politics" movement was really quite simple. Labor unions had mobilized their members not only into active voters but also as party workers. While it was never clear how many of the fifteen million AFL-CIO members were persuaded by COPE to contribute their time and money to partisan activity, many executives were convinced that labor politicians were instru-mental in deciding who were to be Democratic candidates for public office. Moreover, it appeared that trade unions were turning out the votes that elected those candidates in increasing numbers. If this force was to be countered, a new group of citizens would have to enter the partisan arena in an organized and purposeful way. Since the end of World War II, America's large corporations had been aug-menting their white-collar labor force in an unprecedented way. At the same time that technological developments were slackening the

---

[5] Arthur H. Motley, quoted in N.Y. *Times,* Jan. 30, 1959, p. 12, col. I.

[6] Lemuel R. Boulware, quoted in 2 *Editorial Research Reports* 755-56 (1958).

[7] Fenn, "Problems in Review: Business and Politics," *Harv. Bus. Rev.,* May-June 1959, p. 142.

need for production workers, millions of new jobs were being created for clerical, professional, and managerial people. These employees were on salaries rather than wages; they came to work at 9:00 A.M. rather than 8:00 A.M.; they thought of themselves as belonging to the middle class. They were impervious to unionization and not a few of them regarded themselves as businessmen, albeit of the managerial rather than the entrepreneurial variety. If these citizens, hitherto indifferent to and aloof from politics, could be drawn into the parties then a mighty conservative influence would be brought to bear.

The central theme of the "businessmen in politics" programs was to motivate middle-management employees to become part-time politicians. Corporations offered classes, seminars, and workshops which were designed to impart fundamental political lore, the most important lesson being that parties are local in their base. To become influential within a party, a citizen must make a place for himself at the ward or precinct level as a beginning. Students in the company-sponsored practical politics courses were advised to seek out their precinct leaders and to volunteer their services. By virtue of hard work and the expenditure of time they would rise to positions in the party hierarchy. As they labored longer in the vineyard, so would they ultimately participate in the conclaves where candidates for public office were chosen. The theory, in short, was one of infiltration. If businessmen applied themselves to party work, they would in time gain party power. If tens of thousands of white-collar and managerial employees did this throughout the country, then both major parties would be brought to nominate candidates sympathetic to business. Not only was this corps of potential infiltrators available; it was equipped with middle-class talent and middle-management skills. With the expectation that the injection of these new party workers into the political system would pay off, hundreds of corporations gave their white-collar employees released time to take the courses.

As so often happens, national associations entered the scene to give aid and guidance to companies embarking on new ventures. In this instance the United States Chamber of Commerce designed a textbook entitled *Action Course in Practical Politics* that was sold to corporations. The package consisted of eight boxed pamphlets plus a looseleaf notebook containing homework assignments and field-work instructions. By the end of 1959 the Chamber reported that their text had been adopted by 107 corporations in 532 communities and forty-seven states. Among the companies were such names as Aluminum Company of America, American Can Company, Armstrong Cork Company, Boeing Airplane Company, Borg-Warner Corporation, du Pont, Eastman Kodak Company, Esso Standard Oil Company, Ford Motor Company, General Electric Company, H. J. Heinz Company, Hershey Chocolate Corporation, International Business Machines, Inc., S. S. Kresge Company, Monsanto Chemical Company, Mutual of Omaha, Northern Pacific Railroad, Pittsburgh Plate Glass Company, Prudential Insurance Company, Quaker Oats Company, R. J. Reynolds Tobacco Company, Sears Roebuck, Sun Oil Company, Union Carbide Corporation, United States Steel Corporation, and Weyerhaeuser Timber Company. All in all, the Chamber reported that under the auspices of companies and associations, 100,000 people had taken their "practical politics" course.

Some corporations went even further. They appointed, at the executive level, directors of departments of civic or public affairs. These individuals had the responsibility of encouraging white-collar employees to take in-plant courses and then to enlist in local party activities. These executives set up their own national association, the Effective Citizens Organization (ECO), and met at workshops and conferences to exchange ideas and develop techniques. Among the companies establishing such departments and belonging to ECO were (in addition to many of those listed as using the Chamber of Commerce course): Allis-Chalmers Manufacturing Company, American Cyanamid Company, American Oil Company, Armco Steel Corporation, Bank of America, Chase Manhattan Bank, Chrysler Corporation, Dow Chemical Company, Eli Lilly and Company, Ethyl Corporation, General Dynamics Corporation, General Foods Corporation, Gulf Oil Corporation, Inland Steel Company, International Harvester Company, Johnson and Johnson, Jones and Laughlin Steel

Company, Mutual Benefit Life Insurance Company, New York Central System, Richfield Oil Corporation, Shell Oil Company, Standard Oil Company (Indiana), United States Rubber Company, and Western Electric Company. ECO puts out a monthly bulletin, called ECHO, for its civic and public affairs members, detailing the most recent political activities of various companies. Typical reports are entitled "Monsanto Appoints Director of Civic Affairs," "Ford Broadens Program," "Chase Bank Acts," "Weyerhaeuser Platform," "Inland Steel Plans," "Caterpillar Company Workshops," "Scott Paper States Policy," "Union Carbide Urges Party Work," and so on.

ECO estimated that in 1960 as many as 250,000 American adults took practical politics courses under one or another business auspices. These were conducted not only by individual companies but also by local chambers of commerce and similar groups. What is lacking in all of this literature is a serious evaluation of the results of the "businessmen in politics" program. Virtually all of the reports are written by executives who are involved in drawing up and promoting the programs; and they almost invariably emphasize the number of courses given or the number of people taking them or the number of companies sponsoring practical politics activities. What is missing is a systematic follow-up to determine how many of the graduates have actually plunged into party work in a meaningful way. This is curious on its face because it is customary for businesses to take stock of their operations periodically to see if they are "profitable." Clearly when all the expenses and released time for employees are reckoned up, corporations have poured large sums of money into these endeavors. Indeed, the civic and public affairs departments within companies, with their directors and assistant directors and field offices and staffs, have burgeoned into impressive corporate budget items. Yet it is one thing for executives to give speeches about the need for political involvement, to hold conferences and set up courses and expose employees to the facts of political life. It is quite another thing to demonstrate that these white-collar and managerial employees have been taking the lessons to heart. For it must be shown that they are devoting their energies, on their own time and in their own communities, to infiltrating the local party organizations.

The Syracuse Experience

The pioneer in the "businessmen in politics" movement was not a single company, but rather the Manufacturers Association of Syracuse (MAS). As early as November 1957, this Upstate New York group was organizing practical politics courses for the employees of its member firms. The city, with a population of 200,000, or 300,000 including the suburban fringe, contained branch plants of such corporations as Atlantic Refining Company, Carrier Corporation, Crucible Steel Company, Chrysler Corporation, General Electric Company, and Sealtest Foods. General Electric was by far the largest employer in the metropolitan Syracuse area and also the most enthusiastic backer of the MAS program. The organizers drew up their own textbook and put out a complete instructional kit weighing ten pounds and costing $200. This kit contained not only printed class assignments and an instructor's handbook but also four sets of illustrated slides and a tape recording on which Richard Nixon gave his non-partisan imprimatur to the entire project. "Choose the party that comes closest to your political ideas and beliefs," the Vice President told the businessmen-students, "and roll up your sleeves and go to work." During the spring of 1958 employees of twenty-two companies in the area participated in seminars. By July, according to an MAS report,[8] the county chairmen of both major parties were handed the names of "225 alert, aggressive and trained businessmen"; and these course graduates were, the report continued, "eager to participate in any capacity the organizations might use them." By Election Day of 1960 there were 1,500 graduates.

The Syracuse program was given great publicity throughout the business community. Impressive and complimentary articles appeared in *Fortune, The Wall Street Journal, Nation's Business, U.S. News and World Report, Public Relations News, Industrial Relations News,* and *Kiplinger Letters.* Committees of the MAS, in response to invitations, traveled across the country telling the Syracuse story

---

[8] Manufacturers Ass'n of Syracuse, Seminars on Practical Politics, First Anniversary Report 2 (1958).

to large audiences of businessmen. And during the first eight months of operation the organizers received more than 1500 requests for information from companies and associations in every state. If "businessmen in politics" was to become a "movement" it is clear that Syracuse was the prime mover. And an analysis of the Syracuse experience should give some indication of the over-all record of the program throughout the nation. If anything, its performance, due to the early start, should be superior to that of latecomers on the scene.

The tone of the practical politics seminars was set by the slide presentation that opened each course. The set, revised following the 1958 congressional election, stated that "the AFL-CIO had endorsed fifty-four of the ninety-six U.S. Senators now making up the Senate, and a total of 220 of 436 House members. Thus, labor leaders now control a clear majority of members in both houses of Congress." The seminar leader was then told to ask, rhetorically, what was to be done about rectifying this parlous state of affairs. The answer was not money, because business could not compete with the millions of dollars in "union treasuries fattened by compulsory union membership." Nor should businessmen try to best the welfare proposals of their opponents for that would play into the hands of those who aim for "socialistic control of business enterprises." And, attractive as it may sound, it just is not possible to produce hundreds of conservative "ready-made, prepaid, year-round campaign workers." The slide presentation concluded:[9]

> The answer must come from business and industry by tapping our resources of trained and skilled manpower at the middle and junior and top management levels and putting our American business ingenuity to work in the political arena on a continuing, effective, and long-range basis. Business must learn to "speak out" and, we've got to use our leadership where it counts, in both parties.

Ten-week in-plant seminars were the cornerstones of the practical politics program. A typical seminar had about twenty participants, all

[9] "Script of Film Slide," in *Manufacturers Ass'n of Syracuse, Practical Politics Seminars, Political Effectiveness: New Horizon for Management* 12, 20 (1958).

volunteers. At the outset there was a permanent course leader for each ten-week session, with a rotating schedule of chairmen for each weekly meeting of the course. However, this democratic procedure was soon abandoned as the need for expert direction became apparent. Thus the seminar leader took on the additional role of chairman, with some increase in the effectiveness of the teaching. Nevertheless, even the leader was not far ahead of his pupils, as he had only undergone a two-day training session himself on the ins and outs of practical politics. Quite often he was unable to deal with the factual or technical questions on party organization that inevitably arose. Each seminar ran for two hours and half of the ten sessions brought in guest speakers, usually local party officials. The students were given a textbook that had the sterling advantage of gearing its treatment to the vagaries of Syracuse-area politics. They were also presented with various pamphlets and booklets, plus a copy of J. J. Weurthner's *Businessman's Guide to Practical Politics*. This book, written by a General Electric executive and published by the Henry Regnery Company in early 1959, accentuated the business-labor struggle in the political arena.

The sessions covered such topics as party organization, ward and precinct politics, and county government. The pervasive theme was the importance of political participation by individual citizens and this was stressed in the course discussions, the reading assignments, and by the guest speakers. The students were told to visit their election district committeeman after work and to make personal contact with their state senator or assemblyman. Most important each participant was expected to ask his local party officials: "What specific job can you give me for this campaign?" The student was presumably prepared for party work, as one of the out-of-class field-work assignments involved canvassing ten of his neighbors. The course was bipartisan at all times even if the syllabus was less than sympathetic to labor unions. Reprinted in the textbook was G. Mennen Williams' *Harvard Business Review* article "Can Businessmen be Democrats?",[10] the answer being most assuredly that they could. Indeed,

[10] Williams, "Can Businessmen Be Democrats?", *Harv. Bus. Rev.*, March-April 1958, p. 100.

the organizers of the program, departing perhaps from the former Michigan Governor's intention, felt that it was the Democratic Party that especially needed a conservative leaven and that the infiltration of businessmen could achieve this end.

It has been indicated that by the 1960 election there were approximately 1500 graduates of the Syracuse course. In late November 1960, printed questionnaires were mailed to all of these individuals. Enclosed with the form was a letter from a MAS officer explaining that this survey was a Cornell University project, that responses would be anonymous, and asking for the cooperation of the participants. Postpaid envelopes were included in the hope that this would raise the level of returns. The questionnaire had been drawn up at Cornell and revised in cooperation with the MAS; the joint sponsorship was made clear to the respondents. The intention of the survey, quite simply, was to determine how many graduates participated in politics and in what ways. A total of 578 forms were returned. This means that somewhere under a thousand former students did not reply. It could mean, of course, that these graduates were so busy with local party work that they did not have time to fill out a form about their work. Or it could mean, more likely, that the seminar had not motivated them to participate in politics and they had little or nothing to report. The suspicion arises that the response of slightly over one-third contained most of those course participants who did actually embark upon party activity of some sort. Of the respondents 152 indicated that they took the seminar in 1958, 211 in 1959, and 187 in 1960.

A total of 432 out of the 578 replies said they were active in the 1960 campaign. When specific questions were asked about the form that activity took, the responses were as follows:

Donated Money	281
Attended a Political Event	257
Helped or Urged Others to Register	232
Distributed Campaign Materials	203
Canvassed Voters	164
Joined Political Club or Organization	149
Joined a Campaign Committee	134

Solicited Campaign Funds	72
Wrote a Letter-to-the-Editor	37
Served as Election Day Official	32
Ran for Party Office	25
Ran for Public Office	21

How impressive a record this is depends, in the first place, on whether 1500 or 578 is used as the standard for comparison. It also depends on other considerations that will be discussed later on.

The graduates were then asked how many hours of party work they had put in during the just-completed 1960 campaign. This presumably is the most important single question, because its answers indicate how assiduously the former students were attempting to earn a place for themselves within the local party organizations. If the intention of the program was to infiltrate businessmen into the parties, it was emphasized that only by toiling in the political vineyard would such preferment come. The campaign lasted for about nine weeks—from Labor Day through Election Day—and the total hours of work reported for this period were:

None	273
1 to 5 hours	64
6 to 10 hours	71
11 to 20 hours	83
21 to 50 hours	53
51 to 100 hours	16
Over 100 hours	18

Some of these figures may not square easily with the reports on activities cited earlier. For example, 164 graduates said they canvassed voters but only 87 put in more than twenty hours of work during the nine-week campaign. The 164 may have done some canvassing but it is clear to anyone who has undertaken such a job that not many doorbells can be rung in less than twenty hours.

Also emerging from the survey was the fact that no less than 124 out of the 578 respondents had engaged in political activity *before* taking the practical politics course. This is an impressive proportion and it is interesting that these individuals felt the need to take the seminar even though they already had practical experience. However, their existence adds a new dimension to the figures on the number of hours worked. For when it comes to serious party workers —here defined as those putting in more than fifty hours—it seems that most of these were politically active prior to enrolling in the seminar. Of those who worked more than fifty hours, sixty-five per cent were doing party work before taking the course. Put another way, of the thirty-four graduates who recorded over fifty hours only twelve were people who were introduced to practical politics through the seminars. In light of the program's aim of making party workers out of businessmen who had hitherto been aloof from politics, this is rather a scanty record.

One more set of figures will complete the picture. The seminars began in 1958 and ran through 1960. It might be surmised that those who participated in them at the earlier date would lose their enthusiasm and be less likely to show activity in subsequent campaigns. But this was not the case. Indeed the reverse effect could be observed. The respondents were asked, in general terms, whether they had been active in the 1960 campaign:

Active in 1960

1958 graduates (152)	84%
1959 graduates (211)	74%
1960 graduates (187)	69%

The most plausible reason for this decline is that the early students in the course were at the managerial and junior executive level. As the program proceeded the companies ran out of managers and executives and had to descend to clerks and secretaries to fill the seminars. By 1960 the white-collar gamut had been run and the saturation point had been reached. For it became apparent that the lower down one reaches the less likely it is that potential party workers will be found. The point is that clerks and secretaries are not really "businessmen" and do not feel that intensely about entering politics to promote the interests of the companies that employ them. Indeed, it was with recognition that the bottom of the white-collar barrel was being scraped that the MAS decided to curtail the seminar program in 1961.

Those businessmen who did approach their local party organizations were not heartened by the welcome they received. Over two-thirds of those responding in the survey felt that their talents were not being used by the party organizations. Whereas the MAS styled its graduates as "alert, aggressive and trained businessmen" who were "eager to participate in any capacity," the parties wanted not so much executives or policy-makers as envelope-stuffers and doorbell-ringers. As a result comparatively few showed up for a second appointment or asked when they could be used again. This disillusionment was shared by the party officials. One committeeman cited a typical example. He was approached by an executive who offered his services, and this overture was enthusiastically accepted. The assignment was a customary one, to conduct a canvass of a small area in the district. But the canvass was never made, the businessman pleading "lack of time." He subsequently telephoned the committeeman, apologized, and asked if he could come down to the polls on Election Day and help out. Again he failed to show up. Of all this the committeeman said: "He was a really bright and important man. I thought he was a find. And we do need people who will work." Further interviews among party officials revealed that instances such as this one were commonplace. And because of this the practical politics program was viewed skeptically by the party regulars at the local level.

Of the 578 who took part in the survey, twenty-five reported that they ran for party office and twenty-one for public office. Unfortunately, no correlation was made to see how many of these forty-six graduates were people who had been active in local politics prior to taking the seminar; however, some follow-up interviews indicated that some of them were. Of the twenty-five who were candidates for party positions, twenty-two were elected district committeemen. Of the twenty-one who ran for public office, one was elected a town supervisor, three were defeated in races for county supervisor, five out of seven were successful in campaigns for town councilman, and six out of ten were elected to other local offices. The over-all record, therefore, consists of twenty-two graduates in party offices and twelve in public offices. Whether this is a sign of the program's success or failure depends, of course, on the expectations one has for it. The infiltration of thirty-four businessmen into party and governmental positions in a medium-sized metropolitan area may be more significant than first hits the eye. But against this is the fact that Syracuse companies invested uncounted time, energy, and money in training 1,500 employees in the arts of practical politics. And if it is assumed that many of the thirty-four were politically active before the advent of the program, then its dividends are really quite meager.

Several interviews among graduates employed at the two largest corporations gave hints as to why the lessons of the seminars were generally ignored. "If a businessman spends much time in politics, he cannot do his job adequately," one young executive said. "I have been encouraged to take part in local politics, but this will not help me to get promoted." Another manager, while he approved in principle of the aims of the program, had personal reservations. "As men go higher," he said, "they must expect to work greater hours. Company policy tells men to expect this as salary goes up. At the same time there is pressure to be active in politics. How can a man in my position do both?" This last question was posed by most of the people who were interviewed. And these were, for the most part, the kind of alert and aggressive individuals who could have made a mark for themselves in local politics. Another one put it this way: "My job comes first. All one gets for serving on the County Board of Supervisors is $6.00 per day. I recently got a salary promotion for hard work outside company hours. If I had spent this time in politics I would not have gotten the raise." And this attitude was even held by graduates who had engaged in party work. A veteran of several campaigns commented:[11]

> The objectives are excellent and the courses should be continued. Unfortunately, most businessmen are too busy with extra-curricular business activity and "casual" overtime that they do not have the time to spend at politics. In addition,

[11] Interview with Joel Aberbach.

most political parties want doorbell-ringers and are not anxious to delegate other work. After two elections of doorbell ringing, I feel that I've had it.

Finally, it should be added that of those who responded to the survey 479 said that they were Republicans and seventy-four were professed Democrats. The Syracuse area is predominantly Republican and its business community is even more so. One of the seventy-four Democrats expressed his reluctance to get openly involved in politics. "Most Democrats don't want to become too active because of their business relations," he said. "They don't want to be registered as Democrats." Perhaps he and others took the hint when they heard the tape-recorded voice of Richard Nixon, hardly a nonpartisan figure, that opened each of the MAS practical politics sessions.

Conclusion

The "businessmen-in-politics" movement in general and the Syracuse experience in particular raise some interesting questions about recent trends in American political and social life.

The first of these concerns the political anxieties of business. Granted that the 1958 congressional election was a Democratic sweep, the fact remains that the Eighty-sixth Congress remained a conservative body. If anything, its major accomplishment was the passage of the Landrum-Griffin bill regulating labor unions. Indeed, the winds of electoral change have little effect on the composition of either the House of Representatives or the state legislatures, and these remain fundamentally sympathetic to business. Moreover, they are able to check or veto the more liberal proposals of the President, the Senate, and the governors within the states.

In addition, businessmen are making their influence felt in a variety of significant ways. Executives of large corporations on the national level and small businessmen on the local level make substantial contributions to the campaign funds of conservative candidates. If national and local business donations are added together, it is safe to assume that these form a greater total than that provided by labor unions. To be sure, money alone does not elect anyone to office. But it is important as a means of bringing a candidate's name and personality before the public. Business lobbying is also well received, whether by trade or associations or individual companies. Again, it may be assumed that spokesmen for business interests have more prestige and receive a warmer welcome from more legislators than do their labor counterparts. At all events both companies and industries seem to get the laws that they want in no small degree. Furthermore, quite a few corporations are engaged in expensive and extensive public relations campaigns of a political character. These programs, using both the mass media and personal contact at the community level, are aimed at persuading the public that what is good for business is good for America. It is difficult, probably impossible, to measure the ultimate effectiveness of these campaigns. What can be said is that while the public elects the men who make the laws, public relations efforts can have an effect on the kind of laws that are made. That is, these campaigns can build popular sentiment for conservative legislation and thus influence the behavior of all but the most liberal legislators. Finally, businessmen have been coopted into high positions in all administrations regardless of party. The viewpoint of the business community has been well represented in the Departments of Defense, Treasury, and Commerce, plus the Atomic Energy Commission, the Federal Power Commission, and a whole host of lesser agencies. This is far more the case, even under a Democratic President, than is so for trade union spokesmen.

All in all, it is difficult to explain why businessmen have been so worried about the drift of American politics. One answer is that they are chronic worriers and have always been so. Listen to Charles Dickens describing the fears of the businessmen of Coketown over a century ago.[12]

> Surely there never was such fragile china-ware as that of which the millers of Coketown were made. Handle them never so lightly, and they fell to pieces with such ease that you might suspect them of having been flawed before. They were ruined, when they were required to send labouring

[12] Charles Dickens, *Hard Times* 123-24 (1898 ed.).

children to school; they were ruined when inspectors were appointed to look into their works; they were ruined, when such inspectors considered it doubtful whether they were quite justified in chopping people up with their machinery; they were utterly undone, when it was hinted that perhaps they need not always make quite so much smoke. . . . Whenever a Coketowner felt he was ill-used—that is to say, whenever he was not left entirely alone, and it was proposed to hold him accountable for the consequence of any of his acts— he was sure to come out with the awful menace, that he would "sooner pitch his property into the Atlantic." This had terrified the Home Secretary within an inch of his life, on several occasions.

So far as politics are concerned, it is always *Hard Times* in the business community. Businessmen have a habit of looking back to better days when labor was cheap and docile, when profits were generous and markets secure. If they are not satisfied with the outlook of the political parties or the content of legislation it is because they can imagine how things used to be. Yet their dissatisfactions, in mood if not in substance, are shared by most Americans. For the political system gives no one everything that he wants. When it is said that businessmen have done well out of the system this does not mean that they will either acknowledge that they have been successful or that they will cease complaining. Indeed, if they did not complain there would be some reason to believe that something was amiss.

There are also grounds for suspecting that the "businessmen-in-politics" programs were one of those periodic fads that recur in the business community. At one time it was "economic education," the idea being to impart the virtues of free enterprise to employees and the public in general. More recently it has been conferences and courses in "anti-communism," designed to waken an apathetic citizenry to the dangers of internal subversion and external aggression. Chronologically the "practical politics" fad came between "economic education" and "anti-communism." The life of each of these programs is prolonged by full-time staff people within companies and trade associations, who have a personal interest in selling the idea and expanding its operations. It is curious that top executives, allegedly so hard-headed and cost-minded, will pour so much company time and money into programs that pay doubtful dividends. If they are gullible, it is partly because times have been good and there is extra cash available to be spent in these areas. And once the programs, plus their staffs, are entrenched in the organizational chart it is difficult to dislodge them. But, most important perhaps, they stand as a commentary on the lack of sophistication that businessmen have on most matters other than business. Whether it is economic theory or practical politics or communism, most corporation executives and small entrepeneurs seem willing to buy any nostrum that accords with their ideological sensibilities.

The "practical politics" movement never got moving because those who planned it had an unrealistic conception of what motivates people to participate in party activity. The individuals who took the courses were simply not the kind of individuals who want or can be induced to take part in local politics. Two explanations can be given for this.

First of all, local politics are really local. The people who serve as committeemen and precinct workers are, more often than not, longtime residents in their communities. Many of them are locally based, having a business or a professional practice in the area. They know the people in their neighborhoods and they build up a fund of knowledge and goodwill. The American politician is an insider rather than an outsider, and he identifies himself closely with the town or ward or precinct where he was born or brought up. The young people who are in middle-management and technical positions in large corporations are remarkably transient. They are constantly being transferred from branch to branch within the company and they never have time to set down roots in any single community. Of the 578 graduates replying to the Syracuse survey, 404 were not born in the area. This means that they find it difficult to become involved with the political problems of what is, for them, only a temporary residence. And the fact of transiency is all the more true for the kinds of people, for example junior executives and engineers, that were supposed to pitch into party work. It has already been seen, in the responses to the interviews, that these young men on the way up identify with their jobs and their companies. If they have extra time it becomes overtime devoted to furthering their corporate careers. Energy spent in political participation, they figured, would be of no aid in determining their futures. Local, homegrown politicians, in contrast, see a close relationship between party activity and the life they lead as individuals. They engage in party work not because anyone has exhorted them to but because it is second nature to them. The problems of transient residence and corporate careers that face people in middle-management are important if only because they serve to withdraw a significant segment of the population from political involvement at the local level. This tendency will become stronger as the years progress and it will have consequences that deserve serious thought.

A second reason why the response to the program was disappointing was that no one had bothered to assess the general political outlook of the individuals who were to take the courses. Citizens who take the time to participate in party politics are frequently those who have a personal interest in questions of public policy. At the local level, which is always the starting point in party activity, it is very usually lawyers or small businessmen or other professional people who are drawn into committee posts or who run for office. These individuals have coherent interests to promote or defend, and they can see how particular lines of action on the part of governmental bodies will help or harm them. The "politics of interest" has been an integral part of our political fabric since James Madison set down its principles in the *Federalist*.[13] Those who have specific interests of their own have every reason to become active in political life. Whether those interests involve building up a law practice or modifying zoning regulations or advancing the status of chiropractors, these individuals do not have to be told that political activity will be to their advantage. The white-collar employee of a large corporation, on the other hand, does not possess identifiable interests that can readily be promoted through political action. He does have concerns—better schools, a sound dollar, peace with honor—but these are too general and vague

---

[13] *The Federalist No. 10* (Madison).

to be secured by the avenues of political participation open to him. If he is indifferent about working with a party it is because, quite simply, he does not see what he will get out of it. When benefits cannot be visualized it is difficult to become involved. It is this lack of involvement that is increasingly the case with middle-class individuals who are salaried employees of large organizations. The debates of local politics, and often national politics as well, are remote from their own lives. It is not enough to tell them that every piece of public policy, local or national, ultimately affects them. No one likes to think in ultimate terms.

It follows, too, that the people who comprised the student body of the practical politics seminars do not think in ideological terms. In fact, it is not entirely clear how many of them think of themselves as "businessmen" in the traditional sense. With the professionalization of management and the specialization of roles it often seems that they worry less than their elders about the increasing power of government in the economy. Unlike the self-employed entrepreneur or the top corporation executive, the man in middle-management is not as exercised over what appears to others to be the diminution of economic freedom. This is because it is not his freedom that is at stake, and he is not at the point where a wound inflicted on the corporation that employs him is regarded as a personal injury. It is not at all clear that, even if these people were infiltrated into the political parties, they would be a conservative force. Not being concerned with ideology, they might equally as well discover some rationality in policies that call for more rather than less governmental control. As suburbanites many of them have demonstrated that they are not opposed to increasing public expenditures; and as voters, not a few of them cross party lines to support attractive liberal candidates when they appear on the scene. This outlook was illuminated at one Syracuse seminar when the slide presentation depicted labor unions as a mortal threat to all that might be held dear. Not only was the course leader embarrassed by these forebodings of doom, but the students' comments were such that it was clear they were not losing sleep over the prospect of Walter Reuther in the White House. If not personal interest, it takes some measure of ideological commitment to lead a citizen into politics. And this was not in evidence.

As an episode in the annals of American business and as a case-study in political behavior, the "businessmen-in-politics" movement is of more than passing interest. For it raises some vexing questions about the level of political participation in this country at this time. The reluctance to take part in politics that was encountered among Upstate New York businessmen and that persisted despite the urgings of their corporate employers, can plainly be observed throughout the country. If this constitutes a "problem," and opinions can differ on whether in fact it does, then the causes of that problem have deep roots in American society.

The Seven Fallacies of Business in Politics*

MICHAEL D. REAGAN

Michael Reagan, in the following article, raises several important questions as to the proper role of the businessman in politics. He believes far too many businessmen hold misconceptions as to what their proper role is. These misconceptions, therefore, hinder businessmen and their organizations in competition with other groups. Reagan also offers meaningful guidelines for more effective role-playing in the future.

The drive to get corporations into politics is not much more than a year old, yet it has been a precocious baby and has become the center of much concern. Thus:

> The United States Chamber of Commerce is sending out 7,000 sets of political activity primers each month.
>
> Two public relations firms have arisen to specialize in advising corporations on their political problems.
>
> A number of corporations and industrial associations have instituted drives to turn executives into precinct politicians.
>
> Other companies are trying to present their corporate views on public policies to stockholders, suppliers, employees, dealers, and the general public.

Thus, the rash of politics, like June, is "bustin' out all over" in the business community. But the activity may be getting ahead of the thought behind it, and the growth may be too rapid to be healthy.

* Michael D. Reagan, "The Seven Fallacies of Business in Politics," *Harvard Business Review*, XXXVIII (March-April, 1960), 60-68.

As a result of these fears the wisdom of the business-in-politics movement is still being vigorously debated by executives.

Certainly, there are questions to be asked before this new movement hardens into as rigid a dogma as the older notion that business and politics should be separated by a thick and unbreachable wall. Perhaps, as I suggest here, the business-in-politics movement is based on certain assumptions that are more fiction than fact. If so, the entire movement may well produce consequences to business that are both unexpected and unwanted.

Long-Time Interest

In order to face up to the larger problems, let us dispel quickly one rather cloudy but widespread misconception—the belief that business has until now *not* been "in politics." This is nonsense. Where do the campaign funds of both major parties come from, if not predominantly from corporate executives? Do not business associations such as the National Association of Manufacturers and the Chamber of Commerce make frequent appearances before every Congressional committee? Have not institutional advertisements designed to secure a better business climate become an accepted part of our way of life in these days of high corporation taxes? The corporation and the businessman indeed have been in politics for a long, long time.

NEW EMPHASIS

The newness of today's business-in-politics movement lies in its new emphasis on party politics and electoral participation, as additions to the policy-and-legislation kind of political approach which business has generally taken in the past. It represents, in some ways, a shift from the political activities associated with an interest group to those forms of participation directed at selection of candidates and at obtaining a voice in party decisions.

In at least some cases, this change apparently has been motivated by business' growing dissatisfaction with both parties for being too amenable to labor demands. It thus rests on the premise that improvement can only be expected if businessmen become active in party affairs for the purpose of ensuring that they, themselves, or candidates more to their liking are nominated and elected. In other instances, the new direction may stem from the uneasy awareness that legislative deference to business desires lacks the automatic character it once possessed in the happy days when no alternative ideology and no countervailing, organized power competed for the legislator's attention.

A few business groups have learned how to handle modern, sophisticated legislative relations, but most have not. No longer able to rely on wine-and-dine techniques to assure business objectives, many businessmen appear to have turned in desperation to party politics at the grass roots level. On a mass scale, this *is* a new type of political action for business; but it by no means marks the entry of the corporate community into the political process.

REAL QUESTIONS

With the red herring of novelty out of the way, the real questions can be brought forth:

> How deeply does the corporation want to get into party politics?
>
> How wise is it for business to assume other roles beyond its traditional part of being the source of heavy financial contributions?
>
> Furthermore, what types of political participation are best suited to the nature and goals of the corporation?

Clearly both corporation presidents and union leaders have a legal right to use their "voices" in support of their interests. The question is not whether but *how* this should be done. A movement born in desperation and based on questionable assumptions is doomed to failure.

But this is to offer the conclusion before the proof. Why am I so doubtful? From a survey of articles and speeches, as well as the reported activities of corporations, industrial associations, and executives during 1958–1959, I have come to the conclusion that there are seven major propositions underlying the business-in-politics movement, each one of which is to some degree suspect. Admittedly, not all businessmen subscribe to all seven of these propositions; yet the arguments by advocates of a more vigorous political role for business will usually be found to be based on at least several of them.

1. *The interests of corporations are (always) the interests of society; therefore, corporate managers should be trustees for society.*

Another way of stating this is that corporations enter into political persuasion and electoral campaigning purely as a public service, not as an interested group seeking to protect its position against rival groups.

As pleasant as this platitude sounds, it is naive, futile, or dangerous for corporations to strike such a pose. It is especially naive when it is a sincere belief and not a public relations device. Then it indicates a lack of understanding of democratic politics, which is not a process for guaranteeing the dominance of any man's conception of the public interest, but a way of accommodating the conflict of diverse interests. The democratic assumption is that no group possesses all virtue. In the long run various groups often discover that they share a harmony

of interests as to certain goals. In the short run, however, the interests of different occupational and social groups frequently clash—and politics operates in the short run.

It is likely to be a futile belief, because it will not be shared by other groups. The nonbusiness factions, recognizing that in some respects their own interests differ from those of the corporation, will only see hypocrisy in such a claim. It can be dangerous in that widespread public acceptance of such a proposition would mean that one interest out of many would go unchallenged; it would take the pluralism out of *e pluribus unum!* (This is not to say that total submission of everyone and everything to the interests of business is a conscious goal of corporate executives; obviously it is not. But it is a logical deduction from the major proposition.)

As some proponents of more active corporate political activity have suggested, it is probably better for business to assert its own interests frankly, than to wrap all its demands in the mantle of public do-goodism.

The "better business climate" program, which is one of the goals toward which corporate political participation aims, illustrates the problem. Naturally business wants the most favorable climate possible, and in some ways this does promote the public interest in a healthy economy. But labor presumably wants a "better labor climate" too. If the same steps will not equally achieve a better climate for both groups, then who is to say which is the more legitimate claim? The *balancing* of such claims is exactly what democratic politics is all about. Can the balancing be left to a private government? That is what some industrialists assert, and the assertion is related to the trusteeship concept.

The trusteeship or stewardship notion is not a new one, but in the postwar years it has been given a dignity lacking in earlier versions by such writers as Russell Davenport and Adolf Berle, Jr. One of its more recent expressions is that by William T. Gossett, general counsel of Ford Motor Company:

> "We find a new role and responsibility thrust upon management; the adjudication of the conflicting legitimate interests of the groups who are intimately involved with the

corporation. We find management learning to sit in judgment upon itself in those relationships where its power is
preponderant and not subject to ready control or review by
others." [1]

This assertion will not quickly be accepted by all of its intended
beneficiaries in a society that places high on its list of political values
the right of each man to a voice in decisions affecting himself.

2. *Business is at present in a dangerous state of political helplessness.*

This proposition, vigorously advanced in the speeches of Lemuel
R. Boulware, General Electric Company, an early prophet of the
business-in-politics movement, must, in all honesty, be said to result
from self-delusion. Business has never been politically helpless in
this country, and it is not now. Are the Taft-Hartley Act and the
1959 Labor Reform Act the results of business' helplessness? Or
Eisenhower's strong anti-inflation stand and his vetoes of domestic
spending programs?
    What is really meant by this assertion is that business has regularly

[1] William T. Gossett, *Corporate Citizenship,* The John Randolph Tucker
Lectures, 1956 (Lexington, Virginia, Washington and Lee University, 1957).

taken a licking at the polls. This is often true, and should hardly come as much of a surprise to those who realize that a very large majority of the population are not business executives. Even so, it ignores the influence of business on the legislative side of politics. If anything, the election of 1958 and the contrasting record of the First Session of the Eighty-Sixth Congress suggest that access to the legislature is the more vital point of contact, and business has that access.

The picture of giant American corporations as undernourished political underdogs strains credulity past the breaking point for other reasons as well:

> The nation's press is overwhelmingly probusiness.
>
> Institutional advertising and a harmony of interests between business management and communications management give corporations an unmatched opportunity to make their voices heard.
>
> The high prestige of business leaders is attested to by many public opinion studies.

Thus, it is difficult for businessmen to elicit much sympathy when they play the role of poor, pitiful Pearl.

3. *The primary purpose of getting into politics is to put the unions in their place.*

This is the applied version of the second proposition. Its most obvious fault is the implication that when the power of labor weakens, business no longer need interest itself in public affairs. If businessmen are to enter politics with no broader or more permanent reason than to beat down the unions, they can hardly, at the same time, sustain the claim that they have entered politics merely as good citizens.

Somewhat less obvious, perhaps, is the fact that labor's political power is considerably less than its friends hope and its foes fear. Legislatively, this should be fairly clear at the moment; not the AFL-CIO's inability to secure a milder reform bill, a higher minimum wage, adoption of federal standards for unemployment compensation, or major expenditures for public housing.

Nor do the electoral successes of November 1958 prove quite as much as has been asserted. Just as businessmen would be pushed into solidarity by any measure which threatened vital corporate interests—say a peacetime excess profits tax—so also was labor united and pushed into exceptionally vigorous activity by the right-to-work issue.

Further factors overlooked in current corporate estimates of the power of labor are:

> The low proportion of labor union members who bother to vote.
> The fact that at least a third of those who *do* vote mark their ballots in the opposite way from that which is suggested by their national leadership.

Business executives, on the other hand, as is true generally of higher income and educational levels, vote in far greater proportion to their total strength. Thus, even the natural advantage of numbers is not under ordinary circumstances fully available to labor's Committee on Public Education (COPE).

Finally, the attempt by business to ape labor's political tactics is at least as likely to create a reaction of unprecedented solidarity and political effort on the part of unions as it is to increase business power vis-à-vis labor power. In fact, this reaction already shows some signs of being under way. After all, the unions can hardly be expected to sit on their hands in the face of repeated public threats by corporate spokesmen that they are out to cut labor down to political size. The Taft-Hartley Act, it should be recalled, did more than years of intraunion argument to bring the previously apolitical AFL into politics up to its ears.

4. *Business ability is directly translatable into political ability.*

This proposition can be easily inferred from the nature of the political training programs that have blossomed during the past 18 months. Putting all the stress on political techniques, many of these programs emphasize that politics is a field as complicated as business management. They hold that the executive must savvy the structure and operations of primaries, conventions, voter registration laws, and party processes before he makes the big plunge.

Nowhere, however, does one find any recognition that the *sub-*

stance of economic and social issues is also complex and difficult, or that discussion of corporate objectives is at least as important as learning the means by which they are to be defended.

Apparently executives are assumed to have automatically the true answers to all economic and social problems. There is no need to study, investigate, or consider alternative facts, views, or definitions of issues—or anything beyond what is given in the latest issue of *Nation's Business*. A significant exception to the philosophy is that held by the Committee for Economic Development. The CED uses a professional staff and apparently feels a necessity to study a problem before going forth to teach the rest of us. As a businessman's group it has policy predilections of course; however, it does recognize the difference between blind self-interest and informed judgment.

Large affairs are too complex and multifaceted to be susceptible to such off-the-cuff treatment, and the businessman who thinks that he need only learn techniques and not substance will not soon gain the intellectual and political respect of a literate and skeptical public.

This is not a disparagement of the businessman's ability but rather a recognition that his immersion in the particular affairs of a particular concern leaves little time or opportunity for keeping up with public affairs in the outside world. Many executives themselves testify vigorously and constantly to the accuracy of the statement. In a world of specialties, the executive who intends to play an active political role will find it necessary to inform himself deeply on a range of problems far wider than those involved in his own firm's production.

Perhaps the most important obstacle to the translation of business skills into political skills lies in the difference between the corporate and the political environments. The executive lives in a rationalized, hierarchical world in which the major criterion for decision making is: What will advance the long-run welfare of the corporation? Within broad limits, the president of a firm does not have to worry about "selling" his decision to the rank and file of clerk-typists; nor need he fear that he will be turned out of office because of lower-echelon discontent.

The public world—as many dollar-a-year men discovered during tours of duty in Washington—is a vastly different story. Here the legislator is *not* at the apex of a hierarchy; he is accountable to the rank and file of his constituency and can be turned out of office easily. His criteria for action are an inextricable mixture of:

What will this decision mean to me at the polls in November?

What will advance my district?

What will advance the national interest?

The politician faces a multiplicity of demands, some of them conflicting. He cannot ignore any—he cannot please all. He is subject to pressures and temptations, conflicting loyalties nag his decisions, and he must spend much of his time running errands for constituents rather than studying the legislative agenda. In short, his world is one of far more complex and varied relationships than are found in the business world.

Executives of large public corporations occasionally complain of conducting business in a "goldfish bowl." Nothing in business can fully prepare them for the glare of critical publicity that they receive when they step out from behind the comparatively cloistered walls of the corporation into the back alleys of party politics. The primary skill of the politician is bargaining, not administrative management. Vicarious experience in the processes and problems of group bargaining—as through the use of concrete case materials—could make political training programs for executives more realistic and useful in this regard, but few programs have as yet gone beyond the mechanics of government and party structure.

More than knowledge is needed to make the businessman something greater than a political textbook technician.

5. *Electoral activity is the only route to political influence.*

The nine pamphlets of discussion material comprising the Action Course in Practical Politics distributed by the Chamber of Commerce cover party organization, precinct work, the organization of campaigns, party clubs and political meetings, and the selection and

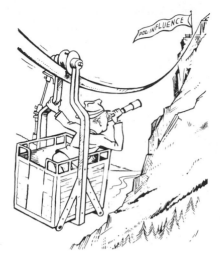

financing of candidates. In its stress on party-electoral politics, the program ignores the problems of influencing legislators and administrators already in office. It also shuns the whole area of *policy politics*, which in our loose party system is at least as important as party politics. By blindly following such programs, business may be ignoring not only its best tools but its accumulated experience, and adopting techniques that are appropriate only for groups that have a mass-membership base.

Business should not forget that some of the most effective political work it has ever done is that of writing legislation—as was apparently the case with Taft-Hartley and the 1954 tax revisions. Nor should it lose sight of the fact that the oil industry—and other extractive industries—did not obtain the depletion allowance by party-electoral activity, but by quiet, unpublicized work with individual legislators. The Congressman needs help in writing legislation and in estimating the impact of proposed measures on his district. The individual businessman who can supply explicit information showing how his plant would be hurt or helped, or who can aid in improving the administrative workability of a law, can have great influence.

Businessmen as a group, whether organized locally or in national trade associations, have a bargaining power far beyond their numbers. Corporate leaders should expend as much effort in devising positive programs to solve evident social problems as they have frequently spent in stubborn opposition to the solutions proposed by other groups. Then they might substantially increase their legislative influence without ever seeing the inside of a ward club.

In a political system whose "liberal" party includes Byrd and Barden, while its "conservative" party embraces Case and Javits, *party* victories are clearly distinguishable from *policy* victories. And policy victories are probably the successes most easily attained by factions such as the business group which lack vast membership but do possess wealth, education, and sophistication in the planning of large affairs. Conversely, labor unions with their mass base frequently may attain party triumphs at the expense of policy aspirations.

6. *What works for the labor goose also works for the corporate gander.*

This is the unhesitating assertion that the way for business to counteract labor power is to follow labor's lead in the strategy and tactics of political participation. This assumption is founded on a

belief in the similarity between corporations and unions as political citizens. But before corporate officers decide to take the plunge into politics, they should give serious consideration to the implications of this analogy.

A trade union is an association of people having officers elected by the membership and removable by them. When the officers act politically in the name of the members—as by editorial support of a party —it is clear whom they are representing. Granted, a disgruntled minority will not approve of political use of its dues money, but majority rule at least provides a rationale for the situation. Direct campaign contributions, by law, come from separate voluntary assessments, and not from regular dues. Should a majority of the membership disapprove, they have a clear legal right to force a change in policy or in leadership.

Where does an attempt to apply a similar analysis to the corporation lead us? First of all, we think of the corporation as an association of capital rather than of people. This is formally true of the only elections held in a corporation, those of the board of directors, where the balloting is on a basis of one share of stock, one vote—not one man, one vote. It is thus the money-ownership that has the vote and to which the officers are accountable.

If the corporation enters politics in the name of the stockholders, then the problem of the minority who may disagree becomes a serious one from the viewpoint of political equality. A majority of stockholders may be a voting minority of stock ownership. Suppose, as one business executive has suggested, corporate entry into politics is made dependent on a stockholders' referendum?

Then the question arises concerning the propriety of voting rights which vary with the amount of property owned by the voter—this in a society that outlawed property qualifications for the suffrage more than 100 years ago! No question is raised about property suffrage when it is applied to the internal affairs of the corporation as a goods-producing agency, but rather when it is applied to the larger political arena in which the *public* citizenship of the stockholders is at stake.

This may be a rather unlikely situation, however. In the era of the managerial corporation, many observers have noted, the role of the stockholder has dwindled to that of a bit player, a simple receiver of dividends who participates in policy decisions even less than do the rank and file of labor unions. Managers have discretionary authority to spend corporate funds on a variety of charitable and educational purposes which have little immediate impact on the balance sheet. Presumably they may exercise the same discretion in political affairs without fear of stockholder insurrections.

But since stockholder pressures have diminished, managers have been able to proclaim that they are acting in the interests of a host of "clients" or "publics," as noted under Proposition #1 above. There are some questions which can be asked that might cause these claims of trusteeship to prove embarrassing:

> If the corporation claims that it acts in the interests of its suppliers, does the ethic of political democracy require that the suppliers have a voice in determining the corporation's political direction?
>
> If the corporation asserts that it is acting also for its employees, then what is to prevent a demand that the corporate leaders be accountable to their members' political preferences?
>
> If, as a final alternative, the corporation foregoes the trusteeship concept to embrace partisan political action and the managers claim simply to be representing the corporation itself as a person created by legal fiction, what then?
>
> Are not serious problems raised concerning the concentration of power?
>
> If the resources of a billion-dollar corporation can be thrown into the political balance by officers who are in effect accountable only to themselves, what happens to the principle of political equality?

7. *The corporation can restrict its participation to the issues it selects.*

In 1958, Richard Bruner, a former labor organizer, spoke his mind as to why unions should get out of politics.[2] One of his major themes

---

[2] "Labor Should Get Out of Politics," *Harper's Magazine,* August 1958, p. 21.

was that the political interests of many unions were too narrow to warrant their playing any role but that of a pressure group. A political movement that places civil rights and foreign policy at the bottom of its legislative list, Bruner states, has no business claiming to be devoted to public rather than private interest and had better stay out of party politics until its view broadens to encompass the nation's problems, not just its own.

Cannot the same logic apply to the corporation in politics? If the corporation wants to play a significant part in partisan affairs, its interests must be as broad as those of a political party. The corporate executive who is acting as a representative of his firm cannot demand to be heard when his party's labor or tax plank is being written and refuse to answer questions about his firm's position on civil rights, summit meetings, or farm policy.

How many corporations are prepared to take a public stand on the full range of public issues? Any that are not ready to do so should do some deep thinking before they mount the political podium.

Guidelines for Action

Faultfinding is fun and relatively easy to accomplish, but I hope that this frank criticism of the assumptions underlying the business-in-politics movement will provide some positive guidelines for politically appropriate action by businessmen and corporations.

INDIVIDUAL PARTICIPATION

Note that my criticisms apply primarily to the corporation as such and to acts by individual officers or employees only as they are part of the individual's corporate duties. They are not intended to apply to businessmen's participation in politics as independent citizens. Clearly the citizen, whether chairman of the board or ditch digger, has the right and obligation to inform himself, to vote, and, if he is to have maximum influence, to work within the party of his choice. As an individual, his right is to participate in any way and to any extent he desires. Most of us would like to see greatly increased participation by persons in all social groups, and especially by the educated middle class from whose ranks political leadership should be arising.

The first step that the corporation can take in politics is to encourage and support political participation by its employees *as individuals*. The register-and-contribute campaign of the Aerojet-General Corporation in 1958, which provided in-plant opportunities to register and to contribute to the party of one's choice, illustrates what might be done. Leaves of absence without loss of seniority for employees and executives who achieve political office, limited time off with pay for employees with occasional local political duties, and arrangements for candidates of both parties to use plant auditoriums to address employee voters—these are some additional ways in which corporations can serve the cause of civic consciousness impartially and without complication.

CORPORATE TECHNIQUES

To go beyond simple good citizenship in an effort to advance their interests and make known their concept of the public interest, corporations are trying a variety of techniques. Among the most common are:

> Letters to employees, dealers, and stockholders setting forth management's side of public issues.
>
> Open advocacy of legislative measures to the general public via speeches and advertising.
>
> Better-business-climate conferences.
>
> Instruction of executives in party processes.
>
> Encouragement of executives to get into party affairs as semi-independents—semirepresentatives of a management viewpoint.
>
> Distributing Congressional voting records with or without comparison of company views.
>
> More numerous contacts with Senators and Representatives by plant managers in each electoral district.

Of these techniques, public advocacy of selected issues tied to election campaigns is perhaps the most questionable from the viewpoint of company welfare as well as public interest. Any company may make known its views to legislative bodies and to the public at large, but for the reasons given under Proposition #7 above it seems dubious that this activity should be tied to party politics. Educating employees to company views through house organs and letters also seems questionable, since it smacks of discredited nineteenth century attempts to coerce employees. The rule of thumb here should probably be that whatever resembles company indoctrination should be avoided. Thus, there is a world of difference between pamphlets presenting *alternative* views of a public policy, written by competent representatives of each viewpoint, and one-sided explanations of a company viewpoint presented as objective and disinterested educational material.

In general, I suggest that it is fine for a corporation to engage in restricted electoral activity of an impartial nature. But when the corporation seeks direct presentation of its views on public policies, it should rely on the traditional techniques of interest groups—appearances before legislative committees and party platform committees, personal meetings with individual legislators, supplying facts and advice to aid legislative judgment, and campaign contributions by individual businessmen.

If corporations do not sensibly restrict their political activity, they run one final and most serious risk: partisan electoral activity by corporations will bring forth redoubled effort by labor. The end result might then be what businessmen have long abhorred—a class conflict in American party politics. And in such a conflict the larger class would emerge the victor. In view of this possibility (if not probability) advocates of a vigorous partisan political role for business had better re-examine the assumptions on which their advocacy is based, and determine for their own satisfaction whether what they think is a political arrow is really a social boomerang.

Organized Labor in Electoral Politics: Some Questions for the Discipline*

HARRY M. SCOBLE

The author of this selection, Harry Scoble, examines the political involvement of organized labor in postwar elections. Past and present political committees of the AFL-CIO have indulged in such electoral activities as candidate selection, infiltration of party machinery and fund raising with mixed success. Working mainly within the fabric of the generally pro-labor Democratic party, labor's fortunes have paralleled those of the Democratic party.

Organized Labor as a System of Electoral Power

The CIO's Political Action Committee was created under and largely by Sidney Hillman in 1943 for the purpose of "nonparty, nonpartisan" politics. The American Federation of Labor hesitated just long enough, in its traditional reluctance to turn away from "business-unionism," to witness the failure of organized labor to defeat the Taft-

* Harry M. Scoble, "Organized Labor in Electoral Politics," *Western Political Quarterly*, XVI (September, 1963), pp. 666-85. Reprinted by permission of the University of Utah, copyright owners.

NOTE: The present article is the result of a broader research on ideology and electoral action in American politics. That research has been made possible by grants from The Maurice and Laura Falk Foundation through the Eagleton Institute of Politics, Rutgers, The State University; from the Social Science Research Council of New York City; and from the Graduate Research Committee, University of Wisconsin. Obviously, no one of these is to be considered the author, publisher, or proprietor of the present publication; nor are they to be understood as endorsing by virtue of their grants or aid any of the statements made or views expressed herein.

121

Hartley Act in 1946; then it, too, took the path of electoral action, patterning its Labor's League for Political Education on the earlier PAC. (Since 1955 and the merger of the AFL and CIO, these political-action arms have slowly been merged into the joint Committee on Political Education.) These facts, which every politically oriented student of America ought to know, are repeated here to underscore the major point that the most fundamental postwar change in the structure and process of political parties has been the entrance of organized labor into electoral activity at the precinct level and on up.

. . . For tentative organization of the factual matter, it is convenient to look at organized labor from the standpoints of the following areas of electoral behavior: the national conventions and legislative recruitment; the party apparatus itself; and vote mobilization in terms first of registration drives, get-out-the-vote drives, and the direction of the vote, and then in terms of labor money in elections. These categories are convenient only; it should be clear that they are not mutually exclusive.

The National Conventions and Legislative Recruitment

. . . If one takes the date of the creation of the PAC as the proper starting point of the entrance of unions into elections, it is clear that nine national elections have now passed in which organized labor has participated; four of these were presidential elections. It seems not reasonable to hypothesize that mass-membership interest groups will seek to seat their officers-members in the state delegations to the national nominating convention of that party with which the overwhelming majority of the interest group members identify. For example, Key noted that "around 200 unionists attended the Democratic National Convention as delegates or alternates in 1952,[6] and anyone attending to his television set in 1960 could learn that there were 42 officers-members of the United Steel Workers alone among the total

[6] V. O. Key, Jr., *Politics, Parties and Pressure Groups* (4th ed.; New York: Crowell, 1958), p. 73, quoting Max M. Kampelman.

Pennsylvania delegation to the Democratic Convention. Further-more, it is common knowledge among political scientists that the Brookings Institution has expended large sums of money and has produced several massive descriptions of national party conventions and of presidential elections; and in all that body of description, it is possible to learn that in 1948 labor union representatives constituted 2.1 per cent of the total Democratic delegations as against 0.2 per cent of the total Republican delegations while 1962 data include in-formation on the annual income, the education, and so on of the delegates . . .

. . . Labor's League for Political Education announced in 1949 that it would henceforth subsidize labor members of those state legislatures in which salaries were extremely low.[8] The proposal was patterned on the long-standing practice of the British Labour party; its purpose was to increase the availability of labor union candi-dates by organized compensation for social-structural processes noted at least as long ago as the time of Max Weber.[9] Within the limits of the institutional and demographic gerrymander against the union vote in all state politics, the LLPE proposal *might, if carried out,* have had some measurable counterbalancing effect. . . .

. . . "[L]aborers and craftsmen" constituted 5.5 per cent of all lower-house members and 2.5 per cent of all state Senate members in 1949; the combined percentage was 5.0, and such *possibly* union legislators were most *numerically* frequent in the legislatures of Rhode Island, Minnesota, Connecticut, and Pennsylvania, in descend-ing order; on the other hand, in the most heavily industrialized states of Massachusetts, Michigan, New York, and New Jersey "rep-resentatives of labor were so few that in numerical terms they were of little significance, although in these states there were more labor leaders."[11]

---

[8] See John P. Roche and Murray S. Stedman, Jr., *The Dynamics of Demo-cratic Government* (New York: McGraw-Hill, 1954), p. 70.

[9] See "Politics as a Vocation" in H. C. Gerth and C. Wright Mills (eds.), *From Max Weber: Essays in Sociology* (New York: Oxford University Press, 1958).

[11] Belle Zeller (ed.), *American State Legislatures* (New York: Crowell, 1954), p. 72.

Labor and the Party Apparatus

Suppose that one asks what is known concerning organized labor and the party apparatus, again with relation to the Democratic party. If it could be demonstrated that organized labor *is* sometimes the political party at city, county, and/or state levels, political scientists could finally turn away from the foolish distinction about nominations and begin to ask the more important questions: Under what conditions, with what tactics, and with what consequences do mass-membership interest groups become the party apparatus? The trend questions also then become appropriate.

To illustrate: in Rockford, Illinois, the CIO-PAC organized to elect precinct captains in order successfully to swing the election of the Democratic chairman for Winnebago County.[12] Concerning *local* elections, the evidence—such as it is—is an odd mixture. In New Haven, Connecticut, the city itself is the fifth largest employer, most of its employees are now unionized and, along with other union members and union families, now constitute about 36 per cent of the electorate; these people have apparently voted as a bloc in at least one important election (1945)—but unionist activity has not become the apparatus for local nominations and elections, and the trade union leadership's activity and involvement is largely that of traditional lobbying "only on questions of the wages, security, and working conditions of city employees."[13] A survey of the politics of education in Massachusetts also suggests that labor union leaders and members have not yet perceived local electoral activity as a means to their ends, relying instead on ineffectual traditional lobbying to promote the addition of pro-labor courses to the public school curriculum, to protest the politico-economic views of teachers, and to protest the use of NAM-supplied "educational materials" in the school system.[14] In

[12] Cited in Hugh A. Bone, *American Politics and the Party System* (New York: McGraw-Hill, 1955), p. 113.
[13] Robert A. Dahl, *Who Governs?* (New Haven: Yale University Press, 1961), pp. 76 and 253-54.
[14] Neal Gross, *Who Runs Our Schools?* (New York: Wiley, 1958), pp. 50, 52, and 53.

Madison and Kenosha, Wisconsin, on the other hand, evidence exists of direct and increasing union activity in local educational elections.[15] The best available survey of New York City politics suggests the following: The Central Trades and Labor Council (AFL and representing about three-quarters of a million unionists) had initially de-emphasized its political purpose, but had "an almost unbroken history of endorsing the major candidates of the Democratic Party for city office" (with, however, an occasional split to a Republican candidate for Borough President and City Council in the last decade). Its electoral activity locally was directed primarily toward a broad concern for personnel and policy in the limited interests of the building trades, teamsters, and longshoremen's unions. Meanwhile the authors expected that the 1959 merger (with a million-and-a-half unionists) would lead to slow change in the direction of "greater and more unified influence" because of the CIO's greater concern for electoral action and also because of the 400,000 votes quadrennially mustered by the Liberal party (largely ILGWU).[16]

The evidence that is available thus suggests that organized labor has not yet become the party apparatus of the community with regard to community or local politics; on the other hand, lacking "community political systems" analyses of Akron, Cicero, Gary, or Pittsburgh, it is wisest to suspend judgment on this point.

. . . Recent studies of the successes of the Democratic party in such widely separated states as Maine and Wisconsin provide brief generalized descriptions of union activity; at the lowest level of analysis, therefore, one may infer some effect.[17] More directly descriptive of the relations between organized labor and the growth of successful party organization are recent studies of the Minnesota and Michigan Democratic parties. Mitau indicates the present importance of union-member identification with the Democrat-Farmer-Labor party in the

[15] Unpublished material of the author.
[16] Wallace S. Sayre and Herbert Kaufman, *Governing New York City* (New York: Russell Sage Foundation, 1960), pp. 508-14.
[17] See John C. Donovan, *Congressional Campaign: Maine Elects a Democrat* (New York: Holt, 1958) and Leon D. Epstein, *Politics in Wisconsin* (Madison: University of Wisconsin Press, 1958).

former state[18] while the studies of the Michigan Democrats by Calkins, by the Sarasohns, and by Eldersveld and his associates[19] particularly highlight the role of unions in creating a party apparatus. In Michigan, for example, it is estimated that 821 of 1,000 members filing in 1948 for Wayne County precinct delegate were stimulated to action by their union-membership; shortly after that (the year of the first Williams victory) it was estimated that 64 per cent of all money donated to the Democratic State Central Committee and directly to statewide candidates came from United Auto Worker and other CIO-union funds. And, by the mid-1950's, evidence existed for concluding that CIO-PAC electoral action not only exceeded that of the regular Democratic organization in much of Wayne County but that "in fact, in a few of the Detroit Congressional Districts the regular organization has been largely supplanted by the CIO-PAC."[20] More broadly, Heard has cited evidence indicating that in 1952, somewhere in the neighborhood of 1,000 unionists were active as full-time campaign workers in the closing weeks of the election in California, while in 1956 in the Detroit area 1,549 UAW temporary election workers were hired with dues money paid to local unions.[21] Additional evidence of the integration of union structure and Democratic party structure comes from a study of precinct committeemen in Gary, Indiana; for the study by Rossi and Cutright indicates the importance of membership in and identification with the union, particularly the United Steel Workers, in leading into precinct political work. In the

[18] G. Theodore Mitau, *Politics in Minnesota* (Minneapolis: University of Minnesota Press, 1960).

[19] Fay Calkins, *The CIO and the Democratic Party* (Chicago: University of Chicago Press, 1952); Stephen B. and Vera H. Sarasohn, *Political Party Patterns in Michigan* (Detroit: Wayne State University Press, 1957); and Samuel J. Eldersveld *et al.*, *Political Affiliation in Metropolitan Detroit* (Ann Arbor: Bureau of Government, University of Michigan, 1957). Arthur Kornhauser *et al.*, *When Labor Votes* (New York: University Books, 1956), also provides useful information on the political activities of the United Auto Workers.

[20] Eldersveld *et al.*, *op. cit.*, p. 87.

[21] Alexander Heard, *The Costs of Democracy* (Chapel Hill: University of North Carolina Press, 1960), p. 205 and n. 108. Heard did not identify the California labor leader source, nor did the latter indicate whether these election workers were union-paid. The 1956 data derive from the 1957 report of the Senate Special (McClellan) Lobby Committee.

sample, 20 per cent of the white Democratic and 23 per cent of the Negro Democratic precinct committeemen gave union (or class-interest) responses as the "self-activating motive" for entering political work. Among Republican precinct workers the comparable precentages were zero.[22] From such facts one may infer that since World War II union leaders and members alike have in large numbers come to the conclusion that political activism within—and public identification with—the Democratic party is an efficient means to personal and organization goals.

Vote Mobilization

Vote mobilization is the third area of inquiry in this review of the scant factual material available about organized labor in electoral politics. Labor unions have carried out registration drives and get-out-the-vote drives in both primary and general elections and have done everything else that a political party does, including provision of free baby-sitting service on election day. . . . Campbell and Cooper present data for 1948, 1952, and 1954 indicating that unionists voted 6.7 per cent more frequently than others—but the comparison is with the general population;[27] but when union members are correctly compared only with non-union workers of comparable occupation, education, income, and status—for the two presidential elections on which data are available the unionists voted at an average of 16.0 per cent more.[28] Both of these figures suggest that important differences in volume of political activity are associated with labor unions and that

[22] Peter H. Rossi and Phillips Cutright, "The Impact of Party Organization in an Industrial Setting," in Morris Janowitz (ed.), *Community Political Systems* (Glencoe: Free Press, 1961), p. 88. These union, class-motivated Democratic committeemen were also reported to be the most issue-oriented—at both local and national levels—of all their fellows. Curiously, in their report, Rossi and Cutright do not trace out the specific nature of the organizational ties of their respondents (see their Table IV and related text, pp. 91-92).

[27] Campbell and Cooper, *Group Differences in Attitudes and Votes, op. cit.,* Table III—11 at p. 31.

[28] Campbell and Kahn, *The People Elect a President, op. cit.,* for 1948 (an observed difference of 15 per cent); and Campbell and Cooper, *op. cit.,* for 1952 (17 per cent).

these differences between unionists and non-unionists (whether generally or specifically compared) *increased* between 1945 and 1955.

This brings us to the second point of inquiry. It is hardly esoteric social science knowledge that organized labor, at least since 1936, has consistently voted more Democratic than have other sectors of society. But all knowledge beyond this seems to be highly esoteric in the sense that it is extremely difficult to find intelligent appraisals of *how much* more Democratic and of trends. Illustratively, union families in Elmira, New York, whether of skilled workers or unskilled, were at least 24 per cent more Democratic than non-union families in both categories in the 1948 election;[29] but that was an unusual election, as Dr. George Gallup and other commercial pollsters have revealed. Its uniqueness is evident in the 1948 "Iowa Poll" of the *Des Moines Register and Tribune,* which indicated that union members were 9 per cent more likely to report having had conversations concerning the election and were 18 per cent more "certain of vote" than the general Iowa sample *even with education controlled.*[30] It is appropriate, therefore, to turn away from the "unique event" which plagues social science just as much as it does Dr. Gallup, although in somewhat different ways. Gallup data for the entire period 1936 through 1960 have recently been published [31] indicating that "union families" voted an average of 6.7 per cent more Democratic than "all manual-worker families." An earlier Gallup analysis, covering only 1936 through 1948 *but* more directly comparing "non-union labor" with "union members," indicated that the latter were on the average

[29] Bernard R. Berelson *et al., Voting* (Chicago: University of Chicago Press, 1954), pp. 46-47. Their analysis also indicated that CIO members were most Democratic, IAM next, and AFL least. Such intra-union differences also show up in Eldersveld *et al., op. cit.,* p. 99.

[30] This was also revealed too late. I infer from this that PAC and LLPE activity had some effect. See Norman C. Meier and Harold W. Saunders (eds.), *The Polls and Public Opinion* (New York: Holt, 1949).

[31] In V. O. Key, Jr., *Public Opinion and American Democracy* (New York: Knopf, 1961), p. 523. As usual, the academic social scientists must have some reservation concerning the precision of comparative analyses by the Gallup organization; that is, the data reported in the text constitute a comparison of "union families" with "all manual-worker families," and there is no indication that the latter catagory is *exclusive* of the former. I suspect that it is not and that, for the reasons given in the text and drawn from SRC data, it unnecessarily deflates the extent of Democratic-orientation of unionists.

12 per cent more Democratic than nonunion labor.[32] Furthermore, if in the depressing discontinuities of social science research it is permissible to consider four successive data points as constituting trend data, the spread between unionist and non-union has increased with the political activity of organized labor; for the 1936 and 1940 differences are the same (8 per cent) and only half the 1944 and 1948 differences. My belief that an *increasing* differential has occurred simultaneously with increasing electoral activity by unions is supported by the most recently published Survey Research Center data, in that a comparison of union members in 1956 with "a '*control*' group of non-members that matches the '*test*' group of members on all important aspects of life situation save the fact of membership" [33] indicated that the unionists were more than 20 per cent more Democratic than the control group, while union families were 17 per cent more Democratic than the matched control group.

These figures have been patiently reconstructed, and the bases of choice and comparison perhaps laboriously verbalized, in order to test the assumption of E. E. Schattschneider that the net electoral impact of organized labor is just under one million votes.[34] My estimate is presented in Table I. It suggests that the net gain of the Democratic party in presidential elections as a consequence of the existence of unions is perhaps as much as 2,800,000 votes; furthermore the *gross* impact of unionization may be estimated by alternatively hypothesiz-

[32] George Gallup, "How Labor Votes," in *Annals*, 274 (1951), 124. Heard, *op. cit.*, p. 205, n. 110, cites unpublished Survey Research Center data from 1956 indicating that among Stevenson-voters, members of union families more frequently indicated having engaged in actual campaign work than did members of non-union families (the reverse was true for Eisenhower-voters). Furthermore, 21 per cent of union members reported having used campaign buttons or car stickers, whereas this figure was only 13.5 per cent for non-union respondents. Stricter controls would undoubtedly reveal greater spreads in rates of "higher forms" of political action as well as in the act of voting alone.

[33] Campbell *et al.*, *The American Voter, op. cit.*, pp. 301-06, at p. 304, original emphasis. A less rigorous comparison with "the residual, non-member portion of the total sample" revealed the following Democratic deviation in the two-party vote division percentage: for union families, +35.8 (1948), +19.8 (1952), and +18.1 (1956); for union members only, no separate comparison was available for 1948, but 1952 showed +24.9 and 1956, +21.4 deviation.

[34] Schattschneider, *The Semi-Sovereign People, op. cit.*, pp. 49-52.

ing what the Democratic vote would be if *all* 31,000,000 workers were unionized (over 16,000,000 votes) and what it would be if *none* of them were (just under 10,500,000 votes)—that is, the total variation for the relevant labor force could be as much as 5,848,700 votes at the present time and under projections of available data as to both turnout and Democratic-preference. And this is why my estimate is almost three times what Schattschneider's was: he assumed that the voting rate was "only about half of the membership" (i.e., for unionists); he assumed that there was no spread between unionists and non-unionists (the data available indicate it is about 16 per cent); and

TABLE I

PROBABLE NET DEMOCRATIC VOTE IMPACT OF ELECTORAL ACTION
OF ORGANIZED LABOR IN LATE 1950'S AND EARLY 1960'S

	ORGANIZED LABOR	UNORGANIZED LABOR
Total numbers	15,000,000	16,000,000
Mean voting rate	75%	59%
Probable turnout	11,250,000	9,440,000
Mean Democratic per cent of the two-party vote	70%	56%
Probable Democratic vote	7,875,000	5,381,000
Probable Democratic vote with assumptions reversed:		
1. if organized labor behaved politically like unorganized labor	5,044,500	—
2. if unorganized labor behaved politically like organized labor	—	8,400,000
Democratic gain as consequence of unions	2,830,500	—
Republican avoidance of loss as consequence of lack of unionization	—	3,019,000

NOTE: This table is based on probable presidential vote: the 1960 Labor Force figures have been approximated; the turnout rates and the party-vote rates for union members have been averaged from Survey Research Center data . . . the differentials between union member and non-union member have been averaged between the SRC (higher) and the Gallup (lower) data.

he lastly assumed a party-preference differential of only 10 per cent (whereas the conservative estimate used here is only 13 per cent, to compromise the differences between Survey Research Center and Gallup data).

•   •   •

Magnitude and Method of Financial Involvement

The analysis of voter-mobilization by labor unions in the preceding section leads to the conclusion that the *net* gain to Democratic presidential candidates during the 1950's was something under one-eleventh of the total popular vote necessary for election.[35] But voter-mobilization is also the end-purpose of the flow of money into elections; therefore it is appropriate to examine in this section what is known concerning the extent, methods, and impact of labor money in politics.

To begin with, it is extremely difficult to obtain any reliable and comparable data that span more than two elections—as Alexander Heard, the author of the most exhaustive treatment of money in politics, has carefully noted.[36] However, it is possible to examine a variety of alternative data presented by Heard in an attempt to establish the upper limit of the extent of spending in elections by labor unions. A first, and perhaps the best, measure is that of direct expenditure (for goods and services consumed during a campaign) by national-level campaign groups. For 1952, labor money constituted 15 per cent of all direct expenditures in behalf of Democrats, and in 1956 this proportion was 11 per cent.[37] At a second and quite different level, Heard estimates that the *voluntary* political giving by some 17,000,000 unionists in 1956 constituted about $2,000,000 which in turn just about balanced the voluntary contributions in amounts of $500 or more recorded by 742 officials of

---

[35] Based on an assumption of an average of 33,000,000 popular votes to win, derived from the last three presidential elections.
[36] Heard, *op. cit.*, chaps. i and ii especially.
[37] *Ibid.*, p. 20.

the 225 largest business concerns in the nation.[38] Approximately one union member in eight contributed voluntarily during this period, with the average contribution something less than $1.00 and with considerable variation: in highly politicized unions such as the UAW or the ILGWU, both the rate and the average amount of contribution were considerably higher (e.g., one in two members and an average of $2.57 in the latter union). But voluntary contribution is only part of the process, as Heard notes; for dues-money may flow into election campaigns through one or more of a wide variety of activities: donations (e.g., the ILGWU donated an average of $15,500 annually to the ADA in 1953-56); the maintenance of political departments, such as the "political shop-steward" program of the ILGWU; the creation of special "Citizenship Funds" (in the UAW, 5 per cent of the member's dues goes into such a fund maintained by the international and another 5 per cent into a local fund); the development of "education and information" programs, such as the IAM training classes on the relation between legislation and political activity; or undertaking communications and public service activities (e.g., the AFL-CIO sponsors Edward P. Morgan on ABC nationally, while the UAW sponsors the radio-television newscasts of Guy Nunn in the Detroit metropolitan area). In addition, it should be obvious that electoral purposes may be served through union expenditures on: public relations and research; union legal departments; union-executive expense accounts; general administrative costs; and, of course, salaries. All of these account for some hard-to-measure but nonetheless real methods for organized investment in the electoral process by unions. In an effort to provide some estimate of the dollar magnitude of such investment, Heard has taken organized labor's numerical membership as a proportion of the potential electorate—

---

[38] *Ibid.,* pp. 195-96. Heard estimates this to be 0.3 per cent of annual union dues; the significance of such money does not, however, lie solely in its magnitude but in its legal status as well; i.e., opponents of organized labor have sought to restrict the use of union-dues by a variety of legal controls; for example, the Taft-Hartley Act of 1947 sought to prohibit unions from *expenditures* as well as contributions in *nominations* as well as general elections for federal offices.

roughly 17 per cent—and concludes that "labor money in politics from all sources pays *a much smaller share* of the nation's campaign-connected costs than union members constitute of the population of voting age.[39] However, such an estimate may unintentionally conceal the significance of such labor money to the Democratic party. For example, one might arbitrarily take 10 per cent as labor's actual share of the roughly $165,000,000 in cash-and-kind costs for financing all the electoral activities entailed in a presidential election year; but that 10 per cent of the *total* would be highly significant in Democratic party finance for two reasons: very close to 100 per cent of all labor money goes to the Democratic side (see below) *and*, for the period under review, the two-party division of resources and expenditures was roughly 60-40 in favor of the Republicans; therefore the 10 per cent over-all share of labor actually would constitute close to 25 per cent of all Democratic funds. Whether the empirical basis for testing this tentative conclusion will ever be unearthed seems highly problematical; such a project would require even more time, money, and effort than were put forth in the heroic labors of the University of North Carolina (Heard) project. Meanwhile one may infer that the apparent autonomy, decentralization, and disarray of the organizational structure of unions provide national labor leaders with a convenient excuse for saying that they simply do not and cannot know all the facts,[40] and one might equally suppose that some, perhaps many, Democratic (and Republican) candidates also prefer not to know too much about the entire process of money in elections.

When one turns from the *magnitude* of labor's financial involve-

---

[39] *Ibid.*, pp. 196-208, at p. 208; my emphasis. The estimate of others occasionally runs higher than this. See for example Ivan Hinderaker, *Party Politics* (New York: Holt, 1956), p. 585. The evidence is sketchy; but to judge from data assembled from the *Congressional Quarterly* and Heard, it seems likely that longer-term analyses will show that organized labor—unlike most party and non-party groups—is able to sustain its level of operation from one election to the next, i.e., it does not suffer post-presidential atrophy.

[40] See Heard, *op. cit.*, pp. 183-84, on the Gore Committee experience in 1956. Furthermore, as seems true in almost all aspects of the study of American politics, information is most full and accurate at the national level and least at the local level—yet six-sevenths of all electoral expenditures are incurred at the state, district, and local levels.

ment in elections to the *method* of its involvement, three additional aspects of Heards analysis of labor money become relevant. Heard's available evidence on the geography of labor support in 1956 indicated that such support was concentrated within the ten states whose populations include two-thirds of all organized labor.[41] His next analysis, focused on the partisan recipients of funds transferred by labor committees, showed the almost exclusive support of Democrats. In 1952, for example, $833,000 could be traced, and $5,450 had been transmitted to one senatorial and five House Republican candidates (an average of $908 each); the analysis for 1956 of $1,616,000 of national-level and of $430,000 of state-local-level. Labor committee transfers showed a total of $3,925 going to eight House Republican candidates (about $491 each).[42] A final aspect of the method of labor's financial involvement as depicted by Heard is contained within the data of Table II. The major point of interest in the table is the clear indication that labor union leaders desire to, and primarily do, deal directly with Democratic *candidates* (or their personal committees); they deliberately bypass the established Democratic party committees at both national and state-local levels. Heard also indicates the obverse of this, in that there is evidence that union leaders have frequently sought to prevent Democratic party solicitation within and among their local memberships.[43] In the broader context of my analysis, these data on voter-mobilization are further indications of the tendency of interest groups to expend such potential resources as exist within the electoral process and to expend them at such a rate and with such efficiency that the group takes over *all* of the *relevant* functions of the political party.

•   •   •

. . . Does a strongly held and economically based ideology—for business or for labor—lead to efficiency in electoral action? Does a left-oriented *labor* ideology incorporate, ignore, or conflict with the central cultural concept and value of "efficiency" in the first

[41] *Ibid.*, pp. 173-75 and 187-88.
[42] *Ibid.*, recomputed from footnotes to Table 23, p. 185, and text at p. 187.
[43] *Ibid.*, p. 193, n. 58.

TABLE II

TYPES OF RECIPIENTS OF TRANSFERS OF LABOR FUNDS FROM NATIONAL LEVEL AND STATE-LOCAL LEVEL COMMITTEES IN 1952 AND 1956*

Election Year, Type, and Number of Labor Committees Transferring Funds

TYPES OF RECIPIENTS	1952 14 N-L AMOUNT	PER CENT	1956 17 N-L AMOUNT	PER CENT	1956 155 S-L AMOUNT	PER CENT
At national level		26		25		9
Labor and other non-party committees	$119,000		$297,000		$ 34,000	
Democratic party committees	98,000		109,000		3,000	
At state-local level		74		75		91
Labor committees	268,000		236,000		95,000	
Democratic candidates or their committees						
for the Senate	100,000		326,000		43,000	
for the House	80,000		334,000		136,000	
Other (non-party) and miscellaneous	101,000		272,000		27,000	
Democratic party committees	67,000		42,000		24,000	
State-local candidates or their committees	—		—		68,000	

* Simplified and recomputed from data presented in Heard, *op. cit.,* p. 185, Table 23.

place? Furthermore, to what extent is organized labor activity confined to *general* elections? Are the electoral practices of organized labor similar in disbursement and endorsement to those of the party groups and of other non-party political groups? Does organized labor in its electoral action normally aid established incumbents, or do its major efforts go into support of non-incumbent challengers? Lastly, to what extent has political science analysis provided intelligible answers to these questions?

. . .

What precisely have political scientists stated about the electoral impact of organized labor? One text[44] notes that organized labor

[44] Roche and Stedman, *op. cit.,* p. 71.

spoke of Election Day 1946 as "Black Tuesday" because only 73 of 318 House candidates and only 5 of 21 Senate candidates endorsed by labor won—but it is impossible to learn whether these were Democrats or Republicans, incumbents or non-incumbents, or how well labor did relative to, say, the Democratic party itself in that Republican year. One author has taken the analysis of 1946 somewhat further, however, in noting that California Republicans uniformly centered their campaign attack on CIO-supported Democratic candidates; that this attack on "CIO-PAC package" candidates became a campaign theme for Republicans almost everywhere in the nation; and that CIO-PAC endorsement of some congressional candidates proved to be a "kiss of death" under certain circumstances.[45] That is, in a number of constituencies the PAC leaders made only a public announcement of endorsement of the candidate and either did not think it important to, or in fact could not, commit labor to any other campaign activity; as a consequence, the labor endorsement in those constituencies provided an issue to opponents of the candidate and permitted them to activate their members and sympathizers with no offsetting gains for the labor-endorsee. As for 1948, which was critical in many ways, slightly more information and analysis are available. Hugh A. Bone pointed out that after the 1948 election the new Labor's League for Political Education (AFL) claimed 172 "friends" of labor elected and 106 "enemies" retired (i.e., now ex-incumbents). Interestingly the most sophisticated analysis of 1948 is to be found in Truman's book—published eleven years ago.[46] Noting generally that the CIO-PAC had endorsed 215 House candidates in 1948 and that 144 of these were elected, the author breaks down the 144 victories in several ways: first, 64 were of incumbents, 74 involved defeating incumbents, while the remaining 6 were in non-incumbency situations; next, 57 of the labor-

---

[45] Hugh A. Bone, "Political Parties and Pressure Group Politics," in *Annals*, 319 (1958), 73-83; also Bone, *American Politics and the Party System, op. cit.*, pp. 146-49.

[46] David B. Truman, *The Governmental Process* (New York: Knopf, 1951), pp. 315-16, citing his earlier data and analysis in Frederick Mosteller *et al.*, *The Pre-Election Polls of 1948* (New York: Social Science Research Council, 1949).

endorsed incumbents re-elected had voted against the Taft-Hartley Act of 1947 while all 74 of the incumbents defeated had voted for it; and finally, a partial analysis of such factors as the two-party division of the popular vote at the last election and the partisan control of the constituencies leads to the conclusion that "the changes in 1948 were of major importance. Presumably the CIO-PAC efforts had something to do with them."

. . . And there is some evidence that labor, especially in its allocation of funds, may be inefficient in such races. For example, organized labor *reported* expenditures of $180,880, Senator Taft *reported* expenditures of $243,740, and probably more than $2,000-000, was spent in that one 1950 contest.[50] As for 1958, the close reader of the *New York Times* found that "Rumor has it that the national COPE organization has been pouring money—as much as $400,000—and political workers into Arizona to defeat Senator Goldwater. . . ."[51] COPE officials and Arizona labor leaders immediately denied this, of course, indicating that labor's financial involvement would be about the same as the $33,000 expended in Arizona in 1956; but when the battle had ended, labor's reported contributions to McFarland (Goldwater's opponent) interestingly totaled only $3,500.[52] Meanwhile, Goldwater's re-election effectively obscured the fact that two other COPE-endorsed Arizona candidates had been elected with impressive vote-margins.[53] The focus upon one great personalized contest at a time may also result from the facts that organized labor, even the AFL-CIO, has no centralized endorsement machinery and that it is therefore difficult, though hardly impossible as indicated below, to learn what the state, district, and

[50] The labor figure is given in the *New York Times*, November 25, 1950, p. 8, and includes $74,470 reported by the secretary-treasurer for the Ohio CIO-PAC; the Taft figure may be found in *ibid.*, November 17, 1950, p. 30. The over-all estimate is that of the Senate Committee on Rules and Administration, Subcommittee on Privileges and Elections, 82nd Cong., 1st and 2nd sess., *Hearings on Investigation into the 1950 Ohio Senatorial Campaign* (1951 and 1952). The *New York Times*, November 8, 1950, p. 1, characterized Taft's re-election as "the worst labor defeat since 1932" and most readers, political scientists included, probably agreed.

[51] October 15, 1958, p. 1, article by Gladwin Hill.

[52] *Congressional Quarterly Almanac*, 15 (1959), p. 809.

[53] *New York Times*, November 6, 1958, pp. 22.

local political units of labor are doing; and as a general rule in this country, that which it is difficult to learn normally goes unreported and necessarily unanalyzed.

But at least one political scientist has provided interesting clues concerning the behavior of organized labor in endorsements. In a tentative survey of CIO-PAC activity in the Detroit area, Nicholas Masters has generalized that "the PAC attempts to endorse the candidate who most nearly meets the claims of the group and who commands the greatest prestige, but it will endorse the medicocre or weak candidate if he is opposed by a candidate who is closely identified with business groups."[54] Thus there is evidence of the push and pull of ideological stereotypes in electoral behavior. Furthermore, Masters has noted that the Democratic partisanship of the candidate is the primary criterion for PAC endorsement in Wayne County, with liberal position coming next in importance; and—

> The term "liberal" does not puzzle PAC leaders as it does academicians. A candidate may prove his liberalism by allowing the PAC to evaluate his stand on ten or twelve key and current issues with which the CIO is concerned. *The usual method for evaluation of a candidate, however, is to tabulate his recorded votes on such issues. Thus the incumbent has the inside track for endorsement. . . .*[55]

This in turn is evidence—if tentative and subject to further testing—that the influence of organized labor, even in a labor-dominated area, may be inoperative or ineffectual until *after* the candidate has established himself; it may also mean that organized labor operates as a conservative force in the limited sense of freezing out challengers and preventing intraparty conflict; at the minimum Masters' evidence suggests that repeated endorsements of incumbents is the major factor in explaining the high rate of success of the CIO-PAC in the 1946-55 period.[56]

[54] Nicholas A. Masters, "The Politics of Union Endorsement of Candidates in the Detroit Area," *Midwest Journal of Political Science*, 1 (1957), 136-50.
[55] *Ibid.*, p. 149; emphasis added.
[56] *Ibid.*, p. 149, ". . . the PAC endorsement average was 67.5 per cent in primary elections and 91.2 per cent in the general elections for Congressional, state, and county offices."

More information is available concerning the national level of politics and especially concerning the 1960 election. For example, that election is the first in which data both on the Senate campaign committees and on labor endorsements and disbursements are readily available to the political analyst. Using such data, then, Table III compares the Democratic Senate Campaign Committee and the AFL-CIO. Labor made only approximately half as many major-support decisions (defined as allocations of $5,000 or more)[57]

TABLE III

RANK-ORDER COMPARISONS OF MAJOR-SUPPORT DECISIONS
(OF $5,000 OR MORE)
MADE BY THE DSCC AND BY THE AFL-CIO RESPECTIVELY
IN 1960 SENATE ELECTIONS

	DSCC			AFL-CIO	
RANK	NAME	STATE	RANK	NAME	STATE
1	Frear (Delaware)		1	Kefauver (Tennessee)	
2	Anderson (New Mexico)		2	Humphrey (Minnesota)	
3	Bartlett (Alaska)		3	Douglas (Illinois)	
4	Humphrey (Minnesota)		4	McNamara (Michigan)	
5	Whitaker (Wyoming)		5	Neuberger (Oregon)	
6	Neuberger (Oregon)		6	O'Connor (Massachusetts)	
7	Pell (Rhode Island)		7	Pell (Rhode Island)	
8	Metcalf (Montana)		8	Knous (Colorado)	
9	McLaughlin (Idaho)		9	Metcalf (Montana)	
10	McNamara (Michigan)				
11	Burdick (North Dakota)				
12.5	Knous (Colorado)				
12.5	Kerr (Oklahoma)				
14	Randolph (West Virginia)				
15.5	Long (Missouri)				
15.5	McGovern (South Dakota)				
17	Douglas (Illinois)				

SOURCE: *Congressional Quarterly Almanac*, 17 (1961).

[57] The assumption is that a contribution of less than $5,000 is considered to be relatively insignificant by most senatorial candidates. This cut-off is un-

as did the DSCC in 1960; sight inspection of this figure also shows that the order of preference varied considerably between the two groups; and a rank-order correlation coefficient (Kendall's *tau*) of the candidates appearing commonly in both the DSCC and the AFL-CIO lists was only + .143—quite close to full independence—for the particular election.

We may also compare the disbursement practices of the AFL-CIO with those of the political party Senate campaign committees (in Table IV). These data for 1960 show several interesting behavioral differences. First, as many political scientists have long suspected, the DSCC in 1960—at least—operated to the distinct advantage of incumbent members of The Club—by a mean difference in excess of $2,400. The Republican National Campaign Committee, secondly, contested the greatest number of races at the level of major-support and, also presumably reflecting the mathematical decline of Republicans in the Senate since 1952, the party allocation policy actually worked to the slight advantage of their non-incumbent candidates. In between these two, the AFL-CIO concentrated its activity— disbursing a much higher mean contribution to a much reduced total number of candidates. Furthermore, for an established electoral interest group such as organized labor, 1960 must be regarded as a year of consolidationist effort. That is, the AFL-CIO devoted its major efforts to helping re-elect five preferred incumbents,[58] disbursing to them almost three times the mean amount contributed to non-incumbent Democratic candidates.

The question of electoral efficiency (and power) can be dealt with least satisfactorily here. At best, until comparable data for a sequence of elections become available, I can only illustrate the

realistically low for states like New York and probably too high for states like Vermont or New Hampshire; presumably electoral costs bear some observable relation to numbers of constituents. Thus when political scientists get about their proper business, the analyst will finally be able to make class discriminations of senatorial constituencies similar to those the Senate itself makes with regard to allocation of office expenses.

See George B. Galloway, *The Legislative Process in Congress* (New York: Crowell, 1953, pp. 391-94.

[58] Because of the recent history of the Oregon constituency and the Neuberger-Lusk-Neuberger sequence during 1960, I have classified the 1960 Oregon contest as the re-election of a Democratic incumbent.

TABLE IV

MAJOR-SUPPORT DECISIONS (OF $5,000 OR MORE) OF
SENATE-ORIENTED PARTY AND LABOR POLITICAL GROUPS
IN 1960 ELECTIONS—ANALYZED BY INCUMBENCY AND
NON-INCUMBENCY SITUATIONS

| | All Major Support | | Incumbent Support | | Non-Incumbent Support | |
POLITICAL GROUP	MEAN AMOUNT	NO. OF RACES	MEAN AMOUNT	NO. OF RACES	MEAN AMOUNT	NO. OF RACES
DSCC	$ 9,880	17	$10,876	10	$8,457	7
AFL-CIO	14,511	9	20,980	5	6,425	4
RNCC	8,327	22	8,119	10	8,500	12

SOURCE: *Congressional Quarterly Almanac,* 17 (1961).

types of assumptions that seem immediately relevant to this question. The crudest measure of efficiency, of course, is whether the endorsed-supported candidates of the electoral interest group in fact win their elections. By one form of this measure—examining the proportion of all disbursements (not just major-supported allocations) according to the final division of the two-party total vote in the constituency—Table V indicates that the AFL-CIO was more efficient than either party campaign committee, for it allocated 81 per cent of all 1960 disbursements to winning candidates whereas its closer competitor (the DSCC) could claim only 61 per cent here. But the data previously given, regarding incumbencies, suggest that this very primitive assumption on which Table V is based is appropriate only where one has a very limited number of cases with which to deal. When the number of cases has increased significantly, the analyst would do well to invoke a second assumption here, already implied by the construction of Table V, that devoting group efforts to "close" contests is more efficient—in terms of the psychology of indebtedness—than either winning too easily (presumably by backing only incumbents) or losing too badly. As the number of cases becomes truly adequate, a third and more important assumption is necessary: that it is more efficient to help a non-incumbent challenger defeat an incumbent than it is merely to aid an already-incumbent candidate win re-election. Furthermore, in this context, efficiency is a function of *net* impact of the distribution of legislative seats (i.e., victories minus losses) rather than of *gross* (victorious) behavior alone. But such more sophisticated and, it is believed, realistic analysis clearly requires detailed information on individual constituencies not now available in any numbers.[59]

TABLE V

RELATIVE EFFICIENCY OF SENATE-ORIENTED PARTY AND
LABOR GROUPS IN 1960 ELECTIONS—MEASURED IN TERMS
OF PROPORTION OF DISBURSEMENTS TO "CLOSE" AND
"NOT CLOSE" RACES

SENATE RACES: DIVISION OF TWO-PARTY TOTAL VOTE	Party and Labor Political Groups		
	DSCC	AFL-CIO	RNCC
"Not close" — more than 55 per cent	39	52	23
"Close" — 50+ through 54 per cent	22	29	27
"Close" — 46 through 50 per cent	23	8	25
"Not close" — less than 46 per cent	16	11	25
Total	101*	100	100

* Errors due to rounding.
SOURCE: *Congressional Quarterly Almanac,* 17 (1961).

To conclude this section, then, one must presently fall back upon fragmentary and discontinuous *aggregate* data such as have been brought together in Table IV. This table provides a framework for summary analysis of four aspects of the electoral activity of organized labor. A first cluster is indicated in Table VI: for example, the magnitude of organized labor's electoral involvement in House races has significantly diminished in the past fifteen years; and I infer from this that labor strategists have acquired experience in limiting labor money to the lesser number of constituencies in which it can make a difference. . . . As for the Senate, analysis of the geography

[59] I have been able to obtain sufficient data to permit invoking these assumptions in the case of the National Committee for an Effective Congress. The analysis of the efficiency of that electoral interest group is presented in my *Ideology and Electoral Action,* forthcoming in 1964.

of endorsements indicates that labor now participates in virtually the full 100 per cent of contested general elections, reflecting the greater advantage of statewide constituencies for labor's electoral resources. And, lastly, labor's electoral efficiency—measured solely by percentage of victories—has closely paralleled the ebb and flow of Democratic party fortunes in the past fifteen years.

TABLE VI

TYPE, NUMBER, AND FREQUENCY OF VICTORY
OF ORGANIZED LABOR ENDORSEMENTS
IN SELECTED CONGRESSIONAL GENERAL ELECTIONS

YEAR	House of Representatives			Senate		
	CON-TESTS	VIC-TORIES	PER CENT	CON-TESTS	VIC-TORIES	PER CENT
1946 (CIO-PAC)	318	73	23	21	5	24
1948 (CIO-PAC)	215	144	67	—	—	—
1954 (CIO-PAC)	256	126	49	26	16	61
(AFL-LLPE)	—	154	—	30	18	60
1956 (AFL-CIO)	288	159	55	29	12	41
1958 (AFL-CIO)	199	—	—	34	24	71
1960 (AFL-CIO)	193	106	55	21	12	57

NOTE: This table has been pieced together from the sources previously cited in this section plus *Congressional Quarterly Almanac,* 15 (1959), and 17 (1961).

A related aspect, not revealed by Table VI, is the fact that labor money is almost wholly concentrated within the Democratic party, probably more so recently than Heard's earlier figures indicated. For example, of 199 money-endorsements for House seats in 1958, only 6 were of Republican candidates. In 1958 senatorial races, only 2 of 34 candidates supported by labor were Republicans; one of these (Knight of California) received less than one-twenty-fourth the sum contributed to his Democratic opponent, while the other (North Dakota's Langer) was noted as a domestic Democrat. In 1960's Senate races, 3 of 21 labor-endorsed candidates were Republicans; 2 of these received relatively token contributions of $500 each (incumbent Cooper of Kentucky and successful challenger Boggs of Maryland) while in the third contest, in New Jersey, incumbent Case received $2,500 to the $1,000 given to his Democratic opponent.

The influence of incumbency may be treated as a third aspect of analysis, in that endorsements of incumbents seem to account for a greater proportion of labor victories in the House than in the Senate. The data are not extensive, but they indicate following: 10 of the 24 Senate victories in 1958 and 7 of the 12 in 1960 involved support of a successful incumbent, while in the case of the House, 95 of the 106 victories claimed in 1960 were of re-elected incumbents.

A final point may be gleaned from the available data, namely the fact that labor-money activity is *not* confined, as the limited data that Heard had available seemed to indicate, to those seventeen states in which three-quarters of all unionists reside. In 1960, for example, a full half of labor's major financial efforts for the Senate fell outside those seventeen states; despite the artificialities of federalism, money is a highly mobile political resource, and the recent extension of this activity by both business and labor would seem both a cause and a reflection of the nationalization of electoral politics in America.

Between the Depression and the end of World War II, business unionism essentially achieved its three major goals of union recognition, shorter hours and higher wages, and control of the job market. The Employment Act of 1946 should be viewed as symbolic of the transition from business unionism to political unionism—in the sense that unions have been able to survive as a social movement in America by the development of a logical succession of goals. Since 1946, labor's goals have been employment, security, and peace.[60] But business unionism could not directly contribute to the achievement of such goals. Each of these new goals was significantly affected by what the national government would or would not do. Therefore business unionism has now been replaced by a political unionism

[60] See the anticipation of this change from business to political unionism in Eli Ginzberg, *The Labor Leader* (New York: Macmillan, 1948), pp. 173-87.

based upon the realistic and realizable premise that political action is necessary to control the government that in such a major way conditions achievement of the newer and broader goals of organized labor.

. . .

The Organized Labor Bureaucracy as a Base of Support for the Democratic Party*

NICHOLAS A. MASTERS

Professor Nicholas Masters examines various electoral activities by organized labor in behalf of the Democratic party. He says that the Democratic party cannot automatically expect the support of labor leaders at each election. Labor unions are not organized for political leadership and their electoral participation varies. This, coupled with declining memberships and public distrust, places limitations on labor's political role.

With the announcement of official top level labor support for the reelection of Franklin D. Roosevelt in 1936, the Gomperian dictum of neutrality in politics received a mortal blow. Labor's neutrality, which had long been an equivocal tradition anyway, was laid to rest in 1955, with the merger of the politically aggressive Congress of Industrial Organizations (CIO) with the less politically oriented American Federation of Labor (AFL). These and other much-publicized events, such as organized labor's role in the 1948 Truman victory and the 1958 congressional elections, have contributed to a widely-held popular belief that labor represents a monolithic force on the American

* Nicholas A. Masters, "The Organized Labor Bureaucracy as a Base of Support for the Democratic Party," *Law and Contemporary Problems*, 27 (Spring 1962), 252-65, published by the Duke University School of Law, Durham, North Carolina. Copyright 1962 by Duke University. Reprinted with permission from a symposium, *The Electoral Process, Part I.*

political scene, capable of placing a massive vote at the doorstep of the Democratic Party. Yet recent scholarly studies demonstrate that, despite increasing political involvements of union leaders, particularly in campaigns, there are a substantial number of union members who vote contrary to the public endorsements of their leadership; who note with disapproval, as detracting from the vital business of contract and grievance negotiation, any display of political activity by union leaders; or who remain politically apathetic, leadership exhortation to the contrary notwithstanding. Moreover, within the union movement, a substantial number of union leaders still attempt to stay out of partisan election campaigns, and refuse to allow their unions to become closely identified with any political party or its candidates.

The intention of this paper is to discuss, first, the generalization that union organizations and their members occupy varying positions on a continuum of political opinion and activity, and that as a result the AFL-CIO cannot *guarantee* a substantial bloc of votes for candidates in national campaigns. In the light of previous studies, this point does not merit detailed documentation and analysis. And second, the major focus of this discussion is on an analysis of organized labor, particularly the AFL-CIO nationally, as a base of support for Democratic candidates for presidential and congressional offices. Such analysis involves two questions: Why is labor sought as a base of support? What are the effects, positive and negative, of such support?

I. *Diversity in Labor Support*

While union leaders have over the years fought for the right to strike, to organize, to bargain with employers, and to engage in the collective promotion of their economic and social welfare by means of the ballot-box and lobbying, they seldom agree on candidates, parties, or issues. It is not a novel proposition to point out that "the American labor movement is a highly complex social phenomenon with myriads of dissimilar features at lower levels. These diversities are multiplied in the alliances and organizational arrangements improvised for political purposes within organized labor and between organized labor and other political groups."[1] For example, the bulk of the political activity carried on by the AFL-CIO in national campaigns is supported extensively by only a few unions, namely, the United Automobile Workers of America (UAW), the United Steelworkers of America (USW), the International Ladies Garment Workers Union (ILGWU), and the International Association of Machinists (IAM). And even within this group, there are some variations. The UAW in Michigan is openly partisan and for all intents and purposes is an integral part of the Democratic Party in that state. In New York State the ILGWU's political arm is the Liberal Party, which occasionally nominates it own candidates, but usually gives its support to the Democrats.[2] A more moderate approach is taken by the USW which, under President David Mac-Donald's leadership, has stopped short of *open* affiliation with the Democratic Party and extensive participation within the Party's internal framework.

Furthermore, a substantial part of the union movement has been conservatively oriented politically. Conservativism among unions might be defined in the following manner: (1) apathy toward or avoidance of national election activity; (2) an overwhelming concern with the political and economic problems of their own union, with little or no interest in the problems of other unions or other segments of society; (3) tight control from the top, with few avenues open for membership participation in policy decisions. Dominated by the late William Hutcheson, a Republican, the United Brotherhood of Carpenters and Joiners of America has a reputation for headquarters control and political conservatism and disinterest. Building and other skilled trade unions have manifestly turned their energies toward control of jobs rather than concern with political issues, and have avoided direct participation in election campaigns. This is not to suggest that conservative unions are politically apathetic and never press for legislation or participate in the determination of state and

[1] Alexander Heard, *The Costs of Democracy* 176 (1960).
[2] Seidler, "The Socialist Party and American Unionism," 5 *Midwest J. Pol. Sci.* 207, 228 (1961).

local governmental decisions. On the whole, however, this type of union deliberately and carefully avoids *partisan* commitments. In brief, organized labor is not unified politically and it is very unlikely that it will be in the foreseeable future. Strictly speaking, organized labor is not, in terms of its organization and leadership, a unified base of support for any candidate or party.

The growing body of union vote analysis supports the point made earlier that the union membership, while characteristically voting for Democratic candidates, is by no means in the pocket of its leadership or the Democratic Party. In the 1956 presidential election, for example, the Survey Research Center found, by dividing their sample of union members according to their one-time AFL or CIO affiliation, that AFL respondents voted fifty-one per cent Democratic, whereas sixty per cent of the CIO members favored the Democrats.[3] E. E. Schattschneider, in his most recent work, points out that although the AFL-CIO membership totals 16,000,000, generous estimates put its normal voter-turnout at about half this figure. The Republican Party's share is estimated at 2,400,000 of the 8,000,000 votes cast, leaving the Democrats with approximately 5,600,000.[4] In brief, the total Democratic vote supplied by organized labor may be only about one-third of the total membership figure. Supporting the implication of Schattschneider's rough calculations are the findings from surveys ordered by George Meany, following the 1952 and 1956 presidential elections. The surveys of union voting conducted in Illinois and New Jersey revealed that the turnout of eligible voters among unionists was below the national average of non-union voters. The AFL-CIO president was, thus, induced to call for a vigorous union-sponsored get-out-the-vote drive for 1960. Another conclusion coming out of the Meany surveys was that while union men had, on the whole, supported Stevenson, their wives had voted for Eisenhower.

Some unions' members, however, are much more solid in terms of voting behavior; and because they back their leadership, these unions become significant bases of support for candidates running

[3] Angus Campbell et al., *The American Voter* 312 (1960).
[4] E. E. Schattschneider, *The Semi-Sovereign People* 50 (1960).

for national or congressional offices in the areas of their membership concentration. The UAW membership in Michigan, for example, strongly supports the Democratic Party, although its membership elsewhere has not been recognized as a unified, potent political force. Kornhauser, Sheppard, and Mayer, and later Sheppard and Masters, found that a majority of union members in the Detroit area consistently support Democratic candidates in state and national elections, and generally approve of and support the UAW's extensive political commitments. Nevertheless, both studies demonstrated that fifteen to twenty per cent of the membership are opposed to the union's political policies and about twenty-five per cent are either apathetic or uncommitted though normally inclined to vote Democratic.[5]

With such disunity in labor's ranks, why all the fuss about labor endorsements? The data supplied by scholarly studies and academic discussions seem to imply that there is little operative political necessity for any elaborate efforts to gain organized labor support except in those areas, such as Detroit, where unionists constitute the bulk of the population and are mobilized through union political organizations. A prevalent belief among some political scientists is that failure to gain organized labor support is not a major disadvantage to a Democratic candidate in the majority of cases, and that the immediate political power of labor at the polls is fairly limited. Unfortunately, the political role of the labor bureaucracy in presidential and congressional elections has not been properly appraised. Although a great deal has been learned about the political variations within the labor movement and the voting behavior of unionists from recent studies, we have neglected to examine why organized labor is sought and what its effects are as a base of support for the Democratic Party in national campaigns. The remainder of this paper is devoted to such an examination.

[5] Arthur Kornhauser, Harold L. Sheppard & Albert J. Mayer, *When Labor Votes: A Study of Auto Workers* (1956); Sheppard & Masters, "The Political Attitudes and Preferences of Union Members: The Case of the Detroit Auto Workers," 53 *Am. Pol. Sci. Rev.* 437 (1959).

II. *Advantages of Labor Support*

A. VOTES

The closeness of the 1960 presidential election has again brought home the point to politicians that any strategem that will affect even the slightest sprinkling of votes may be extremely critical to the final result. The same election also showed the tremendous influence of the large urban areas on electoral vote majorities. In view of the concentration of the most politically active and vigorous unions' membership—unions which support the Democratic Party—in the large urban areas within states having the largest electoral votes, AFL-CIO support has come to be regarded as essential for the effect it may have on perhaps only a small portion of the total union membership in these areas. That is, endorsement and active leadership support may persuade a few more unionists and members of their families to vote for endorsed candidates, or simply to vote. Although political scientists have not yet developed precise methods for measuring the effect of open support and related activity, Campbell *et al.* have hypothesized that when individual members of a group begin to get a clearer perception of the proximity of the group and the world of politics—and presumably aggressive political action programs are more likely to generate clearer perceptions—the susceptibility to group influence in political affairs increases.[6] True, politicians may not use these terms or they may not be able to articulate the point at all, but most of them are aware of the fact that the elaborate political activities of unions have had an impact on the voting decisions of *some* members. Consequently, candidates for the Presidency and for Congress in areas of labor concentration want identification with, and the support of, both unions in the area and the AFL-CIO nationally. Support is desired not because union political actionists control a large bloc of votes that they can swing one way or another—they have never had this kind of control—but rather because they may be able to affect the *size of the urban majorities* for the Democratic Party. This fact alone, despite the political variations within the labor movement, gives the AFL-CIO nationally

[6] Campbell et al., *op. cit. supra* note 3, at 311.

a much greater voice in the Democratic Party and governmental affairs.

In politics, power relationships are determined and affected by the resources at the disposal of the participants. An important element of power is control over votes. The bureaucracy of organized labor realizes that this resource, this element of its power, is not an entirely flexible one, that it can be used only in a restricted manner. Labor's political strength lies in cities like Detroit, Chicago, Pittsburgh, New York, Los Angeles, and St. Louis, that produce the large majorities for the Democrats in presidential and state-wide election contests. This means that the AFL-CIO must remain Democratic in order to maintain a strong and viable bargaining position in politics. It is extremely doubtful that the AFL-CIO could directly influence the size of the Republican minorities in these areas, and the idea that an independent third party can be formed in the event of dissatisfaction with the Democrats is ridiculous. The present structure of the labor constituency is a relatively recent development which, in part, may account for organized labor's earlier caution in political affairs and its refusal to identify with either party. In the local arena or in some cities elements of organized labor have long had a strong voice and have participated in elections, but labor's influence nationally did not come until it had the resources of power, namely, votes and money. In the past, particularly before the emergence of the large industrial unions, union membership was not *concentrated* in the cities, and the cities were not as Democratic as they are today. The United Mine Workers Union (UMW) twenty years ago, for example, despite considerable political activity, had little influence on national elections, primarily because its members were not so strategically located as are the members of the industrial unions today. It should be noted also that the conservative unions are the ones whose memberships are sprinkled throughout the nation rather than concentrated in key political areas. Thus, in a desire to attain more influence in government, the AFL-CIO has adopted the political positions of its industrial-CIO type unions rather than those followed by the older craft-AFL type. AFL-CIO leaders have turned to national election activity in addition to lobbying because they know their economic power can be severely curtailed by political actions (Taft-Hartley, Landrum-Griffin, etc.). Bart Cochran puts it this way:[7] ". . . fifteen years of pressure politics have failed to alter the contour of American politics. What is even worse they have been insufficient for labor to hold its own." Labor's influence over votes presumably prevents incumbents from using their power indiscriminately against labor, or guarantees that incumbents will be favorably disposed toward labor's goals. This being the source of its political bargaining power, the AFL-CIO's alliance with the Democratic Party is firm, although not always openly espoused.

In addition to the influence labor leaders may have on the size of urban majorities, organized labor has gained representation at Democratic national conventions. Approximately one-eighth of the delegates to the 1960 Democratic National Convention where unionists. It comes as no surprise that the majority of the union delegates were from the big industrial states, although there were a few from southern and western states. Organized labor, obviously, did not control the convention, but its delegates, coupled with the votes of delegates not directly involved in the labor movement but committed to its objectives, gave labor a strong voice in the choice of candidates, and an even stronger voice in the formulation of platform provisions. The following data illustrate the delegate strength of unions from some of the large industrial states:

Michigan—102 delegates, 50 alternates; 34 union officials
and 7 industrial workers.
Minnesota—62 delegates; 10 union.
California—162 delegates; 16 union.

On the Republican side, only ten delegates to the Party's national convention were unionists.

B. MONEY

Organized labor has been able to extend its influence outside the areas of labor concentration by offering candidates who are pro-

[7] Cochran, "American Labor in Midpassage," in Bart Cochran (Ed.), *American Labor in Midpassage* 1, 42 (1959).

labor a scarce and essential commodity—namely, money. Alexander Heard points out that:[8]

> . . . the two million dollars or so of free funds that 17 million union members gave in 1956 about equalled the reported voluntary contributions of $500 and over made by 742 officials of the nation's 225 largest business concerns.

(The two-million figure is equal to approximately only three-tenths of one per cent of annual union dues.) Candidates for Congress in predominantly rural and non-industrial areas, *e.g.*, Montana and Idaho, where labor identification does not mean the kiss of death, but where local labor unions are not large enough to be affluent, seek labor endorsements "from the East" in order to obtain AFL-CIO money. In such instances, both labor and the candidate may have to play down labor support somewhat because the popular image of organized labor is not entirely favorable, and some of the members of a candidate's own party may resent "outside" influence. Of course, the source of money in campaigns is seldom kept quiet, at least for very long, and opposing candidates have not hesitated to use the labor domination theme. The influx of labor money has resulted in situations today where conservative forces are using a traditionally liberal symbol. Conservatives, rather than liberals, since they are now able to finance their own political activities almost entirely out of local and state sources, are the ones who charge the opposition with "domination of the monied interests from the East."

How extensively national labor money is brought into the various states during a campaign can be noted from data on the 1956 presidential election. In that year, national labor money "went to back Democratic senatorial candidates in 22 of the 33 states from which senators were elected, the remaining 11 consisting of seven Southern and two Northern one-party states plus Arizona and Kansas." In the same election "one or more Democratic candidates for the House of Representatives received national labor gifts in every state but six, all of the latter being one-party states, except New Mexico."[9]

That contributions from *national labor* are more crucial than

[8] Heard, *op. cit. supra* note 1, at 196.
[9] *Id.* at 187.

efforts of local unions in the financing of certain campaigns can be inferred from the fact that in 1956 of $1,024,258 total labor donations to candidates for federal office or to their campaign committees, $831,700 came from seventeen national labor groups, with only $192,558 coming from 155 state and local labor groups.

Heard breaks the figures down further in tabular form, showing that of the money coming from national labor organizations, by far the largest single amounts were spent on behalf of specific candidates for the House and Senate—amounts of $335,155 and $326,045 respectively. In addition, $109,000 was donated to political committees on the national level and $61,500 was given to political committees on the local level. The bulk of the money from local and state labor groups ($138,893) was spent to aid specific candidates for the House of Representatives. Of the remainder of local labor money, $42,863 was spent to aid specific senatorial candidates, $7,678 went to local political committees, and $3,124 was donated to national political committees.[10]

Except for $3,925, which was split among eight Republican candidates for the House of Representatives, all labor money went to Democratic candidates. And, for the years 1952 and 1956 about "one-seventh of the direct expenses of national-level pro-Democratic committees were met with labor money."[11]

C. ORGANIZATION

Party professionals seemingly complain more about the lack of party organization and money than anything else. The AFL-CIO has been able to provide for the Democratic Party one thing business interests have been unable to supply for the Republicans—namely, organization. The most fundamental point to emphasize is the sheer muscle union workers can provide in a campaign. It is easy to say organized labor provides workers, but it takes almost direct involvement to appreciate what this means. "Getting out the vote" involves climbing stairs, driving through heavy traffic, listening to crying babies, pounding the pavements from one block to the next, and performing a multitude of unglamorous tasks which most middle-

[10] *Id.* at 186.
[11] *Id.* at 188 n. 45.

class suburbanite Democrats or ADA-type Liberals will not perform or are physically unable to perform. In the 1960 election, the AFL-CIO launched the biggest effort in its history. An account of some of the steps it took in this election serves to illustrate what organized labor offers as a base of support for the Democratic Party.

1. Registration Drives

Based on the carefully documented assumption that more people are Democrats than Republicans, the Committee on Political Education (COPE), the political arm of the AFL-CIO, assisted by a special committee set up to handle fourteen key states, embarked on an all-out registration drive in each of the fifty states early in 1960. The effort, financed from donations from each AFL-CIO union at the rate of five cents per member, with any deficits to be made up from the general treasury, yielded impressive results. In St. Louis, 407 unionists registered 85,077 new voters in one day. In Allegheny County (Pittsburgh), Pennsylvania, 43,490 new Democrats were registered as compared with 29,724 new Republicans. In cooperation with other groups, labor registered 100,000 new voters in Spanish-speaking sections of California. In addition to manpower, COPE furnished money to help pay for office rent, radio and TV spot announcements, gasoline, baby-sitting, loudspeakers, floats in parades, and other items.

2. Distribution of Literature

COPE published and paid for ten million leaflets on the voting records of congressmen which reported their "right" and "wrong" positions according to AFL-CIO standards with respect to ten issues. In addition, five million leaflets were distributed that revealed Senator Kennedy voting "right" 91.6 per cent of the time as compared with Vice-President Nixon's 76.6 per cent "wrong" voting record on key labor issues.

3. Get Out the Vote

Employing a variety of tactics ranging from transportation to baby-sitting for voting mothers, large crews of union workers, some of them paid from union funds, attempted to get unionists and members of their families to the polls. COPE, for example, in Senator Kefauver's successful battle for Tennessee's Democratic senatorial nomination, made 60,000 telephone calls, mailed 300,000 copies of Kefauver's campaign literature, distributed 160,000 leaflets, and set up a central file containing the names and addresses of 65,000 unionists in the state.

Beyond its organizational efforts in an election year, the AFL-CIO, along with a number of its international unions, conducts political education programs, informs members about the voting records of incumbents, registers voters, and so on.

D. THE LIBERAL SANCTION

Endorsement and support from organized labor, or some segments thereof, frequently help a candidate to rally support from other self-designated liberal groups. Organizations, such as the Americans for Democratic Action, the National Association for the Advancement of Colored People, the American Civil Liberties Union, and their thousands of local chapters or units, usually will not back a candidate whose acceptability to organized labor is highly questionable. Moreover, the National Committee for an Effective Congress seldom supports a candidate with an anti-labor background.

The importance of the liberal sanction is illustrated by the pre-convention struggle among the Democrats prior to the 1960 election. The discussion that follows, however, rests primarily on newspaper accounts, which, although perhaps generally reliable, certainly do not provide a detailed account of exactly what happened. Preliminary discussions of the desirability of union neutrality in the 1960 presidential election ended with the realization that in the impending presidential contest, labor neutrality would increase the chances of a Republican President. In fact, it was soon realized by some union leaders that even though no formal action could be taken nationally before the Democratic nomination, organized labor had to get into the pre-convention fight to insure the nomination of a liberal candidate. Early in that year, Democrats Kennedy, Symington, and Humphrey were busy lining up labor endorsements not only because labor could affect votes both at the convention and in the election, but also because labor support helped to pave the avenues toward other liberal endorsements and acceptability. But failure to attract organized labor as a base of support significantly damaged Lyndon Johnson's bid for the Democratic presidential nomination.

For a number of reasons, Johnson was almost totally unacceptable to organized labor, and even after he received the vice-presidential nomination many labor leaders remained decidedly cool. Unacceptability to organized labor made it difficult for Johnson to gain support from other liberal groups, and without it he was virtually cut off from the large body of delegates representing the Northeastern industrialized areas. Party professionals in these areas, who perhaps may have been sympathetic toward Johnson, simply would not risk the alienation of organized labor. Moreover, leaders within the union bureaucracy who might have felt that Johnson had done a tremendous job as majority leader in the Senate during the Eisenhower years still found it impossible to support him. To support Johnson would require a change of policies; "it would make us seem inconsistent," one AFL lobbyist said. The extent of organized labor's opposition to Johnson was aptly expressed by *The Economist*:[12] "It is doubtful whether the unions could swallow the gnat of Senator Johnson's nomination, even if this refusal subsequently obliged them to digest the camel of Mr. Nixon's Presidency." Johnson was distrusted by labor primarily because he was trusted by Southern Democrats. It was felt, particularly by the UAW in Michigan, that Johnson, despite his New Deal background, had too many commitments to southern legislators and the oil interests of his native state of Texas to use the power of the Presidency to protect and promote the interests of labor. There is little doubt that labor support might have gained Johnson the nomination. Support is a significant input factor in campaigns which functions so that the acts and statements of the endorsee will be accepted and understood by the public. Such support serves to prevent distrust or lack of

[12] *The Economist,* April 9, 1960, p. 151.

confidence in the candidate by those sympathetic to or appreciative of a group's views, and who judge a candidate as to whether he can speak authoritatively in approval of programs advocated by a particular group. Johnson, despite his record, could not speak authoritatively in support of labor goals before liberal groups committed to labor's programs.

It is not intended to imply, however, that organized labor support guarantees that other groups will be similarly inclined. A candidate for the presidential nomination with labor support simply has a better chance than others. And, of course, labor itself is strongly influenced by the acceptability of a candidate to other groups, liberal and conservative alike. In the 1960 pre-convention period, for example, the sentimental favorite of organized labor was Senator Hubert Humphrey. But Humphrey could not convince labor and other liberal groups that he was a winner, and principles alone were not a sufficient ground for support. A long, hard look at the results of the Wisconsin and West Virginia primaries indicated to labor leaders that support for Humphrey would be futile. Today, labor recognizes that its support inevitably involves burdens and obligations that may cause other segments of society to react adversely, or with total disapproval. Thus, an effort is made to generalize its support, endorsing candidates who have broad, across the board approval, and recognizing that they must appeal to other groups. Labor leaders felt that the Humphrey appeal in an election would be confined to what may be loosely termed the organized labor-northern liberal bloc, a combination not powerful enough to capture the nation.

A Symington candidacy, on the other hand, was considered by many labor leaders to be desirable because he had avoided being labeled an extremist, and his background made him acceptable to management groups. Symington's efforts certainly did not ignore labor. Early in the pre-convention campaign, Symington received the endorsements of James Carey, President of the International Union of Electrical, Radio and Machine Workers, and George M. Harrison, President of the Brotherhood of Railway Clerks. Unquestionably these endorsements made Symington's bid for the nomination more acceptable to other liberal groups, as indicated by labor's desire later for him to receive the vice-presidential nomination; but they did not result in widespread support. "Models for industry" was the slogan attached by Carey and Harrison to contracts negotiated by Symington while president of Emerson Electric.

But the Kennedy bandwagon rolled on, not to be upset by a few endorsements for other candidates from within the labor movement. In fact, significant forces within organized labor, not only assessing the potentialities of those who might be acceptable to labor ideologically, but also looking for a sure winner, attached themselves to Kennedy, even though his equivocal stand on McCarthyism and his failure to fight for civil rights legislation dampened their enthusiasm. The UAW, USW, and the Textile Workers Union of America endorsed Kennedy early, and devoted their pre-convention efforts to insuring his nomination.

In Michigan, strong UAW backing was instrumental in convincing party professionals and leaders of liberal groups that Kennedy should receive the state's delegate votes at the convention. Leaders of Negro groups, in particular, who were at first very cool toward Kennedy, were persuaded by union officials to support his candidacy. In effect, these unions and other groups were playing the percentages, fearful of being left out should the Kennedy forces win. With this much pre-convention support, particularly from two of the largest and most politically active unions within AFL-CIO, it was a foregone conclusion that AFL-CIO would give its endorsement in the post-convention meeting of its general board. A few unions still refused to go along (the United Brotherhood of Capenters and Joiners, the International Association of Machinists, and, of course, the International Brotherhood of Teamsters, who are outside the AFL-CIO organization); but the base of support was there.

E. PROPAGANDA ADVANTAGE

A significant part of the success of any candidate is to gain and hold the attention of the attentive public, to make sure that informed people are aware of his candidacy and his position on the various issues in the campaign. The difficulty involved in becoming known is not commonly appreciated. Money is a crucial variable and labor supplies some of the funds necessary for purchasing TV time, radio programs or announcements, and newspaper advertisements. Articles about candidates and their backgrounds in labor publications—and there are hundreds of them—which reach and are read by intermediate level union leaders help to provide a flow of information to the rank and file membership.[13] Invitations to candidates to speak before union meetings, furnishing them with captive audiences, also contribute to the significance of labor as a base of support for candidates for public office. Perhaps of greatest significance, however, is that a candidate can cut into the network of interrelationships among community elites through labor leaders. AFL-CIO leaders, through overlapping memberships, help to do this for presidential candidates. Labor leaders within particular internationals, or who are part of the state and local AFL-CIO bureaucracy, help candidates for other offices. Today labor leaders participate extensively in a variety of civic, fraternal, and political groups in their communities, and they are included in all types of academic, governmental, and business conferences where they interact with the leaders of other groups.[14]

One of the most significant aspects of labor's new status is the silent revolution which has taken place during the last decade [1940-1950] with respect to union participation in local community services. . . . On the Community Chest staffs of most of the cities there are now one or more union persons employed fulltime, acting as liaison between the social agencies and the unions helping on the fund-raising committees and the planning of the programs. Throughout the country there are thousands of union members serving on the local boards of the various agencies. . . . Union participation in these local activities is put into effect through the AFL Central Labor organizations and the CIO Industrial Union Councils, and has become one of the major functions of these central federations.

[13] "The various labor organizations are regularly publishing some 600 papers and journals. . . . [I]t can be assumed that one or more labor papers are now being received regularly in almost 15 of the 43 million households throughout the country." Florence Petersen, *American Labor Unions* 125 (1952).
[14] *Id.* at 132-33.

Labor leaders, acting in these arenas where their opinions are respected, can and do advocate candidates for office.

III. *Limitations of Labor Support*

A. "EXCESSIVE" LIBERALISM

In assessing labor as a base of support it is necessary to look into its limitations. The political education programs initiated and conducted by the various political arms of the labor movement have borne fruit, *but* the fruit is often unsophisticated and the efforts have frequently promoted a rigid, closed-minded adherence to pat liberal solutions for complex issues. Almost necessarily the programs have stressed slogans and been superficial; and the propaganda has insisted on what many regard as an uncompromising liberal, pro-labor commitment. This commitment has frequently made it difficult for Democratic candidates to maintain full labor support and at the same time adjust their positions to what they think or believe are existing political realities. Intermediate and lower-level union leaders have in a great many cases shown a reluctance to support, or have refused to support vigorously, candidates who do not buy in toto *the* "Labor" position on economic and social issues. In the eyes of some veteran observers, "the screaming liberal line" found in the political education programs has made it difficult for labor's top echelon, whenever they desire to take a more practical position, to sell their members on candidates who do not meet all the issues head-on. Moreover, the tough ideological line in some instances has even forced the leadership to narrow its perspective in order to keep faith with the local and intermediate level of the union bureaucracy.[15]

Rigid adherence to the anachronisms of the New Deal ideology has often left significant elements within the labor bureaucracy with no place to go in campaigns and has, in some cases, severely handicapped its efforts to promote the passage of legislation it favors. On the whole, labor, especially the national headquarters of the AFL-

---

[15] The material presented here is based on close observation of and participation in labor's political activities in both Detroit and, to a lesser extent, St. Louis. Also the points are based on numerous discussions with AFL-CIO lobbyists in Washington.

CIO, is moving away from dogmatism and is attempting to offer more generalized support, but seemingly at a less accelerated pace than some other liberal groups. Kennedy's candidacy, for example, raised *serious* doubts in the eyes of those union leaders who supported him most strongly, specifically because of his record on the two issues mentioned previously, and more generally because he demonstrated few ideological commitments.

B. DECLINE OF THE INDUSTRIAL UNIONS?

Labor leaders have begun to express grave concern about the future. For some time they have been talking about the threats of technological unemployment both to the union movement and the national economy. In a few states unions have proposed the creation of some kind of state commission to control the effects of automation. Today, technological unemployment is no longer merely a threat to union; it is a reality with which they must cope. Membership has begun to drop off significantly in some unions, especially the UAW and USW. For the first time, union leaders are accepting the idea that they do not have a self-perpetuating future. Until very recently, labor leaders, somewhat like our early pioneers who thought there were endless forests, looked at all the unorganized workers and felt that they could always maintain their relative power in society through periodic expansion.

But now they can see that before very long their political and economic power will begin to decline unless something happens to alter the picture. Most labor officials are of the opinion that their power is at its apogee at present and is about to turn down. Some years earlier, 1953, to be exact, Daniel Bell, writing for *Fortune* magazine, pointed out that "organized labor has probably passed its peak point" politically and economically.[16] The lifting of the 1959-1960 recession without substantial change in unemployment figures shows the speed with which the new automation and technological revolution is progressing. Although the writer cannot document this, there seem to be fewer jobs today than five years ago that are poten-

[16] Bell, "The Next American Labor Movement," *Fortune*, April 1953, pp. 120, 204.

tially unionizable. One thing is fairly certain, however, and that is that the conflicts among the craft and industrial unions have slowed the merger's fundamental drive to organize unattached workers, and the unions now have a smaller proportionate share of the national work forces than ten years ago.[17]

What does this mean politically? In the first place, the big industrial unions have been hit the hardest by automation. And, as mentioned earlier, these are the unions that are the most active politically, that contribute most of the money and organization in national campaigns, and that have their membership most strategically located in terms of affecting the outcome of presidential elections. If the resources and membership of these unions begin to dwindle, the significance of labor as a base of support for the Democratic Party will dwindle. It is, of course, plausible that union leaders will turn more to pressure group politics and away from party and campaign politics nationally to delay uncontrolled change and to compensate for the economic power slipping from their grasps. Walter Reuther's increasing concern about the outcome of decisions affecting agriculture is, in part, explained by a desire to forge stronger alliances with other economic groups, in this case the Farmers Union, to offset labor's declining political power. But the road ahead for the AFL-CIO looks rough; it may have fewer votes to play with, less money, and a weaker organization. It is little wonder then that the AFL-CIO is giving serious consideration to re-admitting the Teamsters Union, despite the national image the union has, and the antipathy many labor leaders have toward Teamster President James Hoffa.

C. THE POPULAR IMAGE

It is not difficult to substantiate the point that organized labor still conveys a poor image. The publicity engendered largely by investigations conducted by Senator McClellan's Committee has hurt American trade unions to a point where the AFL-CIO has felt

---

[17] Krock, "Three Houses Divided Against Themselves," N.Y. *Times,* July 7, 1960, p. 30, col. 4.

the need to institute a $1.2 million public relations programs.[18] Such adverse publicity has served to confirm in the minds of many the negative stereotype they have of trade unions in general and union leadership in particular.

The image labor conveys, of course, limits and affects its political role. As previously mentioned, in some areas labor endorsement carries the kiss of death, and even in Michigan, where organized labor is recognized and accepted as an integral part of the Democratic Party, elaborate efforts are made by party professionals to make certain that the public does not think the Party is dominated and controlled by the UAW. More widespread participation by labor leaders in community affairs has helped to change the image, but many people in rural and non-industrialized areas still view unions with suspicion and massive distrust and refuse to support candidates prominently identified with them.

[18] Pomper, "The Public Relations of Organized Labor," 23 *Pub. Opinion Q.* 483 (1959).

The Changing Political Role of the Farmer*

GILBERT C. FITE

Although once the staunchest individualist in the nation, in the past generation the farmer has come to be one of the most politically active men. As pointed out by Gilbert Fite *in this reading, this is largely due to the seriousness of his declining economic situation and to responses made by various agricultural organizations. America's technological revolution has created serious economic maladjustments for the farmer causing various farm organizations to pressure for government programs to cure these maladjustments.*

As one looks back over the past 35 years, it is clear that scarcely any domestic political issue has been more important or persistent than the farm problem. With the exception of World War II and the immediate post-war years, farmers and their spokesmen since 1920 have consistently pressed a wide variety of demands upon the federal government. There has been an increasing tendency to look to the nation's Capitol for aid in establishing and maintaining prosperity on American farms. These well-known facts raise a number of interesting questions regarding the role of agriculture in American political life.

What has been the historic position of farmers in the American political system? Who has spoken for them in the past, and who speaks for them today? How effective are the voices which plead the cause of modern American agriculture? These are questions

* Gilbert C. Fite, "The Changing Political Role of the Farmer," *Current History,* XXXI (August, 1956), 84-90.

which command the attention of citizens who are honestly considering the agricultural issue in current American politics.

At no time since the founding of the nation have farmers spoken through a single, united voice. Farmers were not united in the Nineteenth Century; they have not been united in the last few years and are not united today despite the windy talk about farm lobbies and farm blocs. An endless variety of farms and the many different kinds and classes of farmers have produced more diversity than unity in the political objectives of farmers and farm groups. For example, the current interests of a specialized wheat farmer in Kansas who is interested in high wheat prices is far different from those of a New York dairy farmer who wants to buy cheap feeds. Dairy farmers who desire high butter prices find themselves in conflict with cotton producers whose cottonseed oil goes into butter substitutes. To form a unified and effective political voice from the conflicting economic interests among farmers is the principal challenge facing the nation's farm spokesmen. The task is indeed formidable when one remembers that there are over three and one-half million commercial farmers in the United States who produce something over 200 commercial crops. The problem of achieving farm political unity is one which would tax the most ingenious agricultural leadership.

On the eve of the Civil War farmers and people living in rural areas made up about 84 per cent of the total population and, in general, they made their demands known through the regularly elected senators and representatives in Congress. Passage of the Homestead Act in 1862 is a good example of federal legislation which a large element of farmers demanded, legislation which they hoped would be of benefit to American agricultural interests. Although a fairly small group, wool growers were able to exert pressure on Congress in the pre-Civil War years to get a substantial tariff on wool imports. These and other laws which were demanded by sections of the rural population did not result from pressure by special farm groups. They were placed on the statute books by senators and representatives whose constituency was predominantly rural.

Early Organizations

Despite their numerical dominance in pre-Civil War America, farmers were by no means satisfied with their condition. They frequently complained of low farm prices and of high prices charged by merchants for non-farm commodities. They criticized the banking system and attacked the railroads. However, no genuine farm movement developed before the 1860's. Occasionally, someone urged farmers to be more active politically if they expected Congress to heed their wishes, but that is about all. For instance, Professor J. B. Turner of the University of Illinois wrote in 1858:

> Let us besiege our Legislature and besiege Congress, and give no peace till they properly attend to all those interests of agriculture, which they now profess to attend to, and undertake all other enterprises which we so much need.

Advice of this nature, however, went largely unnoticed and farmers did not create any special organizations to promote their particular interests until after the Civil War.

The National Grange, established in 1868, was the first general farm organization founded in the United States. Formed during a period of low prices following the Civil War, the principal objectives of the Grange were to improve the social and economic welfare of rural people through organization and cooperation. However, the Grange turned to politics in the early 1870's and was largely responsible for the so-called Granger Laws which were designed to regulate railroads and other corporations. The political influence of the Grange was short-lived, however, and after the middle 1870's it had relatively little force in politics until it became active politically during the 1920's, nearly half a century later.

Meanwhile, the Greenback Movement was organized with both farm and labor support to promote the idea of solving some of the economic problems through inflationary legislation. The Greenbackers, who reached their height in the midterm elections of 1878, demanded that the federal government increase the money supply by printing and distributing greenbacks. Although the Greenback Party ran a presidential candidate as late as 1884, it had already declined as a political force.

The farm discontent of the late Nineteenth Century was caused to a large extent by the long period of low prices between 1868 and 1896. But farmers also complained of deflation and the scarcity of money, high interest rates, railroad abuses and many other things. The smoldering dissatisfaction culminated in the organization of the Northern and Southern Alliances in the 1880's, and the Populist Party in 1892. Western and southern farmers found a voice for their grievances in the Populist Party which sought to relieve farm ills by legislative action.

The Populist program included free and unlimited coinage of silver, government ownership of telephone and telegraph lines, an income tax and many other reforms. Although the Populists failed to gain political control, they became strong enough to throw a scare into the old parties. Both the Democratic and Republican parties came to support principles advocated by the Populists and their rural supporters. It should be noted that during the Populist uprising, the Grange did not play a prominent political role.

In the post-Civil War generation farmers sought to achieve their objective through third party organizations. Believing that the Democratic and Republican parties were both corrupt and under the influence of special business and industrial interests, farmers tried to make a clean political sweep. Failing in this, they experienced the frustration of realizing their numerical superiority, yet being unable to make their superior numbers pay off in terms of governmental control. Lack of organization and unity in purpose, and disagreement over means of achieving their objectives plagued farmers as they worked to enlarge their political influence to a place where it would be commensurate with their numbers.

Except for the Nonpartisan League which was confined largely to North Dakota, there was no large-scale, organized attempt by farmers to influence governmental policies between the late 1890's and the early 1920's. Nonetheless, Congress was attentive to the needs and demands of agriculture, and passed several pieces of far-reaching legislation to help farmers. One of the most notable of these was the Federal Farm Loan Act of 1916. In any event, the good times from 1898 to about 1912 and the high prices of farm products created by huge wartime demands in 1917 and 1918 dulled the farm militancy so characteristic of the agrarian uprising of the 1880's and 1890's. The National Farmers Union was formed in 1902, but like the Grange, its emphasis at this time was less on political action and more on education and cooperation.

The postwar agricultural depression which began in 1920 stimulated a strong demand among farmers for some kind of federal action to help solve the ills of agriculture. By this time there were three general farm organizations, all national in scope, which were dedicated to caring for farm interests in Washington and elsewhere. Besides the Grange and the Farmers Union, the American Farm Bureau Federation was founded in 1919, and early the next year it established a Washington legislative office in charge of Gray Silver. The Grange and Farmers Union also kept representatives in Washington either full or part time by the early 1920's. With three national farm organizations active, the average dirt farmer could reasonably expect that Congress would listen when organized agriculture spoke.

But if the sons of the soil expected that they would now have a single, united voice in Washington, they were doomed to disappointment. From the early 1920's to the present time there has been a weakening lack of unity among the organizations which are supposed to speak for the nation's farmers. The National Grange has for many years been strongest among the dairy farmers, and the fruit and vegetable growers. The organization's largest membership developed in the northeastern states and in the Pacific Northwest, and it has been essentially conservative in its approach to solving farm problems.

On the other hand, the Farmers Union found its greatest strength in the Great Wheat Belt from Texas in the South to the Dakotas in the North. It has been characterized by militant leadership, especially under John A. Simpson, who was president in the early 1930's, and [under] James G. Patton. It represents the Left Wing of the farm movement. One of the Union's most cherished objectives has been to maintain the rather loosely defined family-size farm, and many of its members always have been among low income farmers.

The Farm Bureau gained its greatest strength in the Corn Belt—from Indiana west to Minnesota—and among the cotton producers in Alabama, Mississippi, Arkansas and other sections of the central South. Corn and cotton farmers have made up a large percentage of the Farm Bureau's membership.

Discords

The three major farm organizations were made up of farmers specializing in different crops, and to some degree each tended to dominate a particular geographic region. Moreover, each of the organizations have had sharp internal conflicts, not only in the 1920's, but down to the present time. Thus the old problem of getting a united political voice for farmers is still unsolved.

The lack of unity among farmers and their organizations was well demonstrated in the fight over the McNary-Haugen bills during the 1920's. No other farm legislation so gripped the imagination of farmers in the Harding-Coolidge era. The main idea behind this scheme was to remove the price-depressing effect of surplus crops on domestic prices by segregating the amount produced in excess of domestic consumption, and permitting the domestically marketed commodities to rise behind a tariff wall.

The surpluses were to be sold abroad for whatever they would bring and any losses sustained on exports were to be paid from a tax on each unit of a commodity sold. This was called an equalization fee. By this means it was hoped to increase farm prices enough to give them a "fair exchange value" with industrial products. This was the parity concept which was later written into the Agricultural Adjustment Act of 1933.

When the McNary-Haugen bill was first introduced in 1924, the major farm organizations were sharply divided over it. For example, Oscar E. Bradfute of Ohio, who became president of the Farm Bureau in 1922, strongly opposed any government tinkering with the farm price mechanism. He believed that cooperative marketing would solve farm ills. On the other hand, Sam H. Thompson, Charles Hearst and other leaders of the Farm Bureau threw their support behind passage of surplus-control legislation. Likewise, there were those in the Farmers Union and Grange who both supported and opposed the McNary-Haugen bill. This internal division and conflict within the various farm organizations left the farmers with many voices, none of which were powerful enough to command obedient attention in Washington.

American Council of Agriculture

To remedy this difficulty a number of farm leaders got together in St. Paul in July, 1924, and organized the American Council of Agriculture. The main purpose of creating a new organization was to provide one which could devote itself strictly to national farm legislation, especially the McNary-Haugen bill, and which would cut across party and farm organization lines. It was hoped by this means to avoid the jealousies, bickerings, and differences within and among the regular farm organizations, a condition which had greatly weakened their influence. The main objective of the American Council of Agriculture, said the Declaration of Purpose, was

> to make it possible for the existing agricultural organizations of whatever character to speak with one voice through a united leadership wherever and whenever the general well-being of agriculture is concerned.

George N. Peek, who headed the Council, claimed that he represented some 2.5 million American farmers. Before long offices were set up in Chicago and Washington, money was solicited, and strong pressure was brought to bear on Congress to pass the McNary-Haugen bill. Never before had farmers been so ably and powerfully represented in Washington. Peek and Chester C. Davis were among the most effective workers, although they received support from some of the leaders in the regular and other special farm organizations.

Modern farm lobbying really dates from middle 1920's when those who favored the McNary-Haugen bill organized to push their measure through Congress. For the first time, substantial sums were raised for the special purpose of passing particular legislation. Scattered and incomplete records in the files of Chester C. Davis show that the special farm groups spent around $50 thousand between 1924 and 1928 on salaries, literature, travel and other items. The Farm Bureau, Grange and Farmers Union spent thousands of dollars more through their state and national offices.

The power of the farm lobby became clear when the McNary-Haugen bill was passed over stiff administration opposition. Tremendous pressure was turned on reluctant congressmen and senators. For instance, when Representative Charles E. Fuller of Illinois indicated he would not vote for the bill, Chester Davis asked an Illinois farm leader: "Will it be possible for you to see that a particularly warm fire is lighted under him in his own district?" The political fire was indeed lighted and Fuller voted for the measure.

Just before Congress voted on the 1928 bill, one congressman said that he must vote for it even though it was against his better judgment. "I am for it," he said, "I have got to support it, because the crowd at home are on my trail." The Wichita *Beacon* claimed that a majority had been obtained for the bill "under the bludgeoning of one of the most persistent and skillful lobbies ever seen in Washington."

This may have been an exaggeration, but, in any event, there was no question but that farmers were better organized and spoke with more authority on governmental matters affecting their interests than ever before.

After President Coolidge vetoed and killed the McNary-Haugen bill in 1928, the American Council of Agriculture and some of the other special farm organizations ceased to exist. Again farmers had to rely chiefly upon the Big Three. The constant conflicts among these groups, however, continued to weaken their efforts on behalf of farmers. The closest which the Grange, Farm Bureau and Farmers Union came to agreement was at a National Agricultural Conference held in Washington in January, 1932. By that time the severity of the depression had practically forced the major farm organizations to join hands, and "it was the first time in the history of organized agriculture," said one writer, "that the 'big three' have ever reached unanimous agreement on a project of such momentous significance to the industry." The conference agreed that the Agricultural Marketing Act should be amended by adding the equalization fee or export debenture plan.

Unity in Parity

The critical situation in agriculture by 1933 brought a fair degree of unanimity among the farm organizations, although many agricultural spokesmen opposed the acreage restriction provisions of the Agricultural Adjustment Act. However, there was general agreement on the principle of parity prices which would give the producers purchasing power equal to that which they had received in the base period from 1909 to 1914. Ever since 1933, the major farm organizations have stood firmly behind the parity principle despite sharp differences of opinion whether farmers should get 100, 90, or some lesser per cent of parity.

Although the Grange, Farm Bureau and Farmers Union have continued to be agriculture's main political spokesmen, these organizations too often spend more time and energy fighting one another than they do trying to work together to solve general farm problems. The Farmers Union claims to speak for about 750 thousand farm families. In recent years under the energetic leadership of James G. Patton, the Union has fought unceasingly for "mandatory federal farm income protection legislation at 100 per cent of fair parity for the family farm production of all farm commodities." The Farmers Union has also urged setting up a national food allotment plan similar to the stamp plan of New Deal days.

On the other hand, the more conservative Farm Bureau which represents some 1 million farm families has bitterly opposed high rigid price supports. It was the Farm Bureau which backed most strongly the flexible price support plan adopted by the Eisenhower

Administration in 1954. The principle of flexible supports was based on the belief that farmers would cut down the production of surpluses voluntarily if they were threatened with lower support prices in the event of continued excessive surpluses. Although the history of farm production emphatically refutes this concept, it has been popular in some quarters. In order further to reduce surpluses the Farm Bureau has promoted the "soil bank" plan which is currently the center of national attention.

The Grange has not given its full support to the views held by either the Farmers Union or the Farm Bureau. Speaking of the opposing views of the other major farm organizations over rigid and flexible price supports, Master Herschel D. Newsom said early in 1956: "The Grange is standing more or less aside while these two opposing viewpoints battle it out." The Grange has placed heavier emphasis upon restoring foreign markets for American surpluses.

This emphasis has caused the organization to revive the old Domestic Allotment Plan advocated in 1931 and 1932 by Henry A. Wallace, Dr. John A. Black, M. L. Wilson and others. Now called the Domestic Parity Plan, the Grange believes that a two-price plan should be implemented, at least for wheat. Under this arrangement, that portion of the crop consumed at home would be supported at the parity price, but the surplus would go to world markets at the world price.

Enough has been said to show that today, as in the past, farmers lack a strong, united voice in governmental affairs. This situation is no different than it has been for over a century, but today the differences among farm leaders and organizations create a more serious problem than ever before. This is true because of the very rapid decline in farm population. In 1910, for example, 34.9 per cent of the American people still lived on farms; by 1954 farm population had dropped to 13.5 per cent.

Declining Influence

The political implications of a rapidly declining farm population are of utmost importance for agriculture. It is true that during the last 30 years farmers have become much better and more power-fully organized. They have pressed their demands upon Congress with greater vigor and persistence than ever before. But while farmers have been improving organizational methods by which they can gain attention from the federal government, time and the great city migration have been working against them. As more people leave the farms—and 2 million more left in 1952 than returned—politicians have less and less to fear from an aroused and angry rural population when the country as a whole is considered.

Farmers have been slow to face up to their declining political power, and the noise made by farm leaders has actually camouflaged the growing political weakness of farmers. The farm organizations secretly and fearfully recognize the situation, but only infrequently do they bring the matter into the open. However, Homer L. Brinkley, Executive Vice President of the National Council of Farmer Cooperatives, said early in 1956 that

> the lessening political influence of farmers may be forecast by the declining number of farms and the growing popula-tion trends toward cities and urban areas.

He urged support of the idea presented in Congress that the electoral college system be revised in such a way that farmers would have a disproportionate influence in presidential elections. It has been reported that the major farm organizations plan to present a more united front through regular meetings of their representatives in Washington. Herschel Newsom, Master of the Grange, said that many views held by the different organizations could not be reconciled, but he added: "If the farm minority is going to cope with the power of other groups, it must present a united front wher-ever possible."

Thus a few farm leaders are openly recognizing that the long period during which agriculture was politically strong by sheer weight of numbers is a thing of the past. And it should be emphasized that the major farm organizations are not actually as strong politically as they seem to be. Most farm organization members join because of some particular service which the organization provides, rather than because they believe the organization will best represent their political interests in Washington. One of the chief drawing cards is the privilege farmers have to buy cheap insurance. Without this many local units of the Big Three would not even exist.

Despite what has been said, however, farm political power is much stronger than the ratio of farmers to the total population would seem to warrant. This is true because, first of all, the Constitution guarantees each state two United States senators and the most rural state is equally represented in that legislative body. Furthermore, there is still a very strong feeling of agricultural fundamentalism in this country, even among city dwellers who would not think of living or working on a farm. The idea that farming is somehow more pure and virtuous than other occupations and that farmers are God's chosen people is widely believed today as well as in the days of Jefferson.

Then there is another aspect of what is labeled "agricultural fundamentalism." Millions of Americans subscribe to the idea that agriculture is "the base of the economic pyramid" and that the nation's prosperity rests upon a prosperous agriculture. This was one of the great cries of the 1920's and the 1930's as friends of agriculture sought federal aid. It may be a doubtful assumption in the 1950's, but President Eisenhower repeated it in his farm message to Congress on January 9, 1956. He referred to agriculture as "our basic industry," and called "economic reversals of farmers" "a direct threat of the well-being of all our people."

It must be remembered that millions of Americans are only one generation, or less, removed from the farm, and many of these people have a nostalgic affection for their childhood experiences and homes. In addition, large numbers of city people still own farms and therefore have a personal interest in agriculture's welfare. The 13.5 per cent of Americans who live on farms are not alone in fighting the farmers' battles.

This brief discussion of the changing role of farmers in American political life points up at least one significant fact. The population make-up of the country has so changed within the last half century that farmers and farm leaders must reassess their political place and adjust themselves to a minority position. The success of this adjustment will be seen in how well farmers and farm leaders are able to achieve their political objectives. Despite their minority position, it appears that farmers will be able to wield a disproportionate political influence for many years to come because of the effectiveness of their organizations, and the structure of the federal and state governments. Farmers will be aided, too, by a widespread belief in agricultural fundamentalism and by a strong agrarian tradition.

National Farm Organizations and the Reshaping of Agricultural Policy in 1932*

WILLIAM R. JOHNSON

In the wake of the stock market crash of 1929 and the deepening economic plight of farmers in the years immediately thereafter, demands came from leading agricultural organizations for governmental accommodation through some subsidy plan. William Johnson's following selection illustrates various techniques used by three leading farm organizations to influence governmental accommodation of group claims. Pressures directed toward a newly elected President and upon a more sympathetic Congress produced a farm policy in line with group goals and objectives.

I

The Great Depression which began with the stock market crash in the autumn of 1929 was especially hard on farmers who had never enjoyed a high degree of prosperity in the 1920's. In 1929 the average net income of American farmers was only $847; in 1930 it fell to $556; and in 1931 it dropped further to $342.[1] The rapid decline in prices and income was an economic catastrophe for millions of farmers, and, in their desperation, these erstwhile "rugged individualists" demanded

[1] *Yearbook of Agriculture,* 1933 (Washington, 1933), p. 44.

* William R. Johnson, "National Farm Organizations and the Reshaping of Agricultural Policy in 1932," *Agricultural History,* 37 (October, 1963), 35-42.

that the federal government do something to bring equality to agriculture.

The demands of agriculture were voiced by the three national farm organizations—the American Farm Bureau Federation, the Patrons of Husbandry, or Grange, and the Farmers Educational and Cooperative Union of America. With a membership of one and a quarter million in 1932, the AFBF was the largest of the three national organizations: it claimed forty-two state federations, 1,800 county organizations, and 15,000 local bureaus.[2] Its dynamic leader, Edward A. O'Neal, an Alabama farmer who was born in 1875 and educated at Washington and Lee University, had come up through the local and state ranks. He was elected president of the Alabama Farm Bureau in 1923, vice-president of the national organization in 1924, and president in 1931.[3]

In the legislative fights of the 1920's the Farm Bureau supported the McNary-Haugen plan. This scheme, developed by George N. Peek, was designed to bring equality to agriculture by "making the tariff effective." A government corporation would buy price-reducing surpluses and dump them on the world market, while the domestic price level would be maintained at or near a parity figure behind the tariff wall. The loss incurred by the government in removing the surplus would be paid by the producer in the form of an equalization fee levied on each unit of production. With the passage of the Agricultural Marketing Act in 1929, the Farm Bureau temporarily dropped the equalization fee and gave nominal support to Hoover's marketing plan, involving the stabilization efforts of the Federal Farm Board.

In August, 1931, a meeting of several state Farm Bureau leaders was held in Madison, Wisconsin. The state leaders, O'Neal reported to the press, had agreed that since the Agricultural Marketing Act had failed to control agricultural surpluses, the Farm Bureau must once again press for the equalization-fee plan.[4] Accordingly the

[2] House Committee on Agriculture, Hearings, *Program of National Farm Organizations*, 72d Cong., 1st Sess., 1932, p. 14.
[3] For a biographical sketch of O'Neal see Orville M. Kile, *The Farm Bureau Through Three Decades* (Baltimore, 1948), pp. 170-176.
[4] New York *Times*, August 12, 1931.

Farm Bureau, in its annual meeting held in December, resolved to support the equalization fee before Congress.[5]

The National Grange, the second largest farm organization, in 1932 claimed 800,000 organized into thirty-three state granges.[6] Its president, since 1923, was Louis J. Taber. Born in Ohio in 1878, Taber was Master of the Ohio Grange from 1914 to 1921, and Director of Agriculture for the State of Ohio in 1921-1922.

The Grange favored the export debenture plan, first devised by Professor Charles L. Stewart of the University of Illinois in 1924. Two years later a bill incorporating Stewart's plan was introduced in the Senate by Senator William B. McKinley and in the House by Representative Charles Adkins, both of Illinois. Meanwhile, the Grange gave a firm endorsement to the debenture plan, and three years later the Senate attached this system to the Agricultural Marketing Act. The House, however, refused to accept the amendment, and in conference the Senate committee agreed to drop the measure.[7]

The debenture scheme, like the equalization fee, aimed to achieve equality for agriculture by making the tariff effective. The method, however, was different. A bounty would be offered on those farm commodities which were in surplus. According to the proposal, exporters would receive from the Treasury certificates known as export debentures amounting to about one-half of the tariff rate. Within one year these debenture certificates would be received at face value in payment of custom duties or could be exchanged for cash at ninety-eight per cent of face value. Farmer cooperatives were to handle both the exporting of agricultural goods and the receipt of debenture certificates.[8]

Basically the export debenture system was a direct governmental subsidy to agriculture, a factor often criticized. The Farm Bureau, in comparing its proposed farm relief system to that of the Grange,

[5] *Ibid.*, December 10, 1931.
[6] House Committee on Agriculture, Hearings, *Program of National Farm Organizations,* p. 14.
[7] Joseph S. Davis, *The Export Debenture Plan* (Stanford, 1929), p. 1. President Herbert Hoover also strongly opposed the plan.
[8] *Ibid.*, pp. 8-12.

pointed out that the equalization fee would be financed by the farmers themselves. Farmers, they claimed, had never wanted a subsidy from the federal government.[9] Friends of the debenture plan had no adequate answer. They could only point out that use of the system undoubtedly would bring about a general price increase. Farmers, they felt, would not sell their goods on domestic markets at a price lower than the world price, plus the export bounty. The Grange still supported this scheme in 1931.[10]

The Farmers' Union, the third largest national farm organization, was organized in twenty-six states, and, according to its president, John A. Simpson, had a "potential" membership of 500,000.[11] The actual number of dues-paying members probably was a good deal less than half of that figure.[12] When testifying before a House committee Simpson was asked to reveal the number of paid-up members in his organization. He replied that he could not supply the information because "under Hoover, they have not been able to pay."[13]

The Nebraska-born leader of this militant organization, studied law at the University of Kansas, and in 1901 moved to Oklahoma Territory to become a farmer and banker. In 1930, after many active years in the Oklahoma Farmers' Union, Simpson was elected president of the national organization.[14]

Of the three men—O'Neal, Taber, and Simpson—Simpson was by far the most radical. He was quick to voice his ideas, and made no effort to veil his deep-seated economic convictions. His remarks in a radio speech in January, 1932, are representative of his economic philosophy. According to Simpson there are two basic

[9] *Ibid.*, p. 29.
[10] New York *Times*, September 28, 1931.
[11] House Committee on Agriculture, Hearings, *Program of National Farm Organizations*, p. 23.
[12] *Minutes of the Twenty-Seventh National Convention of the Farmers' Educational and Co-operative Union of America* (Kankakee, Illinois, 1931), pp. 8-9.
[13] House Committee on Agriculture, Hearings on H.R. 7797, *Swank Agricultural Bill*, 72d Cong., 1st Sess., 1932, p. 33.
[14] See Gilbert C. Fite, "John A. Simpson: the Southwest's Militant Farm Leader," *Mississippi Valley Historical Review*, XXXV (March, 1949), 563-584.

systems under which men live: the capitalistic system and the cooperative system. "The capitalistic system is of the devil's making," Simpson asserted. "It has, as its foundation principle, selfishness, greed, avarice; it leads to theft, robbery, murder, suicide and war." On the other hand, said Simpson, "the cooperative system is based upon service instead of profit. It has as its attributes, unselfishness and the brotherhood of man. . . . I say to you," continued Simpson, "that no man who is a Christian has a right to want more than the average could have."[15]

Not surprisingly the Farmers' Union's plan of agricultural relief differed materially from those supported by its rival organizations. Simpson's proposal, although termed the domestic allotment plan, did not resemble the proposal of the same name sponsored by Milburn L. Wilson, which later became the basis of the Agricultural Adjustment Act. The Farmers' Union scheme first adopted by the organization in 1930,[16] was essentially a proposal to fix prices based upon the cost of production. A resolution passed at the annual meeting of the Farmers' Union in late 1931, demanded that farmers be guaranteed "a price based upon the cost of production plus a profit as computed by the Department of Agriculture," for all products domestically consumed.[17]

It is quite apparent that as the 72nd Congress met in December, 1931, the major farm organizations remained divided on specific proposals to correct the ills of American agriculture. Throughout 1931 each organization continued to favor its own particular approach, frequently criticizing solutions advanced by the other organizations. However, in order to present a united front before the approaching session of Congress, farm leaders endeavored to agree upon one plan which at a meeting of minds in December they decided would be the Federal Farm Board. They further agreed that, since none of the organizations would abandon their own farm relief

[15] John A. Simpson, "A Discussion of Unsolved Problems and Real Remedies," Simpson Papers, University of Oklahoma Library Archives, Norman.
[16] Fite, "John A. Simpson," p. 566.
[17] *Minutes of the Twenty-Seventh National Convention of the Farmers' Union,* p. 41.

principles, they would push all three methods at once.[18] This unity, as later events proved, was more apparent than real.

II

Early in January, 1932, when O'Neal, Taber, and Simpson went before the House Committee on Agriculture, O'Neal offered the following general resolution supported by the three farm leaders:

> We insist that the Agricultural Marketing Act should be continued in force as a principal method of stimulating cooperative marketing and advancing the cause of disposing of surpluses so that they will not depress the domestic price.
>
> The marketing act should be amended immediately by the inclusion of the debenture plan, equalization fee, or any other method which will make it effective on farm crops and in securing for American farmers cost of production on those portions of their crops sold for consumption in our own Nation; nothing less is a remedy for the agricultural marketing problem.[19]

O'Neal then explained the equalization-fee plan to the House committee, and indicated that his organization still favored its adoption. However, he also expressed a desire to see the ideas of the three organizations incorporated into a single measure which would permit the Farm Board to put any of the alternatives into effect. Taber, following O'Neal before the committee, first stressed the unity of the three organizations and then briefly explained the export debenture system. When asked a question about the equalization fee he declined to answer. "I am not as familiar with it as our Farm Bureau friends. We believe that the debenture is the best. We are not quarreling with them at all, but we believe that the debenture is the best."[20] Finally Simpson also spoke of unity and then presented his own program. His position was made perfectly

[18] New York *Times*, December 8, 1931.
[19] House Committee on Agriculture, Hearings, *Program of National Farm Organizations*, p. 3.
[20] *Ibid.*, p. 21.

clear when he declared that "the one thing that got us together was the statement, 'to get for the farmers cost of production on those portions of the crops sold for consumption in our own Nation'."[21]

The three organizations, therefore, as much as they might agree on a common objective, differed over the means to be enacted, and subsequently backed separate measures which would put their own ideas into effect. In February Simpson appeared before the House and Senate committees on agriculture in support of the Thomas-Swank bill. Although entitled A Bill to Abolish the Federal Farm Board and Secure to the Farmers the Cost of Production, Simpson, who had drafted the bill, declared that the Farmers' Union was not interested in abolishing the Farm Board.[22] Undoubtedly, Simpson, a bitter critic of the Farm Board, could not obtain support from the other organizations on this point. The indispensable portion of the bill, said Simpson, was not which agency administered the bill, but the cost of production feature.

Simpson's proposal called on the Secretary of Agriculture to determine the yearly amount of farm production necessary for domestic consumption, and to ascertain the cost of production for each commodity including wages and interest on investment. This figure would then be the price at which each producer's domestic allotment could be sold. Simpson preferred that the portion of farm production above the "salable" domestic allotment—the surplus— be held on the farm. However, he did not consider this vital to the operation of the scheme and was willing to have the export debenture apply to it.[23] Further, Simpson opposed acreage restriction by government mandate. "The control of acreage," he said, "is very impracticable. We had better let the farmer produce what he wants to, but control the part he can sell and get the cost of production for what he can sell."[24]

The other two groups gave only qualified support to Simpson's

[21] *Ibid.*, p. 24.
[22] Senate Committee on Agriculture and Forestry, Hearings on S. 3133, *To Abolish the Federal Farm Board and Secure to the Farmer Cost of Production,* 72d Cong., 1st Sess., 1932, p. 4.
[23] *Ibid.*, pp. 4-5.
[24] *Ibid.*, p. 8.

proposals. Fred Brenckman, Washington representative of the Grange, endorsed the cost-of-production scheme as a general principle. "However," he said, "there may be differences of opinion regarding the plan or methods to be pursued in accomplishing the desired purpose. I have not been authorized specifically to endorse the provisions of this bill."[25] Chester H. Gray, Washington representative of the Farm Bureau, also spoke in favor of the general aims of the Thomas-Swank bill, but avoided supporting the price-fixing provisions.

Later in February, L. J. Taber also appeared before both agricultural committees in support of a measure (H. R. 7236) that would implement the export debenture plan. The author of the bill was Representative Marvin Jones, Chairman of the House Committee on Agriculture. During the course of his testimony Taber pointed out that, although the Grange was asking for the export debenture, it was ready to accept not only the debenture, but also the "equalization fee, and/or any other constructive method of lifting prices. . . ."[26] In answer to critics of the bill Taber said, "Objection has been made again and again that the debenture is a bounty or subsidy. From our viewpoint, it is neither. It is a complement of the tariff structure. It is a drawback for the farmer. It is a method of equalizing tariff costs and increased production costs."[27]

Taber's proposed measure, as well as Simpson's, did not have enough supporters to gain congressional approval. The debenture bill was rejected by the Senate 46 to 33,[28] and the domestic allotment bill died in committee.

The most significant legislative effort of the three farm organizations in 1932 was a composite bill called the Three-way Farm Relief Plan. Sponsored by Senator Charles McNary and presented to the agricultural committees late in April, it combined the three

[25] *Ibid.*, p. 29.
[26] House Committee on Agriculture, Hearings on H. R. 7326, *Farm Marketing Program,* 72d Cong., 1st Sess., 1932, p. 4.
[27] Senate Committee on Agriculture and Forestry, Hearings on S. 3680, *Amendment of Agricultural Marketing Act,* 72d Cong., 1st Sess., 1932, p. 8.
[28] New York *Times,* May 25, 1932.

different schemes. According to its provisions the Federal Farm Board would select one of the ideas, or a combination of the different plans, to use in dealing with farm surpluses. The bill was as close to unity as the farm organizations could come. They still did not agree upon specific methods, they could only agree to submit their various ideas and let someone else make the final decision as to which would be used. However, the organizations acclaimed the newly achieved unity, and in a joint letter sent to Congressman Marvin Jones laid the responsibility for action upon Congress.[29]

Thus the three national leaders placed their last hopes on the plans they had supported in previous years. They were opposed to M. L. Wilson's domestic allotment proposal which in its modified form advocated cash benefit payments to farmers who would agree to cut production.[30] This scheme gained popularity after 1929; and in 1932 Wilson presented it before Congress, but received little support. Farm leaders remained opposed to Wilson's ideas until late in 1932.

Now that the major organizations had achieved a measure of unity, at least on the surface, the Three-way bill was reported out of committee essentially as they had written it, and was debated in the Senate in June.

On the floor of the Senate the Three-way bill had two vigorous supporters. Senators Elmer Thomas of Oklahoma and Lynn Frazier of North Dakota. Both Thomas and Frazier pointed out that since the major farm organizations had finally agreed upon a single proposal they should be listened to, and the bill should be passed. Influential Senators such as William Borah and Peter Norbeck gave less than wholehearted support. Borah favored the export debenture scheme, while Norbeck leaned toward the Wilson domestic allotment proposal.

Opponents of the bill were led by Senator William H. King of Utah. He and others who spoke against the bill concentrated their heaviest fire on what they considered to be its weakest part—the price-fixing domestic allotment portion. Their argument centered

[29] U. S. *Congressional Record*, 72d Cong., 1st Sess., 1932, pp. 11967-11968.
[30] Gilbert C. Fite, *Peter Norbeck: Prairie Statesman* (Columbia, 1948), pp. 162-163.

on claims that Simpson's plan was clearly unconstitutional. Most of the Senators who spoke agreed with the opponents of the bill on this point.

On June 15, the final day of debate, Senator Thomas, continuing to fight for the Farmers' Union section of the Three-way bill, read into the record a letter from John Simpson. The major difficulty, Simpson wrote, was that the Senators did not understand the measure. He attempted once again to explain his domestic allotment proposal and finally suggested that "if any amendments to the bill would make it read more clearly," Thomas should offer such amendments.[31]

Senator Borah was convinced that the measure could not be further clarified by amendments. It was already all too clear, so clear in fact, that it was sure to receive a veto. Therefore, he offered an amendment to strike out the allotment provision hoping that the rest of the bill would pass.[32] A short time later, however, he reversed his position and withdrew the amendment. He had offered the amendment, he said, because he was "quite sure that the allotment plan is not workable as presented in this bill, and I am quite sure it is not constitutional." He now had decided to withdraw his motion because the friends of the measure had insisted that the entire bill should "go up or go down together."[33]

Immediately after Borah withdrew his amendment Senator King moved to recommit the Three-way bill. After a "last-ditch" effort by Norbeck to secure amendments failed, the bill was recommitted by a vote of 38 to 28 with thirty Senators not voting.[34]

Thus, what farm leaders felt was the best opportunity for legislation in 1932 was lost. The Three-way bill was the culmination of all their efforts. Many days had been devoted to lobbying, but they failed. They failed, first, because they had talked more unity than they had actually achieved. It is clear that each organization continued to support its own favorite plan, damaging even the shallow

[31] U. S., *Congressional Record,* 72d Cong., 1st Sess., 1932, p. 12980.
[32] *Ibid.,* p. 12981.
[33] *Ibid.,* p. 12987.
[34] *Ibid.*

unity they had found. Furthermore, the Democrats in the Senate were reluctant to do anything which might increase Republican prospects in the coming election. And, the conservative Republicans were not in favor of any new farm bill, but stood with Hoover and the old Agricultural Marketing Act.

III

With the adjournment of Congress, attention was completely devoted to the coming presidential campaign. In general the Republicans, in their platform, did not come to grips with the problems facing agriculture and did not give their support to any of the plans advocated by the farm organizations. Their platform attempted to defend the record of the Federal Farm Board and included a statement supporting voluntary crop reduction already sponsored by the Board.[35]

The brief Democratic platform contained nothing which might alienate any group of farmers. Couched in general phrases, it condemned the Federal Farm Board, supported better financing of farm mortgages (without naming the Frazier bill), and promised "the enactment of every constitutional measure that will aid the farmers to receive for their basic farm commodities prices in excess of cost."[36]

Several months before the platform of either party was written, Governor Franklin D. Roosevelt of New York began to line up support among farm leaders. In March he wrote to Simpson asking him to visit Albany to discuss certain matters.[37] The visit was made early in April. Roosevelt, seeking such support as Simpson could swing, indicated that he was willing to have the Democratic platform contain a statement committing the party to the principle of cost of production. This was all that was necessary to bring Simpson into the Roosevelt camp.[38]

---

[35] New York *Times,* June 16, 1932.

[36] Henry S. Commager (ed.), *Documents of American History* (New York, 1958), pp. 418-419.

[37] Franklin D. Roosevelt to John A. Simpson, March 7, 1932, John A. Simpson Papers, University of Oklahoma Library Archives, Norman.

[38] Simpson to Roosevelt, April 11, 1932, Simpson Papers.

In July the president of the Farmers' Union made his support of Roosevelt known to farmers by means of a nationally broadcasted radio speech. After comparing the agriculture planks in the party platforms, of which only that of the Democratic Party was acceptable, Simpson compared the candidates in his own expressive language. "Mr. Hoover," he said, "is influenced by those years and years of training in developing big business. In promoting giant corporations he has unconsciously reached a place where he looks at everything from the angle of bigness and greatness. . . . To our President, the importance of saving a railroad company overshadows the importance of saving the farmers of the Nation."

Then Simpson spoke of Governor Roosevelt. He had visited Roosevelt and had found him living on a farm "just out of the little town of Hyde Park." The Governor, he said, was a member of the Grange, hastening to point out that there was no Farmers' Union organization close by. Furthermore, it was well-known that big business everywhere was against Roosevelt. What better reason could a farmer find for supporting the New Yorker? For Roosevelt, in spite of his upper class background, was still close to the soil, while Hoover, by implication, was allied with the "international bankers."[39]

William A. Hirth, influential editor of the *Missouri Farmer,* also made the trek to Hyde Park early in 1932. Since Hirth had been a vigorous opponent of Hoover's agricultural policy, it was logical that he would be drawn into Roosevelt's fold.[40]

Edward O'Neal, of the Farm Bureau, did not visit Roosevelt as early in the year as some of his colleagues. Speaking to an audience of farmers at a July 4 celebration at Ottumwa, Iowa, O'Neal criticized both parties for showing indifference to the needs of agriculture. He did find, however, that the Democratic platform was "a bit more definite,"[41] and there was no question as to where the Alabama Democrat placed his personal support.

[39] U. S., *Congressional Record,* 72nd Cong., 1st Sess., 1932, pp. 15687-15688.
[40] Theodore Saloutos, "William A. Hirth: Middle Western Agrarian," *Mississippi Valley Historical Review,* (September, 1951), p. 225.
[41] New York *Times,* July 5, 1932.

Roosevelt did not confine his campaign efforts to leaders of organized agriculture. Besides Hirth, he conferred with such men as M. L. Wilson and Henry A. Wallace. The latter, editor of *Wallace's Farmer,* had a great deal to say about the election of 1932 on the editorial page of his journal. Eventually, Wallace, a Republican, came to support Roosevelt. Perhaps his major reason for doing so is explained by a remark made in August, 1932. "President Hoover," he wrote, "apparently is not inclined to experiment with any new method for increasing the prices of farm products. He condemns, by inference, the equalization fee, the debenture plan, and the domestic allotment plan." On the other hand, "Governor Roosevelt accepts the principle the farm organizations have supported, indicates the domestic allotment plan appeals most strongly of those measures discussed and shows a willingness to follow the guidance of the major farm organizations in drawing up the relief bill."[42]

During the course of the campaign Roosevelt demonstrated evidence of the master politician as he worked to secure the support of major farm organizations and the farmers themselves. He always spoke in general terms, advocating the principles which all organizations favored, and did not publicly declare a preference for one plan to the exclusion of the others. Each organization could see in Roosevelt's statements evidence that the Governor was committed to its own way of thinking.

Roosevelt's major campaign statement on agriculture was delivered at Topeka on September 14. Here Roosevelt indicated that he supported the domestic allotment plan of Wilson and John D. Black. Although Roosevelt did not name his preference, and again spoke in general terms, it seems clear that the conditions he presented for his plan best suited the domestic allotment scheme—indeed that part of the statement came from the pen of M. L. Wilson.[43] At the

[42] Editorial, *Wallace's Farmer,* LVII (August 20, 1932) 7.
[43] Gilbert C. Fite, *George N. Peek and the Fight for Farm Parity* (Norman, 1954), p. 239. A comparison of Roosevelt's Topeka speech with a statement made by Wilson before the House Committee on Agriculture the previous May is illuminating. Roosevelt's six points are almost identical to conditions expressed by Wilson, i.e., any plan which would satisfy the needs of agricul-

heart of the Topeka speech, Roosevelt listed factors he felt were basic to any agricultural relief plan. They were: first, agriculture should receive a tariff benefit equal to that received by industry, and it must be applied in a manner so as not to stimulate increased production. Second, the plan must finance itself. Third, any new system of agricultural marketing must not result in European retaliation caused by dumping American surpluses on European markets. Fourth, it must be decentralized, *i.e.,* controlled locally and must not create a new bureaucracy. Fifth, it should strengthen the cooperative movement, and finally, it should be voluntary and should not go into effect until a reasonable percentage of the producers of a given commodity had accepted the system.[44]

In the last weeks of the 1932 campaign Herbert Hoover did his best to counteract the drift of farm voters to the Roosevelt camp. On October 4 one of his best campaign speeches was delivered at Des Moines, Iowa. Hoover presented a twelve-point program advocating, among other things, a repeal of the price stabilization activities of the Farm Board, the inauguration of a program of land utilization intended to "divert land from unprofitable use to profitable use," relief from long term mortgage payments, and the use of foreign debt payments in aid of agriculture.[45]

Despite these belated Republican efforts, the Democrats polled heavily in farm areas. Iowa, which had not returned a majority for for a Democratic candidate since the Civil War, went heavily for Roosevelt. The other states of the Midwest and Farwest, with significant farm votes, joined Iowa in a Democratic victory.

Undoubtedly, Roosevelt's personal contact with farm leaders and his policy of expediency, was an important factor in winning the support of agriculture. However, in great part the Democratic victory in farm areas resulted from the record of four previous years.

---

ture. House Committee on Agriculture, Hearings, *Farm Marketing Program (Voluntary Domestic Allotment Plan),* 72nd Cong., 1st Sess., 1932, p. 2.

[44] New York *Times,* September 15, 1932.

[45] "Hoover's Fight of the West," *Literary Digest,* (October 15, 1932) pp. 7-8.

The old order, if one may borrow a phrase, had not been responsive to the demands of agriculture, especially organized agriculture. Farmers, along with the great majority of the rest of the country, were eager for a change in leadership. This, however, is one of those historical situations which can be perceived by hindsight, but was certainly not something upon which the politically wise candidate could depend. The fact is that Roosevelt sought, by any expedient means, to turn farmers away from the Republican Party.

After the election, farm leaders began to re-evaluate their long-held ideas. Although they had been unable to unite behind a single scheme in 1932, they began to unify their efforts behind the leadership of "the farmer from Hyde Park." In annual meetings held late in 1932, the Farm Bureau and the Grange appeared to accept the voluntary domestic allotment plan proposed by Wilson. The Farm Bureau committed itself firmly to the scheme,[46] and the Grange, although still favoring the debenture plan, felt that the alternative proposal had significant merits.[47] The Farmers' Union was the only major group that refused officially to accept the Roosevelt supported Wilson plan, and, instead, continued to advocate the Thomas-Swank bill that had embodied Simpson's proposals.

On December 12 and 13, at a meeting held in Washington, D. C., the leaders of the major organizations worked out a legislative program. Driven by the desperation which accompanied the sorrowful economic plight of late 1932, farm leaders temporarily relaxed their insistence upon favored schemes to rally support for the Wilson plan and with it the promise of action. The Farm Bureau, solidly behind the voluntary domestic allotment measure, led the way to an unprecedented degree of unity. Only Simpson, holding out to the end, still did not accept the plan,[48] but did not attempt to block it. Thus, whatever reservations the national farm organizations had concerning the principles of the Wilson plan were held in abeyance. They could not afford to repeat the failures and frustrations of 1932.

[46] New York *Times,* December 6, 1932.
[47] *Wallace's Farmer,* (November 26, 1932), p. 617.
[48] Fite, "John A. Simpson," p. 577.

Other Interests

In our pluralistic society, occupational organizations are only one of many possible types. Man and his neighbors have attitudes and interests beyond the essentially economic ones. We find, therefore, other organizations today that include memberships based upon social classes, religion, race, ideology, or political affiliation.

Two of the more prominent organizations appearing on the political scene in recent years are the John Birch Society and CORE. The John Birch Society is a special-purpose pressure group of the political right, ideologically speaking. It has emerged to oppose socialism, communism, and left-wing politics in general. Through selective recruiting, the Society has become a vehicle of expression for many Americans who remain basically unreconciled to many political and social changes in the nation and the world since the 1930's.

CORE is one of the more recent organizations established to gain greater economic, social and political rights for American

Negroes, who because of decades of discrimination and segregation were forced to set up an almost separate existence within a predominantly white society. More militant than its predecessor, the National Association for the Advancement of Colored People (NAACP), and working on a narrower front, CORE has infused new blood into the Negro political movement to end segregation as soon as possible. Its tactics include freedom rides, sit-ins and street demonstrations. CORE sponsorship has produced another Negro civil rights group, the Student Non-Violent Coordinating Committee (SNCC), which coordinates its activities quite closely with CORE and other civil rights groups.

The Congress of Racial Equality and Its Strategy*

MARVIN RICH

This short selection by Marvin Rich, *Executive Director of the CORE Scholarship, Education and Defense Fund, deals with the founding, history and activities of CORE. It mentions some of the tactics used by the organization and their success. Further it underlines the deep commitments of its members and the extreme sacrifices they have made in the past.*

A few of us try harder. A few try not at all. Yet the story of CORE is the story of an effort—sustained and sustaining—to put ourselves out of business.

Origin and Early History

James Farmer started it all, in 1941, when he went home again to his native South. He walked up the steps to the "crow's nest" reserved for Negroes in the local movie theatre. Perhaps for the first time, he fully realized that though he believed "Jim Crow" was wrong, he and most of his friends were actually supporting it by their daily actions. He wrote a memo posing this dilemma and called for the formation of a dedicated group of individuals who would combine mind and body in an effort to take personal nonviolent direct action to end discrimination.

This memo was widely circulated among student and religious groups, liberals, pacifists, and socialists in the spring of 1942. One such group was composed primarily of University of Chicago

* Marvin Rich, "The Congress of Racial Equality and Its Strategy," *Annals,* 357 (January, 1965), 113-18.

students. One Sunday afternoon following a session, the group wandered too far from the campus and was refused coffee at a restaurant. They tried to negotiate with management, but were unsuccessful, in spite of the fact that Illinois law forbade discrimination. They then began the first race relations sit-in in America. They were successful in changing policy. The first CORE chapter was formed out of Farmer's memo and this incident. Ever since, CORE chapters have been adapting the techniques of non-violent direct action to different sections of the country and to different forms of discrimination.

The first CORE chapters were college-centered. They included as members students, teachers, ministers, and trade unionists. They were small and elitist. Only a very few individuals were willing to make the sacrifices of time, energy, and reputation demanded of CORE members, for chapters usually met every other week, and committees met on the alternate weeks. There were negotiating sessions with management, training sessions for new members, and workshops before major actions. Then there was the radical nature of our action—picket lines and sit-ins—and the ever-present possibility of arrest. But if the chapters were small, they were also inclusive. It requires discipline and some training to sit-in and to respond to insults with good will. It does not require an advanced degree. CORE chapters have increasingly involved persons from every walk of life in their membership and in their leadership.

The first CORE chapters were located in the North and concentrated on public accomodations—yes, two decades ago throughout the North many restaurants, bowling alleys, skating rinks, and barber shops refused to serve Negroes. There were some experiments with interracial housing co-operatives and some successful efforts to open up job opportunities. But the main thrust was in public accommodations and in the North. It was in the late 1940's and early 1950's that CORE moved into the border states of Maryland, Missouri, and Oklahoma. It was only in the middle 1950's that the radical idea of direct action was able to secure a base in the South as a whole.

As time went on the emphasis in the North turned increasingly to jobs and to open-occupancy housing. The housing efforts included efforts to negoitate with realtors and to open tract housing in new suburbs to meet the needs of individual Negro families. This approach represented the largely middle-class base of these early CORE chapters. The effort to secure jobs, on the other hand was primarily centered on semiskilled occupations in consumer-oriented industries which were amenable to CORE-type pressure. Successes in this field inevitably drew in more Negroes with a working-class background and subtly changed the character of the middle-class and predominantly white Northern chapters. In the South, almost from the beginning there was a far higher percentage of black members, even though the first emphasis was upon public accommodations.

Growth and Expansion

CORE had grown in the early 1940's. However, the groups were small. They had many student members who graduated and moved away. Further, many had been formed to combat a specific instance of discrimination and, once this was eliminated, they would often disappear. In the 1940's and early 1950's there was no paid staff, and CORE was entirely an organization of volunteers, but, by 1956, the organizations began to develop a nucleus of solid chapters and a trained staff. In the late 1950's, CORE developed a series of summer training institutes for leaders of local groups. Those who participated in these institutes were to play important roles in the 1960 student sit-ins.

CORE staffers negotiated at the national level with the variety store chains involved in the 1960 sit-ins and provided workshops at the local level for the thousands of students. These efforts helped the organization to secure the allegiance of many in every section of the country and to secure firm roots in the upper South. The 1961 Freedom Rides, which were initiated, financed, and organized by CORE, brought CORE to the hard-core areas of the South. Today, CORE has a membership of over 80,000. It has approximately doubled in size and budget every year for the past five years. Thus, in the year ending May 31, 1959, CORE's income was $62,000.

Five years later the income was $900,000. There are now 124 chapters affiliated in every section of the country. In 1959 there was a staff of seven. Today there is a professional staff of 137.

Some Results of CORE Activity

The sit-ins and the Freedom Rides were dramatic, and they were successful. Within a year of the first sit-in in Greensboro, North Carolina, on February 1, 1960, more than 140 communities had desegregated at least some restaurant facilities. Most of these were of the chain variety and department stores and could thus be readily identified by the Negro shopper who wanted service without embarrassment. The Freedom Rides secured the Interstate Commerce Commission order which made possible effective enforcement of the Boynton decision. Further, CORE followed up with the Freedom Highways campaign, in the spring and summer of 1962, which opened the Howard Johnson and Holiday Inn chains, so that by 1962 it was possible for a Negro to travel from one end of the country to the other with dignity.

The successes of these campaigns brought into CORE thousands who wanted to share personally in bringing about the civil rights revolution. They have taken action individually which has brought about change. They negotiated with management, leafleted, picketed, and sat-in. And then, they have used the newly opened facilities. That first cup of coffee and that first hamburger have tasted better than any others for thousands. For these people, talk by columnists, politicians, and some civil rights leaders of returning the civil rights struggle to the courts and the legislative halls and out of "the streets" is a way of saying that they are not needed or wanted, that they are to be relegated to the status of dues-payers. This status they will no longer accept.

Direct action plays an important role for the country as well. The Emancipation Proclamation, the First, Fourteenth, and Fifteenth Amendments have been the "law of the land" for some little time. Most Northern states have had civil rights laws for more than eighty years, and these laws have been strengthened since World

War II. And, yet, these laws are as honored in the breach as in the observance. The nonviolent activists know that their demonstrations which caused people to say: "Aren't they going too far, now?" also brought about the Civil Rights Act of 1964. They know that Act is as strong as it is only because of their pressure in the streets of Birmingham, Greensboro, and Jackson. When they went to talk to congressmen they could say: "It really happened in America; it happened to me." Zev Aelony told his congressman about facing a death penalty in Americus, Georgia, on a charge of insurrection. Jerome Smith could tell of being brutally beaten in McComb, Mississippi, while law enforcement officials looked on. And the congressmen responded by strengthening the bill. And the American people have responded—reluctantly, slowly, hesitatingly—but they have responded. When forced to make a choice between making a mockery of the American creed and making it a reality they have chosen the course of equality. Surely, there has been a backlash. It used to be called prejudice, but now there is a new term. But most of the American people and their representatives have chosen to go forward. We in CORE believe that when forced to make a choice, they will continue to make the choice for progress.

The willingness to sacrifice of CORE members has also played an important role. The first sit-in students who actually served their full jail terms in the 1960 sit-ins were members of Tallahassee CORE. The first of the Freedom Riders to serve their full jail terms rather than appeal were members of New Orleans CORE. After the first bus of Freedom Riders was burned in Anniston, Alabama, a second bus proceeded to Birmingham only to be met by a mob. Here Jim Peck, editor of the *CORE-lator,* was brutally beaten. Walter Bergman of Detroit CORE is still partially paralyzed three-and-one-half years later as the result of the injuries suffered then. It was a CORE member, William Moore, who was ambushed and murdered at night on an Alabama highway in April of 1963. A few months later the vice-chairman of Cleveland CORE, the Reverend Bruce Klunder, was killed in a demonstration against the construction of a segregated school. And then CORE staff members James Chaney and Michael Schwerner and their student companion Andrew

Goodman were abducted and murdered in Philadelphia, Mississippi, on the night of June 23, 1964. The sacrifices and the determination to go on in spite of them have struck a responsive chord throughout the nation. The fact that three of the four CORE leaders who have given their lives are white has re-emphasized the essential interracial character of the organization.

There are other forms of sacrifice and commitment. CORE Task Force members live on a meager $44.89 every two weeks, are occasionally cold or hungry, often harassed by local registrars, police, and night riders, and frequently discouraged. They must win the confidence of a people whose only protection is their seeming apathy. CORE Task Force members have picked cotton and worked in tobacco fields to win the confidence of local people and to earn a few dollars for a new shirt. They have given years of their lives while friends have taken the first steps on more rewarding careers. Their day-to-day dedication and sacrifice have played a decisive role in the growth of CORE.

Future Goals and Problems

But the new recruits who have been attracted to CORE because of its militancy, its dramatic successes, and the desire to share in the sacrificial struggle have also brought new problems. Their very number has made it difficult to train them in methods and in the philosophy of nonviolent direct action. When a staff doubles in size each year, very few can have had much training themselves. This past year CORE began a series of area training conferences. In the coming year these will be augmented by larger institutes as well as by regional workshops on specific problem areas.

During the past year CORE has emphasized in the North and in the South a program of community service to develop community roots, indigenous organizations with the ability to help themselves economically and politically. In the North there has been door-to-door canvassing in the sprawling urban ghettos to determine the complaints that most concern the people themselves. This has led to major programs to secure housing-code enforcement through rent strikes, demonstrations before the offices of building commissioners and mayors, and tours of the slum buildings with community leaders. It has also led to successful demonstrations to secure play streets and traffic lights. These kinds of demonstrations, if effectively followed up, can lead to permanent and significant community organization. In Mississippi, Louisiana, and northern Florida, CORE has developed a series of community centers that not only house the voter registration offices, but also have libraries, game rooms, sewing classes, and art activities.

The voter registration efforts of the past have begun to pay off with significant numbers of new registrants in most of the Southern states—excluding Mississippi and Louisiana. For example, during the past two years CORE staffers in South Carolina have co-ordinated registration drives that have put 31,000 Negroes on the books—this in spite of the fact that for most of the year the registration books are open only one day a month and in spite of prolonged slow-downs by some of the registrars. The voter registration effort which has been part of CORE's Southern activity since 1956 is now firmly rooted in the North as well. In part, this has been a natural outgrowth of the effort to service local communities more effectively. It has also been an outgrowth of the effort to defeat Goldwaterism. Soon, the national organization will establish a political action department to co-ordinate and develop local action programs.

The struggle for an increased share in the economy continues to receive major effort. CORE works under the assumption that there cannot be fair employment unless there is relatively full employment. However, we also know that even in a full-employment economy there need not be fair employment. Negroes could and probably would be the last hired and the first fired, confined to the menial and the dead-end jobs. So CORE continues to work to end discrimination by employers and unions. Our major concern has been among consumer-oriented industries where we can be most effective and to secure unskilled and semiskilled jobs where the largest reservoir of unemployed and underemployed manpower is available. There have been some notable examples of success. The First National Bank of Boston, after several weeks of picketing and previous months of negotiations, moved to hire Negroes. We believe that this will mean approximately 1,000 jobs. To do this the company re-evaluated its personnel policies and changed requirements for many jobs. For example, they decided that a messenger really didn't need a high school diploma. In New York, we were able to get the A&P to reverse a long-standing personnel policy and agree to hire hundreds of full-time Negro employees, whereas they had increasingly resorted to part-timers. These victories point to a concern and a direction. To use direct action effectively with primary manufacturers, such as steel and aluminum, will be more difficult than with consumer-oriented companies, but not impossible.

CORE has changed to meet new situations and new demands. It will continue to do so. However, it will also continue to emphasize nonviolent direct action methods which involve people from every status level, to be interracial and interreligious, to be national in scope, youthful in membership and outlook. We believe that it will continue to be the cutting edge of the civil rights movement.

The John Birch Society

Fundamentalism on the Right*

ALAN F. WESTIN

Professor Alan Westin's essay is an analysis of the champion of American right-wing fundamentalism, the John Birch Society. The Society emerges as a semi-secret organization with a monolithic structure and an authoritarian personality under the control of its founder—Robert Welch. According to the author, the Society's image of national politics is conspiratorial; government and its institutions and political leaders, along with established religions and public schools have been infiltrated by Communists. And it further believes only a radical change in our governmental form as prescribed by the Society can save the nation from communism. The essay concludes by raising several points as to why right-wing fundamentalism will continue to exist in the country.

Last April, the Gallup Poll asked a nationwide sample of Americans whether they had heard of the John Birch Society and found that thirty-nine million persons—an extraordinary number, according to Gallup—had read or heard of the Birchers. Of these, 47 per cent had an unfavorable estimate of the Society, 8 per cent were favorable, and 45 per cent had not yet reached a judgment. In one sense, these figures suggest a firm rejection of the Birchers by majority sentiment. But the figures also indicate that at the moment when the Society was receiving its most damaging publicity—when the

* Alan F. Westin, "The John Birch Society: Fundamentalism on the Right," *Commentary*, XXXII (August, 1961), 93-104. Copyright © 1961 by the American Jewish Committee. Reprinted by permission.

mass media were featuring the charge by Birch founder Robert Welch that President Eisenhower was "a dedicated, conscious agent of the Communist conspiracy"—three million persons still concluded that the Society was a commendable, patriotic, anti-Communist organization. If the undecided 45 per cent were to be divided in the same proportion as those who had reached a judgment (and this would probably underweight pro-Birch sentiment), another two and a half million persons would be added to the ranks of the approving. By this estimate it can be argued, then, that at least five and a half million Americans from among the most public-affairs conscious forty million of our adult population were favorably impressed with the John Birch Society.

One reason for this extraordinarily high degree of support is that the Birch Society has become the most appealing, activist, and efficient movement to appear on the extreme right since the fertile decade of the 1930's. Birch membership at present is probably close to sixty thousand and is distributed widely throughout the nation, with particular strength in traditional centers of fundamentalism like Houston, Los Angeles, Nashville, Wichita, and Boston. This membership provides an annual dues income of $1,300,000. Life memberships at $1,000, special donations by wealthy supporters, and sales of Society literature add perhaps $300,000 more, giving the group a present working fund of $1,600,000 a year. By its own count, the Society has twenty-eight staff workers in its home office in Belmont, Massachusetts, thirty fully salaried and expense-paid traveling coordinators, and one hundred partially paid or volunteer coordinators. Its jabbing forefinger has already been felt in the mid-section of dozens of communities, and some commentators not prone to overestimating fringe movements warn that the Society may become an effective united front for the hundreds of right-wing groups currently operating on the American scene.

All this being the case, it is worth asking what kind of group the John Birch Society is and how it compares with traditional right-wing organizations. Why has it suddenly come into prominence at this particular moment, and what are its prospects in the decade ahead?

I

However much factors like urbanization, the cold war, and status insecurities may have provided a new setting for native fundamentalists, a large and irreducible corps of such people has always existed in the United States. Unlike American liberals and conservatives—who accept the political system, acknowledge the loyalty of their opponents, and employ the ordinary political techniques—the fundamentalists can be distinguished by five identifying characteristics:

(1) They assume that there are always solutions capable of producing international victories and of resolving our social problems; when such solutions are not found, they attribute the failure to conspiracies led by evil men and their dupes.

(2) They refuse to believe in the integrity and patriotism of those who lead the dominant social groups—the churches, the unions, the business community, etc.—and declare that the American "Establishment" has become part of the conspiracy.

(3) They reject the political system; they lash out at "politicians," the major parties, and the give-and-take of political compromise as a betrayal of the fundamental Truth and as a circus to divert the people.

(4) They reject those programs for dealing with social, economic, and international problems which liberals and conservatives agree upon as minimal foundations. In their place, the fundamentalists propose drastic panaceas requiring major social change.

(5) To break the net of conspiracy they advocate "direct action," sometimes in the form of a new political party, but more often through secret organization, push-button pressure campaigns, and front groups. Occasionally "direct action" will develop into hate-propaganda and calculated violence.

At various periods, the United States has experienced both left-fundamentalism (the Knights of Labor, the Wobblies, the Populists, the Communists, the Trotskyites, and the Wallace Progressives) and right-fundamentalism (the Know-Nothings, the Coughlinites, the Silver-Shirts, and America First). Today, right-fundamentalism spans a broad spectrum. At one pole, with its passionate thousands, is the "hate" right, led by the Conde McGinleys, Gerald L. K. Smiths, Admiral Crommelins, Father Terminellos, John Kaspers, and George Rockwells, who offer various combinations of anti-Semitic, anti-Catholic, and anti-Negro sentiment. These groups are thoroughly discredited in contemporary America, and the major problem they present is a matter of defining the line which our law should draw between deviant expression and hate-mongering or advocacy of violence. At the opposite pole is the semi-respectable right. Here we encounter a variety of different political and educational organizations including the Foundation for Economic Education, the Daughters of the American Revolution, the Committee for Constitutional Government, and the White Citizens' Councils of the South. Socially prominent figures belong to such groups, which are well-financed, often have connections with local and national major party factions, and exercise substantial lobbying influence. Their supporters and leaders may long to break with the two-party system and start a rightist party, but they are restrained by the knowledge that this would isolate them and thus diminish their present effectiveness.

The John Birch Society stands between these two poles. In the words of one of its chapter leaders in Louisville, Kentucky, it is a "middle-of-the-road right-wing organization." In order to get a precise picture of its ideology and tactics, I have examined every published word issued by the Society since its formation in 1958: the 1961 annotated edition of the *Blue Book of the John Birch Society*, its operating manual and theological fount; the monthly *Bulletins* which are sent to members and contain the agenda of activities (the 1960 issues of the *Bulletin* are available in a bound edition titled *The White Book of the John Birch Society*); those writings of Robert Welch which have been officially incorporated and reprinted by the Society (e.g., *The Life of John Birch, May God Forgive Us, A Letter to the South on Segregation*); and every issue of *American Opinion*, the monthly publication edited by Robert Welch for the Society.*

Measured by its official materials, the authenticated accounts of

* This was published by Welch before February 1958 under the slightly more modest title of *One Man's Opinion*.

Welch's speeches, and public comments by members of the Society's Council, the Society emerges as a pure-bred specimen of American right-fundamentalism.

(1) *Its image of world events and American politics is wholly conspiratorial.* In the July 1960 *Bulletin,* Welch explains that the "key" to the advance of world Communism "is treason right within our government and the place to find it is right in Washington." The danger, Welch says in the *Blue Book,* "is almost entirely internal." And it is "a certainty," he writes in *May God Forgive Us,* that there are "more Communists and Communist sympathizers in our government today than ever before." As recently as January 1961, Welch was informing his supporters that "Communist influences are now in almost complete control of our Federal Government."

Each year since 1958, Welch and his "board of experts" have published a "scoreboard" rating all the nations of the world according to the "present degree of Communist influence and control over the economic and political affairs" of the country. In 1958, the United States was rated as 20-40 per cent under Communist control; in 1959, the United States went up to 30-50 per cent; and in 1960, the figure climbed to 40-60 per cent. (At that pace, we will reach the 80-100 per cent mark in 1964.) England's rating went from 20-40 per cent in 1958 to 50-70 per cent in 1960. Israel is presently rated as 40-60 per cent controlled; Egypt 80-100 per cent.

Everywhere, the Birchers advise, Communists are at the heart of events, even some events that might seem to less skilled observers remote from Kremlin direction. In an open letter to Khrushchev in 1958, Welch said "your hands played the decisive unseen part" in the run on American banks and their closing in 1933. It was the Communist-contrived recognition of the Soviets in 1933 that "saved them from financial collapse." The "very idea of American foreign aid was dreamed up by Stalin, or by his agents for him." The "trouble in the South over integration is Communist-contrived"; the Communists have invented a "phony 'civil rights' slogan to stir up bitterness and civil disorder, leading gradually to police-state rule by federal troops and armed resistance to that rule." The United States Supreme Court "is one of the most important agencies of Communism." The Federal Reserve system is a "realization" of "point 5" of the *Communist Manifesto,* calling for centralization of credit in the hands of the state. The purpose of proposed legislation requiring registration of privately-owned firearms is to aid the Communists in making "ultimate seizure of such by the government easier and more complete." Everywhere, Welch concludes, the Communists are winning: in "the press, the pulpit, the radio and television media, the labor unions, the schools, the courts, and the legislative halls of America."

All the above descriptions of conspiratorial trends have been cited from official Birch Society literature, what Welch calls the Society's "steps to the Truth." But the picture grows darker when one turns to the *Black Book,* or, as it is more commonly known, *The Politician*— the book-length "letter" which Welch circulated "privately" to hundreds of persons but which the Society has carefully rejected as an official document. *The Politician* is to the Society what Leninist dogma is to the Communist front groups in Western or neutralist nations—it is the ultimate truth held by the founder and his hardcore, but it is too advanced and too powerful to present, as yet, to the "masses" being led. In *The Politician,* Welch names names. Presidents Roosevelt, Truman, and Eisenhower; [the late] Secretary of State John Foster Dulles; [former] CIA Director Allen Dulles; Chief Justice Warren—all of these men are called knowing instruments of the Communist conspiracy.

It is worth noting that Eisenhower and his administration draw the strongest venom in *The Politician,* just as Social Democrats do in full-dose Communist literature. For Welch (a Taft supporter and McCarthy stalwart), the Eisenhower administration was a betrayal which could only have had Communists at its source. "For many reasons and after a lot of study," Welch writes, "I personally believe [John Foster] Dulles to be a Communist agent." "Allen Dulles is the most protected and untouchable supporter of Communism, next to Eisenhower himself, in Washington." Arthur H. Burns's job as head of the Council of Economic Advisers "has been merely a cover-up for Burns's liaison work between Eisenhower and some of his Communist bosses." "The chances are very strong that Milton Eisenhower is actually Dwight Eisenhower's superior and boss within the Communist Party." As for Dwight Eisenhower himself, Welch states unequivocally: "There is only one possible word to describe [Eisenhower's] purpose and actions. That word is treason." "My firm belief that Dwight Eisenhower is a dedicated, conscious agent of the Communist conspiracy," he continues, "is based on an accumulation of detailed evidence so extensive and so palpable that it seems to put this conviction beyond any reasonable doubt." Discussing what he terms Eisenhower's "mentality of fanaticism," Welch refuses to accept the idea that Ike may just be an "opportunistic politician" aiding the Communists. "I personally think he has been sympathetic to ultimate Communist aims, realistically willing to use Communist means to help them achieve their goals, knowingly accepting and abiding by Communist orders, and consciously serving the Communist conspiracy for all of his adult life."

(2) *The Birchers impugn the integrity and patriotism of those at the head of the major social and economic groups of the nation.* In a supplement to the February 1961 *Bulletin,* Welch announced that "Communist influences" are "very powerful in the top echelons of our educational system, our labor-union organizations, many of our religious organizations, and of almost every important segment of our national life. Insidiously but rapidly the Communists are now reaching the tentacles of their conspiracy downward throughout the whole social, economic, and political pyramid." Thus, the National Council of Churches of Christ is Communist-minded, and from 3 to 5 per cent of the Protestant clergy have been called actual Communists. "Treason," Welch further declares, "is widespread and rampant in our high army circles." The American Medical Association has been "took" and can no longer be depended upon for support in the fight against socialism. So too with the United States Chamber of Commerce, which has been preaching dangerously liberal and internationalist doctrines in its courses on practical politics. (When Chamber leaders protested this slur, Welch replied that their outraged

reaction was exactly like that of the State Department in the 1940's when charges of Communist infiltration were first raised.) The leadership of our universities, corporations, foundations, communications media—all are riddled with Communists, or "Comsymps" (a word Welch coined to avoid having to say whether a given person was a real party member or only a sympathizer).

Naturally, Welch and his colleagues are certain that these "Comsymp" elites are out to destroy him and his movement. References to persecution and images of martyrdom abound in Birch literature, ranging from incessant mention of how the patron saint (Senator McCarthy) was driven to his death, to suggestions that Welch may be murdered one day by the Communists.

(3) *The Birchers are convinced that the Communists have gone so far in penetrating American politics that there is little hope in the existing political system.* In his letter to Khrushchev, Welch wrote that the Communists obviously intended to "maintain and increase [their] working control over both our major political parties." We cannot count on "politicians, political leadership or even political action." Though he advocate[d] the nomination, on an American Party ticket, of . . . Barry Goldwater for President and J. Strom Thurmond for Vice President in 1964, Welch . . . warned his followers that even Goldwater—the most "Americanist" figure around in politics at the moment—is "still a politician" and therefore not to be relied upon. Welch . . . also had some things to say about "Jumping Jack" Kennedy. According to Welch, the nation received "the exact Communist line . . . from Jack Kennedy's speeches, as quickly and faithfully as from the *Worker* or the *National Guardian*. . . ." And in 1959, Welch denounced the "Kennedy brat" for "finding the courage to join the jackals picking at the corpse of McCarthy."

A particularly revealing sample of Welch's sense of American political realities is found in his description of the Eisenhower "steal" of the Republican nomination in 1952, one of the "dirtiest deals in American political history, participated in if not actually engineered by Richard Nixon." If Taft had not been cheated of the nomination, Welch predicted:

It is almost certain that Taft would then have been elected President by a far greater plurality than was Eisenhower, that a grand rout of the Communists in our government and in our midst would have been started, that McCarthy would be alive today, and that we wouldn't even be in this mess. . . .

(4) *Most of the Birch Society's positive program consists of advocating the repeal of things or the removal of the nation from something or somewhere.* A partial list of the things that the Society describes as wicked, Communist, and dangerous includes: U.S. membership in the United Nations, the International Labor Organization, the World Health Organization, the International Trade Organization, and UNICEF; membership in GATT (the General Agreement on Trades and Tariffs); reciprocal trade agreements; the "useless and costly" NATO; "so-called defense spending"; all foreign aid; diplomatic relations with the Soviet Union and all other Communist nations; the National Labor Relations Act; social security; the graduated income tax; the Rural Electrification Administration, the Reconstruction Finance Corporation, and TVA; government wage and price controls; "forced integration"; "deliberately fraudulent" U.S. government bonds; the Federal Reserve system; urban renewal; fluoridation; metro government; the corporate dividend tax; the "mental health racket"; federal aid to housing; and all programs "regimenting" farmers.

Some items on this list may be opposed by conservatives or by liberals. But taken together, it adds up to a nihilist's plea for the repeal of industrialism and the abolition of international politics. Such a program can be called rational or even political only by people who do not know what those words mean.

(5) *Finally, the Birch Society advocates both "direct action" and "dirty tactics" to "break the grip of the Communist conspiracy."* Unlike those right-fundamentalist groups which have energetic leaders but passive memberships, the Birchers are decidedly activist. "Get to work or learn to talk Russian," is a slogan Welch recommends to his followers, and they are certainly hard at work. From national headquarters in Belmont, Massachusetts, Welch formulates

a set of complementary national and local action programs, then issues them to members through directives in the *Bulletin* and contacts with chapter leaders. A mixture of traditional and fundamentalist techniques is prescribed. The local programs include infiltration of community organizations such as PTA ("to take them away from the Communists"); harassment of "pro-Communist" speakers at church meetings, political gatherings, and public forums; creation of local front groups (e.g., the Committee Against Summit Entanglements, College Graduates Against Educating Traitors at Government Expense, the Committee to Impeach Earl Warren, and the Committee to Investigate Communist Influences at Vassar College); campaigns to secure endorsement of Birch positions and signatures for Birch petitions in all groups that Birch members belong to (e.g., veterans and business organizations); letters and telephone calls to local public officials, leading citizens, and newspapers who support what the Society opposes or oppose the Society directly; monthly telephone calls to the local public library to make sure it has copies of the five right-wing books recommended by Welch every month.

The national campaigns are carefully pinpointed efforts. They range from letter-and postcard-writing to national advertising campaigns. In the past two years, Birchers have been told to: write the National Boy Scouts director and demand to know why the president of the National Council of Churches addressed their National Jamboree; insist personally and in writing each time a member flies American, United, or Eastern Airlines that they stock *Human Events* and *National Review* on their planes; write to *Newsweek* to protest a "pro-FLN Communist" story (the Society has a crush on Jacques Soustelle), to *Life* protesting the "glorification" of Charles Van Doren, and to the NBC network and the Purex Corporation for sponsoring a TV drama favorable to Sacco and Vanzetti; circulate petitions and write letters on the number one project of the moment, to impeach Chief Justice Warren and thereby "give the Communists a setback." Welch also sends out the copy for punchy postcards to be addressed to national political leaders. To cite instances in 1960 alone: to [former] Ambassador Henry Cabot Lodge, Jr. at the U.N., "Two questions, Mr. Lodge—Who

Murdered Bang-Jensen? And Which Side are You On?"; to [former] Secretary of State Christian Herter, "Castro is a Communist. Trujillo is an anti-Communist. Whose Side are You On?"; and to President Eisenhower, on the eve of the scheduled summit conference, "Dear President Eisenhower—If you go, don't come back."

The last postcard stirred some protests from Society members, who felt that Welch's savage little message to the President was a bit too strong. Welch set them straight in the *Bulletin*: "It is one of our many sorrows that, in fighting the evil forces which now threaten our civilization, for us to be *too civilized* is unquestionably to be defeated." The Communists, he continued, want us to be "too gentle, too respectable . . . [but] this is not a cream-puff war . . . and we do mean business every step of the way." Welch admitted that the technique of planted and loaded questions and the disruption of meetings was a "dirty trick," but he still defended it as another vital tactic.

To stimulate compliance by members with the local and national efforts prescribed each month in the *Bulletin,* Welch has devised the MMM system, or "Member's Monthly Memos." These forms are filled out by the member detailing what he or she has done and including sundry observations on the "Americanist fight." They are then collected by the chapter leader and transmitted to Belmont. Welch and his staff, according to the *Bulletin,* spend much time going over the MMM's.

So far, the Birch Society has been successful in attracting to it some highly substantial figures in local communities—physicians, stockbrokers, retired military officers, lawyers, businessmen (particularly small and middle-sized manufacturers in the Midwest and South), and professionals, many of whom have become local chapter leaders and state coordinators. The Council of the Society is a veritable board of directors of right-fundamentalism: men like Colonel Lawrence Bunker, Cola G. Parker, T. Coleman Andrews, Clarence Manion, and Spruille Braden. Among the contributing editors and editorial advisory committee for *American Opinion* are J. B. Matthews, William S. Schlamm, Kenneth Colegrove, J. Bracken Lee, Ludwig von Mises, [the late] Adolph Menjou, J. Howard Pew, and Albert C. Wedemeyer. In several communities, observers of the Society have noted a significant number of thirty-to-forty-year-olds joining the organization. Welch has stated that half of the Society's membership is Catholic, that there are some Jewish members, and that there are Negroes also—two segregated locals in the South and integrated chapters in the North.

Press reports suggest that most of the Society's members already had strong affiliations with other right-wing groups before the Birch Society was formed. What Welch hopes to do is build a one-million member organization by welding together the masses of right-fundamentalist joiners into the fighting educational and pressure arm of the John Birch Society. In the *Bulletin* and *American Opinion,* Welch continually offers flattering salutes to various right-wing groups, publications, and personalities, stressing that "Americanists" can work in several forums at once for the cause. In May 1961, for example, Welch listed two pages of "other anti-Communist groups" which he endorsed and urged Birchers to support. These included the American Coalition of Patriotic Societies, the American Council of Christian Laymen, the Cardinal Mindszenty Foundation, the Catholic Freedom Foundation, the Christian Crusade, the Freedom Club (of Los Angeles), Freedom in Action (Houston), the Intercollegiate Society of Individualists, the Network of Patriotic Letter Writers (Pasadena), and We, The People! (Chicago). In turn, Welch's appearances are often sponsored by such groups: the Freedom Club of Reverend James Fifield arranged his Los Angeles rally, and the Sons of the American Revolution sponsored his Houston appearance.

To a large extent, Welch's personal selflessness and his salesmanship have already made him a rallying point for the fundamentalist right, and no recent right-wing group comes to mind which has achieved so large and solid a dues-paying and working membership. In a world of Communist advances in Asia and Africa, pressures on Berlin, vast changes in the relation of white to colored populations throughout the world, the Birch Society has developed a thoroughly satisfying way for the thin-lipped little lady from Wichita or the self-made manufacturer of plumbing fixtures in North Carolina to work in manageable little daily doses against "the Communists." The cancer of the unquestioned international Communist menace and the surgery of local pressure on the PTA and public library—here is a perfect appeal for right fundamentalism. This highlights the fact that the Society's most successful efforts to date have not been on the national scene but on the "soft underbelly" of American democracy— those places where a minimum of pressure can often produce maximum terror and restrictive responses. Welch has stressed that school boards, city colleges, local businesses, local clergy, and similar targets are the ones to concentrate on. Above all, Welch has brought *coordination* to the fundamentalist right—coordinated targets, coordinated meetings and rallies, and coordinated pressure tactics. "All of a sudden," the director of a Jewish Community Council in one city reflected, "the right wingers began to function like a disciplined platoon. We have had to contend with precision and saturation ever since."

II

If this is what the Society advocates and how it functions, what are its immediate and long-range prospects? In the short run, the Society has lost one of its most potent weapons—the element of secrecy. Those in local communities who felt the sting of Birch campaigns during 1959-61 report that it was the factor of surprise at these sudden fundamentalist pressures and the unawareness of their organizational source which threw them off balance. Now, however, the Society has been brought into public view. Its authoritarian character and extremist statements have been attacked in both liberal and conservative newspapers; by important Catholic, Protestant, and Jewish leaders; and by political figures as diverse as Richard Nixon, [the late] President John Kennedy, [former] Attorney General Robert Kennedy, [the late] Representative Sam Rayburn, Senator Thomas E. Dodd, and even [former] Senator Barry Goldwater himself. The fact that a prominent leader of the Society who had been chosen as Washington lobbyist for the American Retail Federation was hastily discarded in June by the Federation because of his Birch affiliation indicates that recent publicity has damaged the Society's claim to respectability. One Midwestern Congressman known for his open advocacy of right-wing movements felt it wise recently to seek out liberal leaders from his community and explain privately that he did *not* support the Birch movement. Increasingly, those "solid" figures who joined the group when it was operating privately will have to face public disapproval of the Society, and this will probably cause some falling away among border-line conservatives.

In the longer perspective, however, there are three specific factors which deserve mention in assessing the Society's potential growth. The first is the authoritarian character of the group and the centralized control exercised by Robert Welch (a situation which has led [former] Senator Goldwater to criticize Welch directly). According to the charter of the Society, Welch is the absolute leader; there is no accounting of dues or contributions; there is no representative process or democratic system for selecting programs or defining positions; and Welch has the power (which he has used) to expel any member or chapter for reasons sufficient to him, without right of hearing or appeal on the expulsion. This has produced widespread criticism of Welch as a "little Hitler" and the Society as a group run on fascist lines. However, Welch has stressed again and again that members can disagree with him; that he doesn't expect any member to carry out a project which violates his conscience; and that the Society definitely opposes an "enforced conformity" within its ranks. The controls, Welch explains, are needed to prevent Communist infiltration of the Society (which he believes has already begun or will certainly begin as the Society becomes more effective) and infiltration by hate-mongers. This blend of leader-principle and group self-protection has great appeal to right-fundamentalists and even to some right-wing conservatives. The authoritarian set-up makes fine ammunition for liberal and main-stream-conservative fire, but this is not likely to harm Welch a bit in his recruiting among fundamentalists.

A second factor is Welch himself. The fantastic allegations he has made in *The Politician*—even though the book has not been endorsed by the Council and is, indeed, repudiated by some members —have branded him as an unbalanced figure and convinced many staunch conservatives that Welch is a truly dangerous leader. The conservative Los Angeles *Times* recently did a thorough exposé of the Society and wrote a stinging editorial which read Welch out of the conservative camp. Out of self-defense, Republicans in California joined in with the *Times* (especially in condemning Welch's attacks on Eisenhower), for the Birchers were proving so effective in pulling the Republican party to the far right that some counterattack was felt to be essential. Welch himself has been highly equivocal about *The Politician*. He insists that it was a "private" letter and never published, though he does not deny its authenticity. In the May 1961 issue of the *Bulletin,* he alludes to "questions or criticism from some of our most loyal members" relating to *The Politician*. To these, he replies that "the considerations involved in connection with many such matters are varied, overlapping, involved, and with too many ramifications to be explained in short compass. There are even times when, for reasons of strategy, we take an oblique approach to a specific objective, and fully to explain every step of our course would seriously handicap our effectiveness." Having decided not to say anything at all, Welch assured members that if he "could give . . . the whole background of events" then objections might turn into approval, and with this, he dropped the subject of his *magnum opus*.

Those members and leaders of the Society who find anything to criticize in *The Politician* (and many have fully endorsed the charges it featured) have stressed that Welch is entitled to his personal views and that their disagreement with him on Ike or the two Dulles brothers indicates how free and diverse the Society is.

In all probability Welch's talents as an organizer, salesman, proselytizer, and unifier of right-wing ranks overweigh (for the right-wing aristocracy) his tactical blunder in *The Politician*. Since he controls the Society fully, he is not likely to be replaced, and, indeed, there is no indication that an acceptable replacement is available either in the Society or outside it. As long as he heads the Society, however, *The Politician* will severely limit his credibility outside fundamentalist strongholds.

A third factor relating to the Birch Society's immediate prospects is the question of anti-Semitism. Repeated charges have been made that the Society is a genteel endorser of anti-Semitic persons and literature. Welch has recommended to his members such anti-Semitic publications as Russell Maguire's *American Mercury* and Merwin K. Hart's *Economic Council Newsletter*. Hart—who often talks about a conspiracy of "Zionists and their confederates" controlling America and whose organization was described by a Congressional committee investigating lobbying as one which relies on "an ill-concealed anti-Semitism"—is presently leader of the Birch Society's Manhattan Chapter No. 26. In addition, such openly anti-Semitic spokesmen as Conde McGinley have rushed to endorse the Birch Society. In the March 15, 1961 issue of *Common Sense,* McGinley wrote: "Inasmuch as we have received many inquiries from all over the United States regarding the John Birch Society, we want to go on record. We believe this to be an effective, patriotic group, in good hands."

On the other hand, Welch has always appealed to all religions, has urged Jews to join the Society, and has warned that it is a "Communist tactic to stir up distrust and hatred between Jews and Gentiles, Catholics and Protestants, Negroes and Whites." Much of the April 1961 issue of his *Bulletin* is devoted to a discussion of the allegation that the Society is anti-Semitic, and what Welch has to say there is well worth close examination.

He opens by noting that "the most vicious" charges leveled against him have come from "such notorious anti-Semites as Lyrl Clark Van Hyning *(Women's Voice)* and Elizabeth Dilling (the *Dilling Bulletin)* on the grounds that my various committees and supporters are nothing but a 'bunch of Jews and Jew-kissers.' . . ." He then cites the names of Jewish members of the Society such as Willi Schlamm, Julius Epstein, Morrie Ryskind, the late Alfred Kohlberg, and Rabbi Max Merritt, and indicates that it has been endorsed by the American Jewish League Against Communism (a Jewish right-fundamentalist group). Next, Welch explains that he probably has "more good friends of the Jewish faith than any other Gentile in America." When he was in the candy manufacturing business in Massachusetts, he recalls, he had many Jewish customers; he drank coffee in their kitchens at midnight, borrowed money from them and lent them money in return, and engaged in every kind of business and social activity with Jews.

Turning to some specific accusations, Welch admits that he used a pamphlet by Joseph Kamp as a source for his book, *May God Forgive*

Us, and also paid Kamp a hundred dollars to go through *The Life of John Birch* to find errors. This was in 1954. But later, he says, he became "aware of both the fact and the weapon of anti-Semitism in America, and I wanted no part of the whole argument." He had nothing further to do with Kamp after the 1954 contact, but he adds that he still simply doesn't know enough to say whether Kamp is really anti-Semitic.

Welch goes on to relate that a person who had been trying to convert one local chapter into "a hotbed of anti-Semitism" was dropped from the Society, and he pledges that the Society will never become a haven for anti-Semitic feeling "so long as I am directing its policies." After several additional paragraphs explaining why no member of the Jewish faith can also be a Communist (and pointing out that Karl Marx was "probably the most vicious anti-Semite of all times"), Welch concludes with the following warning:

> There is only one real danger in the charge of anti-Semitism today, to the man who actually is not anti-Semitic. It is that the utter (and in some cases malicious) unfairness of the charge may cause him to react with anger against Jews in general, and then begin to let some of his feeling creep into his writings or his speeches. That brings on even more vitriolic attacks, with a few more straws to support them. And so the development continues until the man in question winds up actually becoming violently anti-Semitic. And he seldom realizes that this was the Communist game and purpose all along, of which the majority of Jews who innocently helped the Reds to implement it were as unaware and innocent as the ordinary Methodist who supports the National Council of Churches. And many an anti-Communist fighter of great promise in America has had his career ruined and his effectiveness destroyed by letting himself fall into that carefully prepared trap.

This will never happen to him, Welch declares; to his "thousands of Jewish friends" he pledges, "I shall remain your friend, no matter what happens. . . ."*

---

* One other bit of information bearing on Welch's attitude is that he has been consistently anti-Nasser, viewing the Arab nationalists as aiding the Communists in gaining control of the Middle East.

All the evidence available at the moment suggests the presence of a certain ambivalence in the Birch Society on the matter of anti-Semitism. Welch himself seems to be personally without bias toward Jews, and he wants the Society to reflect this position. Yet there is no doubt that some local leaders and members are well-known anti-Semites. With one after another of the rabbinical associations and major Jewish civic groups speaking out in complete condemnation of Welch and his movement, there will be rising pressures to respond to the "Jewish attacks." Probably, Welch will continue to allow some light flirtation with the more sophisticated anti-Semitic spokesmen. But it is a testimony to American maturity and the activities of Jewish defense agencies that open anti-Semitism is seen as a dead end today for any "middle-of-the-road right-wing organization."

One final aspect of the Society should be noted. Welch's writings have a remarkable combination of fantastic allegation and sweet reasonableness. Along with his proposals advocating drastic action against the Communist agents all over America will go reminders to be polite while making menacing telephone calls to local officials, to exercise self-restraint when attacked unfairly, and to take no action which violates "moral principles." "It is a major purpose of the John Birch Society," he often explains, one "never to be overlooked by its members, to help in every way we can—by example as well as precept—to restore an abiding sense of moral values to greater use as a guide of conduct for individuals, for groups, and ultimately for nations." If there are some right-fundamentalists to whom this sort of passage sounds a bit like the National Council of Churches, the total blend of warm-hearted, main-street vigilantism is still appealing to the majority of Welch's followers.

III

Whatever the specific prospects for the Birch Society—and I consider them unhappily bright—the 1960's will surely be years of expansion for the fundamentalist right in this country. Several things point toward that conclusion.

First, this will be a decade of immense frustration for American foreign policy. We will witness increased neutralism among the new nations; increased militancy among the non-white peoples over questions of color; constant military and scientific pressures from the Russians and, soon, the Chinese Communists; diminished American influence in the United Nations; greater conflict in Latin America; and continued outlays of foreign assistance which do not "buy loyalties" or "deliver votes" on critical issues. If the United States can simply prevent these situations from exploding, most informed students of diplomacy would think we had done well. But cutting losses inflicted by the stagnant 1950's and preparing hopeful future positions is not going to appeal to the right-fundamentalist masses (or the frantic pacifist variety on the left either). The right is unshakable in its faith in unilateral solutions and its belief that each loss for America can be traced to a Communist agent or "Comsymp" in the CIA, at the New York *Times,* in the Cathedral of St. John the Divine, or at the Yale Law School. And the inescapable strategic retreats of the early 1960's (Laos is a good example) will lend fuel to the fires on the right.

Second, the domestic racial issue also poses a serious threat of a rise in right-fundamentalism. In the 1960's, the struggle for Negro equality will move increasingly into areas outside the South. Lower-middle-class resentments against Negro neighbors and Negro competitors are bound to increase. The crescendo of Negro militancy and the spreading use of government power to enforce civil rights will peel away the already thinned layers of toleration in many sectors of the Northern and Western population. In this area of public policy, groups like the Birch Society—which are not explicitly anti-Negro but oppose compulsory integration—have a promising position, and the reservoirs of white hostility, unless carefully and wisely channeled by both white and Negro liberal leaders, could fill the well of the fundamentalist-right to overflowing.

Third, there exists the distinct possibility of an unprecedented coalition of Catholic and Protestant right-fundamentalists in the 1960's. Only those who know little about the history of American Catholicism would assume that this is a monolithic community. Yet many factors suggest that the 1960's may see an even deeper division of American Catholics into warring ideological factions than has obtained at any time in the past. Already some influential Catholics are complaining bitterly that [the late] President Kennedy . . . joined the "Liberalist Establishment," that he "[sold] out" Catholic Church interests, and that the administration of the first Catholic President may go down in history as the "softest on Communism." This is far from the dominant view among American Catholics. Indeed, it may represent the last thrashing of the old, super-loyalist element in the American Catholic community—a group which will be goaded to extremism by the sight of an a-clerical, literate, sophisticated Catholic liberal in the White House. Under these conditions, and with the magic memory of Joseph McCarthy to help bridge the chasm of the Reformation, the fundamentalist Protestants and the fundamentalist Catholics may enter into an alliance (possibly inside the Birch Society).

. . .

III
PRESSURE GROUPS AND GOVERNMENT

Foreword

Government's most consequential activity is policy-making. It may mean the building of a national highway system, an increase in federal income taxes or federal aid to colleges and universities. It is the process of making relatively routine decisions such as changing governmental office forms to significantly important decisions, such as the passage of Medicare legislation—a law which will eventually affect the lives of millions of Americans.

In a democratic society such as ours, policy-making (a law, a presidential directive, or an agency decision) is both influenced and formulated as the result of the activities of many individuals and organizations. Such organizations as Congress and the executive agencies daily make decisions of varying import. The President and individual congressmen also make decisions which will affect the orientation and thrust of governmental activity. Pluralism, then, is the overriding characteristic of public policy-making. No one individual, no one center within government monopolizes this function. Governmental agencies and individuals are only part of the policy stream. Public policy-making is both fostered and conditioned by certain constitutional arrangements. The constitutional principle of separation of powers, for example, is one of these arrangements. The fact that three branches of government—executive, legislative, judicial—were created allows no one single branch to become dominant in policy-making. Each branch operates both semi-independently and interdependently with the others. The formulation of public policy becomes an interdependent function of all three.

A system of checks and balances is a second constitutional arrangement which allows the power of one branch to be counter-balanced by the power of the others. This concept of "balanced government" is an old one, harking back to the times of the Greek philosopher, Aristotle. The writers of the United States' Constitution, however, adapted it to the American experience to mean that the several constituent parts of government must be kept in balance. Each branch, under the Constitution, has enough power to indirectly affect the operation of the others.

The consequence of this has been a considerable overlapping of policy-making and function among the three branches. For example, treaties do not bind our nation without senatorial ratification after executive negotiation. The Supreme Court may void an executive action as being in conflict with the Constitution, but the President appoints members of the Supreme Court. Public policy-making proceeds, thus, on a pluralistic basis reflecting in whole or in part the decentralized character of our national government.

Policy and policy-making emanates, also, from outside government and its institutions. Individuals and their organizations demand certain services from government: Social Security, Medicare, unemployment compensations, aid to the blind or cheaper home loans. These demands, in the form of pressures, are directed toward government because of its primacy and authority in these and other policy areas. The division of labor, then, between private and public policy-making becomes blurred. Pressure groups will influence and seek access to legislators or executive personnel in order to mold policy-making along the lines of group desires. The NAACP kept unrelenting pressure on Congress in 1963 and 1964 in order to ensure the passage of civil rights legislation.

Pressure groups, as they become more established and politically organized, enjoy greater independence and power. Their independence is bolstered many times by growing memberships and greater financial support. Power grows because a certain relationship becomes established with government which is strengthened with time, resources and support for public officials. This intimacy over the years enhances a group's opportunities to become influential in policy making.

Because many of our top policy-makers are in elective office, they are continually seeking the kind of political support pressure groups can give them. The money, propaganda and membership of various pressure groups are coveted by political parties and candidates. In order to win elections, candidates will pledge themselves to support the platforms and policies of various groups. Once in office, these officials are under an obligation to implement in some way the objectives of their group support.

Policy-making is, thus, a composite or mosaic. Many interacting parts are involved and contribute to its final make-up. Certainly, the presence within our society of hundreds of pressure groups— wielding power and influence—dramatizes the pluralism of the process. The competition and conflict among these various groups to be influential makes policy-making processes a power struggle. Government is an arena in which groups contend for its attention and support at every level. Government has the task of deciding which group demands will be influential and acted upon and which will be rejected.

Pressure Groups in Congress*

EMANUEL CELLER

According to Congressman Emanuel Celler, pressure groups are an indispensable part of lawmaking. The legislator is a message center through which pressure groups, as part of the electorate, make their views known. He must be politically astute enough to incorporate group demands within his constituency demands. Although congressional pressures have been subject to abuses in the past, Congressman Celler believes these will be corrected when more of the electorate becomes concerned with the lawmaking process.

As the result of an amazing new breakthrough in electronics, scientific articles written in Russian can be fed into a machine, a kind of bilingual typewriter, which translates and returns them in English. This marvel is already functioning in a rudimentary way and its perfection will provide American investigators with untold stores of basic science research that are not now available. A side effect, of course, will be to transform the existing shortage of competent human translators into an over-supply.

No doubt within the lives of many readers this new technique will be developed and improved. The next step may be an automatic evaluator capable of grading as well as receiving and translating messages. When that time comes, will Senators and Representatives no longer be required to perform, each for himself according to his lights, the arduous task of ascribing the proper weight and significance to the thousands of messages which come to them annually from the people? Science fiction writers, undoubtedly, will soon envision

* Emanuel Celler, "Pressure Groups in Congress," *Annals,* 319 (September, 1958), 2-9.

an automatic legislator that will supplant the Congress, just as the automatic translator seems to be about to supplant human linguists.

An Automatic Legislature

To me, legislation is the most exacting job in the world, and the most enjoyable. I do not relish the idea of its technological displacement. But neither would I retard the march of progress. So, in anticipation of that perfect state in which legislation can be performed by a machine, and in gratitude for the many years of satisfaction I have had being allowed to participate in doing it the old way, I should like—as the social scientists say—to "construct a model" of the automatic legislator of the future, with special attention to problems of intake.

A word as to the purpose of this machine: it would replace the human—hence imperfect—legislator, whose function, in every political democracy, is to appraise and arbitrate the conflicting demands of the people. Civilized society entrusts the orderly accommodation of these demands to its legislatures as an alternative to strife and chaos. The essentially arbital character of the legislative role cannot be overstressed. Politics is aptly termed "the art of the possible." In its very nature, effective legislation is the fruit of compromise.

Those who decry the readiness of Congressmen to reconcile their aspirations to the demands of particular political situations seem to me to miss this essential characteristic of the legislative process. The "good" representative in Congress, manifestly, is he who effectively accommodates conflicting interests within his constituency; who successfully relates the needs of his constituents to those of the people as a whole; and who, at the same time, harmonizes his responses to the demands made upon him with the dictates of his conscience. Of corrupt or venal influences on legislators, I shall speak presently. But make no mistake about this: the elected representative who *wholly* subordinates the selfish requirements of interest groups to the furtherance of abstract principle, who ignores the felt needs of people in *exclusive* pursuit of high ideals, falls as far short of fulfilling the legislative function as the legislator who sells his vote. And I must add that he enjoys a substantially poorer expectancy of survival in office. In a sense this is justified, for a legislator is not elected in order that he may function exclusively by Divine guidance or personal intuition; he is a message center and reagent in a vast communications system through which the electorate make known their needs.

I should like to appraise the practices which are usually grouped within the concept "lobbying" in their aspect as elements of this communications system—as the "intake" of the automatic legislator of the future. The character and quality of these messages and their impact on legislation have been the subject of century-long public discussion, both in and out of Congress, and have given rise to scores of learned articles. Many of these articles follow a discernible pattern, somewhat as follows: "the right of the people to petition Congress for the redress of grievances is guaranteed by the Constitution, therefore, lobbying cannot be prohibited; there is good lobbying and bad lobbying—open and forthright lobbying is good, venal and deceptive lobbying is bad; Congress may and should curb or prohibit bad lobbying; and this or that remedy will best eliminate the abuses, while preserving the right."

I have no quarrel with any of this. But I believe that it tends to undervalue lobbying by understating its indispensability to the legislative process. We may define lobbying as the total of all communicated influences upon legislators with respect to legislation. So defined, it includes direct and indirect influences. The latter comprise campaign contributions, on the one hand, and so-called "grass-roots" public opinion formation on the other. Even if we restrict our definition to direct importunings of Congressmen, however, lobbying still includes all the messages by which citizens, individually or in groups—that is, in "interest" groups and "pressure" groups, business groups and labor groups, farm groups and veterans' groups, women's groups and reformers' groups, liberal groups and conservative groups, religious groups and teachers' groups, state-wide groups and regional groups—notify the Congress of their needs and wishes. After thirty-six years as a target of such messages, I still regard them as the bloodstream of the democratic process and a *sine qua non* of effective legislation. It is true that these messages come to us in a Babel of tongues. It is true, as Mr. Justice Jackson observed of lobbyists, that "their conflicting claims and propaganda are confusing, annoying, and at times, no doubt, deceiving and corrupting." There is an understandable tendency to blame legislative failures upon lobbying, a tendency that no doubt inspired Senator Jim Reed's quip that "a lobbyist is anyone who opposes legislation I want." But fundamentally, I believe, we all recognize that the touchstone of "good" lobbying and "bad" lobbying is not whether the objectives of persuasion are selfish or altruistic, liberal or conservative, prolabor or probusiness, but solely and simply whether the message conveyed is intelligible, accurate, and informative, or cryptic, deceptive, and obscure.

Upon this premise, our automatic legislator should be programed with a view to enabling translation of the various tongues in which lobbyists speak to Congressmen, irrespective of the content of their messages. First, however, we must identify and eliminate certain existing phenomena with which the machine will have no concern. One of these is venal lobbying, a form of lobbying in which the favor seeker pays for the legislator's vote or advocacy.

Venal Lobbying

Money talks. One writer has attributed the following cynicism to a regional counsel for an oil company:

> "You just put good, green folding money in their lily-white
> hands and be . . . sure they know why you put it there."

I sometimes think that the political maturity of a people is best indicated by the extent to which they insist upon high moral standards in the conduct of their public affairs. The nineteenth century, a period of rapid expansion in America, saw widespread venality in office. The open buying and selling of votes is described in novels dealing with the period. A House committee investigation conducted in 1854 disclosed that the attempts of Samuel Colt to secure extension of valuable patents included the retention of a Member of Congress on a $10,000 contingent fee, numerous gifts of small arms to other Congressmen, and lavish entertainment. Even as late as 1923, when I entered Congress, the halls were still resounding with the scandals brought to light ten years earlier concerning lobbying activities of the National Association of Manufacturers which opposed the Underwood Tariff Bill. These abuses went so far as to include employment of the chief page of the House to eavesdrop and report on the cloakroom activities and personal conversations of Congressmen.

Flagrant abuses such as these are no longer typical. Moreover, this type of abuse is not so much a problem of lobbying regulation as it is one of the enforcement of the criminal laws. I recently asked the staff of the House Antitrust Subcommittee, of which I am Chairman, to prepare a report on the federal conflict of interest and bribery statutes. From this report, it is evident that the gravest abuses of the right of access to Congress are and have long been the subject of direct criminal prohibition and penalty. I wonder how many people realize that the payment of anything of value to a Member of Congress with intent to have his vote or action influenced thereby subjects both the payer and the recipient to fine and imprisonment; that the Member of Congress is also prohibited from receiving anything of value "for his attention to or services" on any Congressional question or for services before federal agencies.

Friendly Lobbyists

More troublesome than outright bribery, because of the obscurity of its motivation and the subtlety of its effect, is the practice of some modern lobbies indiscriminately to befriend influential office holders. In its sophisticated form, this activity never includes *request* for a favor, but limits itself to the extension of amenities and courtesies in the form of free transportation, hospitality, and adjuncts to "gracious living." The sole visible object appears to be the establishment of the amiability of the lobbyist and his client. Effectiveness of this technique to influence legislation is not susceptible of precise measurement and can only be inferred from the extensiveness of the practice. Lately, Congressional committees have been concerned with the impact of this form of social seduction upon employees of the executive branch.

The campaign contribution is another method by which cash is capable of influencing legislation. The furore created two years ago, when [the late] Senator Case of South Dakota reported that an oil lobbyist had attempted to contribute $2,500 to his campaign at a time when his position on the Gas Bill was uncertain, exemplifies the problems which can arise. While no one would dispute a citizen's right to help elect the candidate of his choice, that right is rarely exercised in the absence either of approval of the candidate's past record or a favorable estimation of his future actions. So, too, the candidate himself has difficulty in determining to what extent he owes a campaign contribution to recognition of his qualities of statesmanship and to what extent it reflects approval of his particular past or anticipated action on a matter close to the contributor's heart. It begs the question to say that such contributions are proper when the purpose for which they are given is the election of the candidate and not the purpose of influencing his vote. And what if they are given for both purposes?

The Senate committee which investigated the Case episode recommended that each candidate be required by law to have a fiscal agent whose duty would be to solicit, accept, and make public all campaign contributions. This would provide the advantage of publicity and also some insulation of the legislator from contact with his benefactor.

No special adjustment to protect against bribery or to appraise the motives underlying campaign contributions need be built into the automatic legislator; its lack of human attributes and its immunity from campaigns for re-election will remove all incentive for such payments. Meanwhile, human legislators must continue to meet their problems with common sense and self-restraint.

Recognition of Lobbying by Congress

It has been pointed out that lobbying (whether or not accompanied by venality) is not only as old as government itself, but actually always precedes government. Establishment of any governmental system implies that the conflicting demands of participating groups have been accommodated. In the United States, persistent lobbying to affect legislation has evoked intermittent Congressional interest in the nature of lobbying practices, which in turn ultimately produced legislation to affect lobbying. The earliest federal measure bearing on lobbying was a House rule adopted in 1852 which excluded from seats on the floor of the House newspapermen employed to prosecute claims pending before Congress. The earliest investigations were those of the Colt patent lobby, two years later, and of the Pacific mail steamship scandal of 1872. In 1867, the House adopted a rule excluding former Congressmen from the floor if they were interested in any claim pending before Congress. For a part of the 44th Congress, in 1876, the House operated under a resolution requiring registration of the name and authority of persons employed as counsel or agent with respect to pending measures, on pain of prohibition from appearing in such capacity before any House committee.

Apparently spurred in part by the revelations of a New York State investigation of insurance industry lobbying conducted in 1905 and 1906, the present century saw a marked increase in Congressional proposals to regulate lobbying. This trend was augmented by the Congressional investigation of the Underwood Tariff lobby in 1913, the 1930 investigation of lobbying activities at the Geneva Disarmament Conference of 1927, and the Public Utilities struggles of 1935–36. The latter culminated in provisions of the Public Utilities Holding Company Act of 1935 which required the registration of lobbyists on holding company matters before Congress, the Securities and Exchange Commission, or the Federal Power Commission. Similar provisions were included in the Merchant Marine Act of 1936, affecting lobbyists on matters related to shipping before Congress, the Federal Maritime Board, or the Secretary of Commerce.

Ten years later, Congress enacted the present law governing lobbying—The Federal Regulation of Lobbying Act—as Title III of the Legislative Reorganization Act of 1946.* This enactment re-

---

* The Federal Regulation of Lobbying Act and the Harriss case are treated in more detail in Part IV of this volume (pp. 298-300). [Ed.].

quires those who attempt to secure the enactment or defeat of pending
or proposed legislation to register and to report on their activities.
As construed by the Supreme Court in the landmark case of
United States v. *Harriss* (347 U. S. 612 (1954)), the reporting
requirements are applicable only to persons who solicit or receive
contributions where a principal purpose of the contribution or of
the solicitor or recipient is aiding to influence legislation by direct
communication with Members of Congress. The Court held that
thus construed the Act is constitutional. It is noteworthy that in this
construction the Act does not apply to those who spend, but do not
receive or solicit, funds to influence legislation, nor to those who
seek to effectuate influence by indirect rather than direct methods.
The rationale of the Act was stated by Chief Justice Warren as
follows:

> Present day legislative complexities are such that individual
> members of Congress cannot be expected to explore the
> myriad pressures to which they are regularly subjected. Yet
> full realization of the American ideal of government by
> elected representatives depends to no small extent on their
> ability to properly evaluate such pressures. Otherwise the
> voice of the people may all too easily be drowned out by the
> voice of special interest groups seeking favored treatment
> while masquerading as proponents of the public weal. This
> is the evil which the Lobbying Act was designed to help
> prevent.
> Toward that end, Congress has not sought to prohibit
> these pressures. It has merely provided for a modicum of in-
> formation from those who for hire attempt to influence legis-
> lation or who collect or spend funds for that purpose. It
> wants only to know who is being hired, who is putting up
> the money, and how much.

Operation of the Act was studied by the Senate Committee on
Expenditures in the Executive Departments in 1948, by the Bu-
chanan Committee in 1950, and by a special Senate Committee to
Investigate Political Activities, Lobbying, and Campaign Contributions in 1956 and 1957. As a result of these investigations and in light
of the Supreme Court's construction of the Act in the Harriss case,

legislation introduced in both Houses of Congress would overhaul the Act, clarifying and sharpening its provisions. Principal proposals for amendment provide for administration by the Comptroller General of the United States and clear definition of the persons to whom the Act applies—principally professional lobbyists and their employers and persons who conduct campaigns urging others to communicate directly with Congress. New in these bills is a salutary criminal provision, penalizing the transmission to Congress of communications known to be spurious, that is, "false, forged, counterfeit, or fictitious."

All constructive efforts to improve existing lobbying regulation are to be supported. The task of the Congressman is arduous enough without being complicated by apocryphal or spurious messages. It is sometimes possible to spot such propaganda by the uniformity of its size, shape, and postmark, and of the handwriting in which it is addressed. Not infrequently attempts to reply to this kind of message have been returned "unknown," or have received a response declaring that the writer had not communicated with the Congressman in the first place. More often, the answer is complete silence. Legislators cannot afford to give this kind of message much weight. Nor can they afford to ignore it entirely. The result is a great waste of time counting the idividual letters on each side of the question and in perfunctory attempts to reply. Public disclosure of "who is being hired, who is putting up the money, and how much," and outright prohibition of counterfeit pressures are minimal and necessary protections of the legislative process.

Problems of Evaluation

Even after lobbying regulation has been perfected in these respects, and after venal, social, cryptic, and deceptive lobbying have been eliminated, perplexing problems of evaluation will remain to occupy the legislator and his mechanical successor. Fundamentally, these will be problems created by the disparity in volume, intensity, and quality of the representations that are made to Congress. A number of the modern lobbies operating in Washington are of the highest quality. With plenty of money to spend, they spend it on qualified analysts and advocates and provide Congressional committees with lucid briefs and technical documentation in support of their positions. Nothing is more informative and helpful to a legislative committee than to hear the views of competent, well-matched advocates on the opposite sides of a legislative issue.

It is true that the cost of effective lobbying is ultimately borne by the people. It is also true that the pressures generated by a well-organized interest group can become irritating. But despite this cost and irritation, I believe that too much lobbying is not as dangerous to the quality of the resulting legislation as too little. It is disturbing to sit through legislative hearings at which the conflicting interests who should be heard are unequally represented in the presentation of their views. Worst of all, from the standpoint of a Congressman's desire to legislate intelligently, are those situations in which only the proponents of the suggested legislation are heard from. The Congressman may know or suspect that there are serious opposing considerations, but they are simply not presented. He is faced with a dilemma as to how far he can or should go to supply the omission.

This is not to say that it is necessary to maintain a costly and permanent organization in order to lobby effectively. Excellent presentations are constantly being made on behalf of relatively small lobbies, organized on an *ad hoc* basis, to support or oppose particular measures. These groups must and often do overcome the handicap of limitation of funds by making their blows count. The effectiveness of such presentations lies in stating a position forcefully, clearly, and tersely—without frills. Congressmen are more appreciative than is generally known of lobbyists who respect their crowded schedules and keep representations to a minimum consistent with thoroughness. A potential advantage enjoyed by *ad hoc* lobbies is that they are not inhibited by the need to be consistent with their own former positions, which sometimes affects permanent organizations.

Congressmen also receive many messages from individuals who write to or visit their representatives in person. With respect to lobbying by mail, individual letters expressing honest convictions in a logical and convincing manner are always welcome. Even inspired mail, the fruit of a letter-writing campaign, can be effective if the writers take the trouble to express their sincere views and the reasons therefore individually. At the other pole, of course, are intemperate or extremist messages from overzealous and emotionally disturbed persons, sometimes resorting to threats. These accomplish nothing. Every member of Congress receives both kinds of letters from his constituents. If he reaches the level of committee chairman, moreover, they come to him from every section of the country, representing every shade of feeling on substantially every issue which is or may be within his competence. For there is a marked tendency on the part of individual citizens to overestimate the power of a single Congressman, simply because he is the chairman of a committee.

Personal visits by lobbyists are subject to similar observations. The man who keeps his appointment, presents his problem or proposal, and lets the Congressman get on with his other work comes to be liked and respected. His message has an excellent chance of being effective. The man who feels that it somehow adds to his usefulness and prestige to be seen constantly in the company of one legislator or another, or who seeks to ingratiate himself with Congressional staffs, gets under foot and becomes a nuisance. He does his principal and his cause no good. Every Congressman receives many visits from both kinds of callers. He can only hope that the first kind will increase and that the second kind will gradually disappear.

Better Legislation

It is an unhappy commentary that in lobbying the voice of zealotry and passion is sometimes more insistently raised than the voice of statesmanship and wisdom. This is true of individual lobbyists and of organized interest groups alike. We hear from extremists and the emotionally disturbed; we must hear more fully from the sane and mature. Increased interest and direct intervention by all the people in the working of their government will greatly facilitate the task of legislators, human or utopian. It is the only true guarantee of better legislation.

Lincoln once said:

> Public sentiment is everything. With public sentiment nothing can fail. Without it, nothing can succeed. Consequently, he who molds public sentiment goes deeper than he who enacts statutes or pronounces decisions. He makes statutes and decisions possible or impossible to be executed.

Realization that ultimate power to affect legislation resides in the people has given a significant new direction to pressure group activities, which now seek to influence legislation by remote control. The new profession of public-opinion engineers is engaged in creating public sentiment in favor of or opposed to particular policies. The thought is that once the desired public climate is achieved, the people themselves will do the work.

Aspects of this newly accelerated phase in the struggle for men's minds have a frightening, Orwellian portent. These include recent experiments in so-called subliminal advertising, wherein messages are flashed on a movie or television screen at a speed too great to permit their conscious reception, but long and often enough to condition the viewer without his knowledge that he has been subjected to manipulation—in effect inscribing the advertisement on his brain. They include the increasingly frequent boasts of experimenters that any person can be taught to do anything by conditioning. They include disturbing instances of planted articles and stories in the public press.

As has been noted, the Supreme Court has held that the Federal Regulation of Lobbying Act was intended to regulate only those persons who receive funds for the purpose of *direct* communication with Congress. "Grass-roots" public opinion formation is not included. Despite the potential perils from mass manipulation through use of the channels of communication, I am of the opinion that the high Court's decision was wise. For Congress to attempt to control the formulation of public opinion would be to throw out the baby with the bath. The constitutionality of such an attempt would be highly dubious, and the cure would be worse than the disease.

Social ills affecting our media of mass communications are not to be dealt with by direct regulation or control, but primarily by insisting to the best of our ability that these media shall always remain free. Competition has been the foundation of American economic policy, and the national antitrust laws, which implement that policy by outlawing monopolies and combinations in restraint of trade, are the great bulwark of our private enterprise system. As the Supreme Court has stated, ". . . the widest possible dissemination of information from diverse and antagonistic sources is essential to the welfare of the public." Undue concentration of control and anticompetitive practices in the fields of mass communications—the press, radio, and television—are the essential evil to be counteracted. I am convinced that vigorous enforcement of the antitrust laws in these industries will, by assuring "the widest possible dissemination of information" to the people, most effectively guard against our ever becoming a manipulated electorate.

Pressure Politics and Resources Administration*

ROBERT J. MORGAN

Administrators are subject to the same pressures directed toward legislators. Cognizant of the decision-making powers within the executive branch and its agencies, pressure groups seek to become influential in those decisions. The following article by Robert Morgan is a case study of how local pressure came to influence executive policy-making centers in the field of water resources conservation and development. It illustrates how successful well-organized, articulate organizations can be as opposed to those which are not.

Writing in the tenth and fifty-first essays of *The Federalist,* Madison concluded that the great virtue of the federal union and the separation of powers was that the variety of interests and territory embraced by the United States would render a majority of the whole either incapable or indisposed to invade the rights and interests of other members of the community. Even, however, if a majority were to discover its common motive and power, he thought that it would be difficult for it to act in unison. As a deterrent to democratic government in the eighteenth century, the effectiveness of Madison's proposition does not seem open to serious challenge. The real question is whether, in the twentieth century, it ought to be materially revised to take into account the prolific growth of pressure groups and their special relationships with legislative committees and administrative agencies. Would it not be more accurate to say that at present, be-

* Robert J. Morgan, "Pressure Politics and Resources Administration," *Journal of Politics,* XVIII (February, 1956), 39-60.

cause of the variety of sentiments growing out of the diversity of geographic, cultural, economic, ethnic, and other factors in the United States, particular interests are actually forced to discover their strength and to pursue their objectives, often with little serious regard for a majority or national interest?

Among the current problems awaiting rational public decision, the orderly conservation of water and land resources is caught up in this web. While much of the recent discussion concerning the failure to develop a comprehensive policy has centered in devising workable administrative machinery, one may ask whether the difficulty does not lie much deeper in a constitutional system which was deliberately intended to frustrate majority action.

Many of the obstacles to be overcome in framing legislative and administrative decisions regarding this matter are illustrated by the history of the Salt-Wahoo flood control project in southeastern Nebraska and its relation with the Watershed Protection and Flood Prevention Act of 1954. Hailed initially as an example of true co-ordination between federal agencies and a local interest group in resources development and later damned as an instance of "co-ordination gone sour," the labored effort of four years finally produced agreement on the level of the field services and a local organization seeking to frame a program satisfactory to local interests.[1] The project's history is more than another dreary tale of inter-agency suspicion, jealousy, and acquisitiveness. It is, rather, an illustration of the powerful and perhaps indispensable rôle of pressure politics on all levels of government. Of equal importance, it is again indicative of the interlocking trinity of pressure group, administrative agency, and Congressional committee which has wrought a constitutional revolution not wholly anticipated by Madison.

The innocent central party to this controversy which swirled back and forth between Lincoln, Nebraska, and Washington for more than four years is a normally muddy trickle of a stream called Salt Creek

[1] See *Missouri: Land and Water,* The Report of the Missouri Basin Survey Commission (Washington: U.S. Government Printing Office, 1953), pp. 216-227; and "The Flood Control Program of the Department of Agriculture," House Committee Print No. 22, 82d Cong., 2d Sess., p. 34; Lincoln (Neb.) *Sunday Journal and Star,* November 28, 1954.

and its principal tributary known as Wahoo Creek. Together they drain over 1,000,000 acres of rich, undulating farm land embracing parts of six southeastern counties. They have periodically flooded the watershed, including the city of Lincoln, during the past fifty years; and a particularly heavy flood in May, 1950, cost an estimated $53,000,000 in damages and twenty-two lives in the six counties of southeastern Nebraska.[2] Although this flood and the less extensive ones which damaged Lincoln in May and again in June, 1951, were not as spectacular as the sort which occurs on the mainstream of the Missouri, their destructiveness was real enough to stimulate demands for preventive action.

Capitalizing on the dramatic news of the flood of May 9 to 11, 1950, Raymond A. McConnell, Jr., editor of the Lincoln *Evening Journal,* unleashed a journalistic torrent of feature articles to demonstrate his conclusion that farms on which a high degree of approved soil conservation practices were completed had suffered little or no damage from the heavy rainfall. Judging the public to be especially receptive to his plan at this time, he asserted that if his readers wanted to avoid future loss of life and property, especially the soil, they would have to press "for consideration of the flood program as one to be coped with properly only on a watershed-wide basis, beginning on the land and in the smaller tributaries."[3] McConnell was familiar with the Pick-Sloan plan authorized by the Flood Control Act of 1944, but he was convinced that it offered little prospect of solution to the flood problems affecting areas drained by the small tributaries of the mainstream. He was also aware that the Department of Agriculture had developed a comprehensive program for the Missouri Basin to include the construction of some types of flood control structures, not the least of which were small dams.[4] Whatever may have been the hidden

---

[2] *Missouri: Land and Water, op. cit.,* p. 132; Lincoln (Neb.) *Evening Journal,* May 11, 1950.

[3] Lincoln *Evening Journal,* May 13, 1950.

[4] *Missouri River Basin Agricultural Program,* House Document No. 373, 81st Cong., 1st Sess., 1949. Charles M. Hardin in *The Politics of Agriculture: Soil Conservation and The Struggle for Power in Rural America* (Glencoe, Ill.: The Free Press, 1952) indicates unflatteringly that this program was initiated on the eve of World War II at least in part to make work; p. 90. The watershed flood control program had already been started elsewhere in the

wellspring of motive, a newspaper editor had turned raindrops into a public issue.

With a sure instinct for political realities, McConnell sponsored a meeting attended by 175 local and state civic leaders and office holders as well as representatives of the Soil Conservation Service and the Corps of Engineers. On this occasion E. A. Norton, then Assistant Chief, Soil Conservation Service (Washington), uttered a phophetic warning of coming events. "You'll need a strong organization to press for what you want. Federal agencies are not going to move any faster than you ask them to. Therefore, it is up to you to push this thing."[5] In the light of this warning it may be less than coincidental that those present at the meeting decided on two courses of action. They resolved to form a Salt Creek watershed organization. They also expressed approval of a program of flood control in which downstream flood works would be planned to supplement, and be integrated with, "the most widespread upstream application of water and soil conservation practices on all watershed lands of the tributaries." It was claimed that "experience and research have proved" such practices to be essential elements of flood control.[6] With these actions McConnell and his local supporters were caught up in a bitter struggle between the Department of Agriculture and the Corps of Engineers, centering in the question of proper techniques and administration of flood control.

So far as a mere layman can make out the issue, it amounts in essence to this: the most obvious and sensational sort of flood damage suffered in the Missouri Basin, as in much of the rest of the country, occurs when excessive rains or the melting heavy snows flood low-lying areas bounding major rivers and their tributaries. To reduce, or even prevent, the resulting destruction, large dams and levees have been built, channels have been dredged and straightened. This has

---

country, especially in the Little Sioux watershed in Iowa, in the Arkansas — Red River watershed of Oklahoma, and on the Trinity River in Texas. The status of the program in 1952 is reviewed in House Committee Print No. 22, *op. cit.*, pp. 1-5.

[5] Lincoln *Evening Journal,* June 1, 1950. In 1945 the Corps had surveyed the upper reaches of Salt Creek for flood control but had found no economically justifiable project.

[6] *Ibid.*

been the work largely of the Corps of Engineers. In the western fringes and the upper basin of the Missouri, the need for irrigation water and the electric power to pump it to fields (and, in part, to pay for costly irrigation works) has stimulated construction projects by the Bureau of Reclamation. Differences in uses and consequent differences in construction techniques and payment of costs, not to mention institutional jealousies, led to a conflict between these two agencies with a resulting settlement of sorts in the Missouri Basin known as the Pick-Sloan Plan authorized by the Flood Control Act of 1944. Despite this uneasy truce, many of the flood control projects in the area are multi-purpose structures.[7]

This picture was further complicated when the Department of Agriculture framed its own comprehensive program of development for the Missouri Basin in 1949.[8] Of special relevance here is the portion dealing with flooding, especially as it causes sheet erosion of soil and the overflow of the small tributary streams draining croplands. According to Mr. Brannan, this program would "assure the safe disposal of water in small watersheds and the lesser tributary streams" and "contribute to flood control" by reducing sedimentation behind large dams and by protecting the destruction of lands through gully erosion, bank cutting, and stream sedimentation. The program "contemplates the construction of gully control structures, flood-ways, bank protection works and small retarding basins." This plan, which the Secretary termed "accelerated," would require thirty years for completion and would add "to flood control in all the major and minor valleys of the basin."[9] It would also, he claimed, place primary responsibility for results on the people of the area, provide a unified

[7] 58 Stat. 665. A useful account of the programs proposed and authorized for the Missouri Basin can be found in Marvin Meade, The Missouri Basin Proposals for Development (Bureau of Government Research, University of Kansas, 1952), Citizen's Pamphlet Series Number 11. Three articles dealing with the general problem may be found in Land Economics, XXX, No. 4 (November, 1954): S. Blair Hutchison, "Fitting Big Dams Into Little Economies," pp. 329-332; Walter M. Kollmorgen, "And Deliver Us From Big Dams,"pp. 333-346; Kris Kristjanson, "Institutional Arrangements in Water Resource Development," pp. 347-362.
[8] House Document No. 373, op. cit. Cf. Missouri: Land and Water, op. cit., p. 220.
[9] House Document No. 373, op. cit., p. 25.

comprehensive and multi-purpose plan, and give a balance now lacking because the construction of "engineering works is outdistancing programs for the land." The Department's program would, he said, complement existing mainstream projects as well as any which might in the future be undertaken.[10] In short, stripped of its varnish, the Department of Agriculture's proposal was that it, too, would construct flood control works, including "small" dams, as a logical extension of its soil conservation work. Reduced to a slogan effective on the hustlings, it was to "catch the raindrops where they fall." It was the Department's rejoinder to the claim that effective flood control measures must be limited generally to large dams on the mainstreams.[11] This program did, of course, call attention to the often unspectacular but real flood damage which occurs to our viable top soil both on the uplands and in the lesser floodplains of tributary streams.

Utilizing the initiative which was his, McConnell, with the assistance of other local leaders, set up a committee of twenty-five, including representatives of the three largest banks in Lincoln, several leading farmers from the two counties principally affected, editors of two rural newspapers, two soil conservation district supervisors, and other influential persons, including the mayor of Lincoln. Meeting on June 12, 1951, this committee secured a promise from [the then] Representatives Carl Curtis and Karl Stefan that the House Committee on Public Works would be requested to authorize the Department of Agriculture to make a survey and recommendations for flood works under the Flood Control Act of 1936. When this request

---

[10] *Ibid.*, p. iii. Cf. House Committee Print No. 22, *op. cit.*, pp. 1-5.

[11] The Department of the Interior greeted this program with a coolness evident in its half-dozen major objections. Curiously, however, the Corps of Engineers observed that the plan "includes provisions for *needed measures* to complement the coordinated plan for flood control . . . now being prosecuted by the Corps . . . and the Bureau of Reclamation. . . ." The Bureau of the Budget cleared the program as being in general accord with the President's policy but said that basic data to determine cost-benefit ratios would have to be developed before economic justification could be determined. House Document 373, *op. cit.*, pp. 1-2, 3-5, 6-7 (italics supplied). According to one view, both the Department of Interior and the Corps acting in the Missouri Basin Inter-Agency Committee requested such a program. It was said to have been received by the field representatives with approval which "bordered on the enthusiastic. Their superiors in Washington, however, found little to favor in the proposed plan. . . ." *Missouri: Land and Water, op. cit.*, p. 220.

was granted a month later, the Department of Agriculture was reported as saying that the survey would be completed within four to six months.[12] The watershed association was formally launched on its curious career at a mass meeting at the State Fair Grounds on July 21. On this occasion McConnell assured the public that he had promises of co-operation from every affected federal, state, and local agency. Pointedly, the major address of the evening was made by Bryce Browning of the Muskingum Conservancy District to stir public support for watershed management as a flood control.[13]

The first of much bad blood erupted out of the project when, on October 20, 1950, the Corps announced a plan for the Salt-Wahoo area to include structures to cost $14,000,000 (to be paid 90 per cent by the federal government) and to be built to withstand floods of an intensity likely to occur once every twenty-five years upstream from Lincoln, once in a hundred years around the city, and once in fifty years between Lincoln and the mouth of Salt Creek at Ashland on the Platte River. Professing complete consternation, the Salt-Wahoo Watershed Association responded by chastising the Engineers, calling the plan a piecemeal one which attacked the problem backwards by ignoring the possible benefits of the plan yet to be formulated by the Soil Conservation Service. Charging that the Corps had violated pledges given to the association, it admonished the Corps to reconsider its plans, co-ordinate its future work with the Soil Conservation Service, and present a genuinely integrated plan to the local interests.[14]

The following December, when Governor Peterson of Nebraska raised the issue of inter-agency co-operation before the Missouri Basin Inter-Agency Committee, he was assured by representatives

[12] Lincoln *Journal,* July 20, 1950.
[13] *Ibid.,* July 21, 1950. The friends of the Muskingum District (at New Philadelphia, Ohio) have called it a model of local initiative and co-operation with federal agencies in providing flood control, but it does not lack critics who say that both initial and continued federal support has been necessary, and that it is not an example of watershed management as visualized by the Department of Agriculture. James Lawrence, editor of the Lincoln *Star* and chairman of the Missouri Basin Survey Commission, is one such critic. Cf. Meade, *op. cit.,* pp. 45-52. Cf. Arthur E. Morgan, *The Miami Conservancy District* (New York: McGraw - Hill Book Company, Inc., 1951).
[14] *Missouri: Land and Water, op. cit.,* p. 216; Lincoln *Journal,* Oct. 20 and 31, 1950.

of the two agencies that there was no dispute between them.[15] Since McConnell had raised the cry of non-co-operation in the Lincoln *Journal,* this profession of brotherhood had a counterfeit ring to it. On December 18, however, McConnell announced that the Soil Conservation Service had received an extension of time to complete its survey. Both agencies were now quoted as favoring co-operative effort of the sort which the "House . . . Public Works Committee instructed . . . and both agreed to . . . at the Washington level."[16] Assuring the association that orders had come down from Washington (from whom he did not say) to secure a coordinated plan, McConnell publicy exuded confidence when the two agencies made a report to the Nebraska Coordinating Committee in June, 1951. Although further studies were needed to complete the report for submission to Congress at its next session, the progress to date was "a milestone in federal flood control planning . . . meeting with great success."[17]

Despite the apparently bright prospects for a co-ordinated plan, the association adopted a wholly new approach to secure at least the soil conservation phase of the project, when in August, 1951, it was decided to act on the suggestion of [the late] Senator Kenneth Wherry to press for appropriations to make the Salt-Wahoo area a demonstration project, a model possibly to be copied nationally. Complaining that Secretary Brannan was unrealistic in insisting on the adoption of the agricultural program for the whole Missouri Basin, McConnell urged that it be broken down into small demonstrational watershed projects, saying prophetically, "that is the only way Congress is ever going to authorize it . . ."[18] Such a move was

[15] Missouri Basin Inter-Agency Committee, *Minutes of the Forty-Fifth Meeting,* Dec. 1, 1950, p. 3.

[16] Lincoln *Journal,* Dec. 18, 1950. The Inter-Agency's cover-up of this dispute was not surprising in view of its previous record in such matters. See Arthur Maas, *Muddy Waters* (Cambridge: Harvard University Press, 1951), p. 114.

[17] Lincoln *Journal,* June 11, 1951.

[18] *Ibid.,* Aug. 20, 1951. McConnell's view was most interesting in light of the fact that Secretary Brannan had fought hard to overcome SCS objections to making his program a comprehensive one for the Missouri Basin. SCS preferred to limit the plan to erosion control and physical development. Hardin, *op. cit.,* p. 90.

made in the agricultural appropriations sub-committee in the Senate, but when a request was also submitted to the House appropriations committee, it was rejected. McConnell lamented this failure, saying that one specific trouble was that with the death of Representative Karl Stefan, "Nebraska is without representation on the appropriations committee."[19]

Thrown back upon the original plan, the association awaited the project of the Soil Conservation Service which was revealed to its board of directors in January and March, 1952. There was private doubt that it would be received enthusiastically by the Corps, but McConnell gave assurances that the Engineers would not interfere with it. Thus, the association accepted the agricultural program at this time without any integration with the Corps. Early in July this plan was sent to Congress as a supplemental report to the Missouri Basin Agricultural Program. Significantly it was directed not to the Committee on Public Works which had authorized the Salt-Wahoo survey, but to the Committee on Agriculture.[20]

It was undoubtedly not without strong reason that this curious action was taken, for on March 27, 1952, a sub-committee (the Jones Committee) of the House Public Works Committee had commenced public hearings on a study of civil works, which included an extensive review of the relations between the Corps of Engineers and the Soil Conservation Service, making considerable use of the Salt-Wahoo project for illustrative purposes.[21] On May 8 Representative Curtis introduced Liebers, McConnell, and

[19] Lincoln *Journal,* Oct. 11, 1951. The Department of Agriculture had asked for $1,475,000 for watershed projects in Nebraska and Kansas.

[20] House Document No. 530, 82d Cong., 2d Sess. It should be noted that this program requiring ten years for completion included not only the Salt-Wahoo project, but also three others. Thus, in all probability the regional office in Lincoln was under some pressure from the Washington office to complete its plans regardless of whether co-ordination with the Corps had been achieved or not. For this and other reasons to be noted later, it appears that the desire for local integration of projects was not uppermost in the minds of the highest levels of the Soil Conservation Service. Cf. pp. 38, 45-78 for a description of the project. Cf. *Missouri: Land and Water, op. cit.,* pp. 132-136.

[21] "Study of Civil Works," Hearings Before the Subcommittee to Study Civil Works, of the Committee on Public Works, House of Representatives, 82d Cong., 2d Sess., Parts 1 and 2.

Byron Dunn of the Salt-Wahoo Watershed Association to testify before this committee. Dunn confined his testimony largely to a description of the enormous effort by the Association to educate the Nebraska public in favor of the agricultural program. Liebers summarized the early efforts of his organization to secure co-ordination from the Corps and the Conservation Service, asserting that co-operation had continued until the final stages of program formulation. At this point, however, he averred, "disagreement at the top level of the two agencies caused delay in completion of the report. Seeing that the delay would forbid presentation of the joint report to this session of the Congress, the Salt-Wahoo Association requested the Department of Agriculture to complete its recommendations. . . .

"To date the Corps . . . has not submitted an alternative plan for the Salt-Wahoo Basin."[22] He added that while the organization was favorably impressed with the Department's program, the members were convinced that downstream works constructed by the Corps were necessary to complete an adequate program. For his part, McConnell expressed a fear that the monstrous floods on the Missouri in July, 1951, and April, 1952, would result in what he termed a permanent imbalance of programs frozen into the familiar form of the Pick-Sloan Plan. Moreover, a demonstration of the value of a co-ordinated plan of watershed management, such as in the Salt-Wahoo area, would be of inestimable use to the entire country. Such action, based on plans supported by locally affected interests, he claimed, would be the democratic way of shaping policy. He insisted that his organization stood not for two programs linked by a hyphen, but one genuinely integrated from the top to the bottom of the watershed. He concluded: "The Salt-Wahoo Watershed Association is not anti-Army Engineers. It is not anti anything—except piecemeal and incomplete planning and execution, or either of these that overlooks or brushes aside local problems and local needs."[23]

[22] *Ibid.*, part 2, p. 317.
[23] *Ibid.*, p. 331. At this time Congress had no program before it, but it did receive the agriculture plan on the following July 3, just before the end of

During the summer of 1952 the Jones Committee digested the evidence presented to it and in December released a devastating critique of the Department of Agriculture's attempt to participate in the flood control program. It found that co-operation in the Salt-Wahoo project had officially ended on January 22, 1952, when the Omaha District Engineer informed the Regional Director in Lincoln that joint planning was at an end because the Soil Conservation Service had continued its planning on an independent basis. The Regional Director had replied by saying that the Salt-Wahoo organization had urged both agencies to place their plans before the Eighty-second Congress, although the Corps had indicated its inability to ready its plan before May 15. At this time the Corps felt that questions of cost-benefits and standards of construction had not been resolved satisfactorily. On May 27, the District Engineer wrote the Regional Director, indicating his sympathy with the Soil Conservation Service's lack of funds for survey work and acknowledging its thesis that co-ordination could only follow Congressional authorization for the entire watershed program.

The Jones Committee noted with apparent dismay that "at no time until late in May was the Corps given any data on the Department's study to analyze and perhaps tie-in with the Corps report."[24] For some curious reason the committee did not mention the Corps' eagerness to act alone, when, in October 1950, it had submitted its plan for the area before the Soil Conservation Service could complete its plans. Amazed and chagrined, the Jones Committee also observed that it had authorized the Department of Agriculture's survey for Salt-Wahoo only to have it referred to the Committee on Agriculture, citing the directives of the Public Works Committee merely as incidental authority for the action

---

the session. On April 14, and on May 10, 1952, respectively, McConnell met separately with Secretary Brannan and General Pick (then Chief of Engineers) to iron out the differences on the Salt-Wahoo project, but apparently to no avail. He also attended a Presidential press conference, where he queried President Truman on his attitude toward the agricultural program. He said that Truman approved this program as a supplement to the Pick-Sloan plan. Lincoln *Journal,* April 18, 19, May 11, 1952.

[24] House Committee Print No. 22, *op. cit.,* p. 32.

taken.[25] Denying a rumor that the Corps had deliberately sabotaged the joint approach in the summer of 1951 by claiming that it lacked funds, the committee concluded that the "responsibility for the breakdown rested with the Department of Agriculture's consideration of urgency as paramount."[26] This evident hostility to the Department's program was translated into recommendations which urged that the Department of Agriculture be denied further authority to make surveys under the flood control laws and that it be subordinated to the Corps of Engineers in future flood control planning and construction. The Jones Committee emphatically rejected the Soil Conservation Service's watershed management program as "flood control in the accepted sense of keeping large flows of water from causing excessive damage."[27]

McConnell's response to this virtual death sentence for a joint solution to the Salt-Wahoo problem was a counter-charge that the Jones Committee report was "outdated" and that it had failed to account for "a series of meetings between the two agencies which began in October (1952)."[28] He further chided the committee for accepting what he called the "outmoded" idea that flood control should begin at the bottom of the stream. He admitted that joint planning had stopped late in 1951, but, he said, the new meetings had been called by the Watershed Association at the suggestion of the Engineers. Out of these contacts the Association forged a four-point statement of principle, whereby the enhancement of agricultural values" was to be the responsibility of the Department of Agriculture and the "protection of urban and industrial areas" was

[25] *Ibid.*, pp. 34-35.

[26] *Ibid.*, p. 33, *Missouri: Land and Water, op. cit.*, p. 216. One may speculate whether the Corps displayed interest in the Salt Creek area because Senator Wherry was a Vice-President of the Rivers and Harbors Congress and a member of the appropriations sub-committee for Engineer civil functions before his death. Mass., *op. cit.*, p. 46.

[27] *Ibid.*, pp. 42-43. The Jones Committee actually wished a plague on both Houses, calling the conduct of the two agencies "deserving of high censure for their uncompromising attitudes and actions which have unduly alarmed and confused the residents of many areas and have wastefully delayed efficient and economic prosecution of important programs. Both upstream and downstream works have their place in a balanced conservation program." House Committee Print No. 22, *op. cit.*, p. 40.

[28] Lincoln *Journal*, Dec. 16, and Lincoln *Star*, December 17, 1952.

to be the primary responsibility of the Engineers, who were to recognize the contribution of the agricultural program: co-ordinated flood control works were to be built by the Engineers where watershed treatment would not afford adequate protection to urban property, but these structures should be so located as to minimize the impairment of agricultural values; such works were not to be duplicated by the Department of Agriculture.[29] Despite this apparent agreement in principle among the affected parties, the Soil Conservation Service in Washington reversed a decision reached by field technicians in regard to five dams which had been assigned to the Engineers, and the project again wallowed.[30]

One remaining strand of action proved essential to the success of the Association. On February 2, 1951, McConnell met in Lincoln with several Kansans interested in the watershed movement. It was decided then, or shortly thereafter, that the Lincoln *Journal* should sponsor a meeting of interested groups to discuss ways and means of gaining Congressional authorization for the program of the Soil Conservation Service. The severe floods in Kansas during July stimulated a meeting which was held on August 11 and 12 in Lincoln and was attended by representatives of the watershed groups, the Soil Conservation Service, the Bureau of Reclamation,

---

[29] "Some Proposed Principles of National Policy," mimeographed, Lincoln, Neb., January 20, 1953. The Jones Committee had devoted much attention and criticism to the upstream-downstream controversy which had developed, the members thought, because the Department of Agriculture had encouraged farmers to expect greater flood protection from watershed management than the known facts warranted. See House Committee Print No. 22, *op. cit.*, pp. 12-13, 20. Rep. Jones (D., Ala.) appeared to be a friend of TVA and a critic of the Corps as well as the Department of Agriculture in this instance. See his trenchant questioning of Dwight Payton of the Kansas-Nebraska Watershed Council; "Study of Civil Works," *op. cit.*, part 2, pp. 366-367. Both Gladwin Young, "father" of the Agricultural plan, and Secretary Brannan testified that large downstream dams were necessary and that the controvery was one largely manufactured by those who had something to gain from it. *Ibid.*, pp. 206-207.

[30] Lincoln *Journal* and *Star*, November 28, 1954. In November, 1952, the Salt-Wahoo association, suspicious of the Corps, received assurances from Governor Peterson and Governor-elect Crosby that neither would approve any Corps plan which did not meet with the Association's approval. It is customary for Corps' plans to be cleared in each state by the Governor before they are submitted to Congress; see *Missouri: Land and Water*, *op cit.*, pp. 250-251. Cf. Mass, *op. cit.*, pp. 23 ff.

the Corps of Engineers, and members of Congress, including [the late] Senators Wherry of Nebraska and Schoeppel of Kansas. Representative Clifford Hope wrote to McConnell after the close of the conference, saying that the missing legislative element was specific legislation tying together the programs of the Department of Agriculture with those of the Corps of Engineers and the Bureau of Reclamation. He further expressed hope that a subcommittee of the House Committee on Agriculture would soon conduct hearings on the Missouri Basin program prepared by the Department of Agriculture.[31] On September 5 following, the Kansas-Nebraska Watershed Council was formed to propagandize newspaper editors in the two states through the use of a periodic newsletter and, ultimately, to pressure Congress in support of the Department of Agriculture's program. McConnell personally went beyond this step, however, as he moved in an ever widening circle to form a national pressure group in support of this legislation. He became special consultant on watershed management to the Capper Publications and wrote a series of articles evidencing enthusiasm for a flood control program to include the Department of Agriculture.[32] He arranged for a spokesman to address the National Association of Soil Conservation Districts, an obvious ally, in Jaunary, 1952. He personally addressed the Soil Conservation Society of America on November 6, 1953, and the National Association of Soil Conservation Districts on February 23, 1954. Meanwhile, in February, 1953, he was instrumental in forming the National Informal Citizens Committee on Watershed Conservation. This group of twenty-five members, of which McConnell was made chairman, consisted of individuals nationally active in the watershed movement.[33]

On May 15, 1952, even before the Jones sub-committee had

[31] Lincoln *Journal*, August 11, 12, 20, and 21, 1951.

[32] *Capper's Farmer*, June, July and November, 1953.

[33] The names of most of the members can be found in "Conservation and Watershed Programs," Hearings, House Committee on Agriculture, 83d Cong., 1st Sess., pp. 133 ff. The members came from such widely scattered farm states as Nebraska, Iowa, Kansas, Texas, South Carolina, North Carolina, Georgia, Oklahoma, and California. The committee had a journalistic outlet through the Capper Publications and the Curtis Publishing Company (*Country Gentleman*), both of which had members on the committee.

completed its study, Representative W. R. Poage (D., Tex.), second ranking member of the House Committee on Agriculture, introduced H.R. 7868 to authorize the Secretary of Agriculture to co-operate with states and local agencies to plan and execute works for flood prevention. Referred to the Agriculture Committee and to Poage's sub-committee, this bill died in committee, although the sub-committee did report favorably, of course.[34]

For reasons not obvious on the record, Poage on June 17 introduced another bill, H.R. 8243, with the same stated purpose, and it was referred to the Committee on Agriculture. Two days later it was reported and placed on the Union Calendar, where it died.[35] According to a press report five months later, Poage said that he would again introduce such legislation in the Eighty-third Congress. His bill, he said, was "strongly opposed" by the Public Works Committee and the Rules Committee. A member of the Agriculture Committee's staff was quoted as saying that "we didn't have time to make a fight of it last time; it will be at the top of our agenda next year and we'll fight for it all the way." This "sweeping new flood control bill will involve two House Committees in a jealous fight for jurisdictional supremacy early next year."[36]

With the election of a Republican President and Congressional majority in 1952, the prospect for favorable action authorizing the Department of Agriculture's program brightened noticeably. The foresight by which McConnell had linked himself with the watershed interests in Kansas assured him that he would have the aid of one of the most vigorous Congressional supporters of the Soil Conservation Service, Representative Clifford Hope of Kansas, new chairman of the House Committee on Agriculture. Similar support was expected of Senator Frank Carlson of Kansas, one of the President's trusted advisers at the time. In addition, the inclusion of watershed advocates in Texas and North Carolina assured him of assistance from the minority in Representatives Poage and Cooley. Further entrée to the White House was available through ex-Sena-

[34] 98 *Cong. Rec.* 5292 (cf. Daily Digest, D315, D332), 82d Cong., 2d Sess.
[35] *Ibid.*, pp. 7451, 7663; cf. House Report 2222, 82d Cong., 2d Sess.
[36] Omaha *World Herald,* Nov. 2, 1952.

tor Fred Seaton of Nebraska, who had been a very close campaign adviser to the President.[37] Immediate use was made of this propitious situation by McConnell's high command, the National Informal Citizens Committee on Watershed Conservation, which met with the President on February 23, 1953, to secure his support for the legislation which would authorize the watershed program. As a result the President urged this step in a special message to Congress on the following July 31.[38]

Meanwhile an old project was revived to achieve speed, and possibly finesse. Representative Hope was instrumental in adding an item of $5,000,000 to the Department of Agriculture's 1954 budget to start approximately sixty "pilot" watershed projects to demonstrate the value of watershed management as flood control. Although this amount was omitted by the Senate Appropriations Committee despite the efforts of Senator Carlson, it was restored in conference, as its friends confidently expected it would be. In cloakroom maneuvering Representative Hope and the members of the informal committee secured the pivotal allegiance of [former] Representative Carl Andersen (R., Minn.), Chairman of the House Agricultural Appropriations Subcommittee, who later engaged in the following exchange with J. C. Dykes, Deputy Chief of the Soil Conservation Service, regarding the Jones Committee's recommendations:

> *Mr. Andersen.* Apparently you are not in agreement with that recommendation, then?
> *Mr. Dykes.* I will say we are not in agreement with it if the Department of Agriculture will be taken out of the flood-prevention work.
> *Mr. Andersen.* In the final analysis, the proposal by the House Public Works Committee would put this entire program under the domination of the Army Engineers, would it not?
> *Mr. Dykes.* It certainly would.

[37] The watershed movement in Kansas had particularly attracted the attention of the Kansas delegation because of the bitter squabble over the Tuttle Creek Dam in Northeastern Kansas. Topeka *Capital,* August 9, 1952.
[38] House Document No. 221, 83d Cong., 1st Sess.

Mr. Andersen. I disagree with that proposal, and I thought it well to have something in the record on the subject.[39]

The members of the Agricultural Appropriations Subcommittee were quite proud of the fact that the appropriation "happens to have been almost a piece of legislation on an appropriation bill, however, with the blessing of the legislative committee. So it came in a sort of left-handed way to the Department. . . ." Representative Andersen, in fact, wanted credit where credit was due:

> I want the record to show that when this subcommittee fought through its bill, putting the initial $5 million for the Andersen-Hope program into this bill in spring of 1953, that the Senate refused to agree to that item and struck it out in committee . . . If you will check the record, this subcommittee urged and fought for the retention of that item in conference and I am making this statement here, gentlemen, this morning to show where the credit belongs for actually bringing this thing into being. It was this subcommittee that started this particular program after having it called to our attention by Mr. Hope and Senator Carlson. They sat across the table from us and explained it to us. They had no hopes, however, of its even getting out of the Congress, and I reiterate, had it not been for these seven of us sitting here, that we would not today be already seeing the beginning of a program which I think is seizing the country with its popularity . . . even to the extent where the President . . . has . . . come out publicly in its behalf.[40]

Concurrent with the success in securing a one-year authorization by appropriation for the "pilot" projects, Representative Hope introduced H.R. 6788 which was intended to make the Department

[39] "Department of Agriculture Appropriations for 1954," Hearings before the Subcommittee of the Committee on Appropriations, House of Representatives, 83d Cong., 1st Sess., Part 4, pp. 1902-1903. The appropriation was made by Public Law 156, 83d Cong., 1st Sess., 67 *Stat.* 214.

[40] "Department of Agriculture Appropriations for 1955," Hearings before the Subcommittee of the Committee on Appropriations, House of Representatives, 83d Cong., 2d Sess., Part 3, pp. 1344-1345, 1315-1316. It is of interest to note that the initiative for this appropriation came from outside the Department of Agriculture—from Congress via the pressure groups.

of Agriculture a "partner" with local interests (and with the Corps and the Bureau of Reclamation) in developing flood "prevention" through watershed management. It scarcely need be said that his bill was given a sympathetic ear by the House Agriculture Committee under Hope's chairmanship. Interested groups who supported the bill were invited to send their spokesmen and the "informal" committee, in particular, was given ample time again to present its case. Opposition forces were conspicuously absent (including the Corps) so that the bill was favorably reported and acted upon by the House.[41] The exponents of the Hope Watershed Bill expected that their measure would receive quick and friendly treatment in the Senate. At the request of the President, Senator Aiken (R., Vt.) introduced a companion bill, S. 2549. Senators Thye, Schoeppel, Anderson, Young, and Monroney joined him as sponsors of this bill which, like H.R. 6788, was intended to give the Department of Agriculture authority to survey and to construct flood control works, including dams with a capacity of 5,000 acre-feet, independent of existing flood control laws.[42] To the alarm of some of the friends of the legislation Senator Aiken scheduled public hearings on his bill only to have the Corps of Engineers come out at long last with an emphatic public condemnation of the proposal. In his testimony General Sturgis said that the size of the dams authorized in the bill was too large (5,000 acre-feet); it would continue construction of purely federal and not state projects; local interests ought to

[41] See "Conservation and Watershed Programs," *op. cit.;* and 99 *Congressional Record* 10956. According to one observer, Rep. Hope has been an open proponent of the Soil Conservation Service in the power struggle within the Department of Agriculture and among farm organizations. Moreover, Senator Aiken has, according to Hardin, opposed the Service and this may account for his holding Senate hearings on the Hope Bill. See Hardin, *op. cit.,* pp. 26, 174 ff.

[42] "Cooperative Soil Conservation and Flood Prevention Projects," Hearings on S. 2549, Committee on Agriculture and Forestry, Senate, 83d Cong., 2d Sess., esp. pp. 1-34. Legislation to authorize some phases of watershed management were not new to this Congress. At least fifteen bills were introduced in the House and three in the Senate during the Eightieth, Eighty-first, and Eighty-second Congresses dealing with this matter; see Missouri Basin Survey Commission, *Bibliography of Congressional and Federal Documents on the Missouri River Basin* (1947-1952), Publication No. 1, mimeographed (Lincoln, Nebraska, 1952). In addition two other bills were introduced in the 83d Congress, S. 1916 and H.R. 4877.

share 50 per cent of the costs and should not rely on such federal largess as ACP and SCS payments to farmers in calculating them; and the bill would probably result not in more coordination, but less.[43] Senator Aiken turned the bill over to a subcommittee for study and possible amendment only to have it become lodged there on the objections of Senator Holland, who later opposed the bill on the floor saying that Congress was unwise in hastening this legislation without waiting to observe the effects of the pilot projects. Immediately McConnell invited the proponents of the bill to meet in Lincoln on April 14-15, 1954, to generate pressure for it. As a result the fifty-odd persons who were gathered made use of the usual means of contact with all of their strategically located friends in Congress to force the subcommittee to report the bill. While the bill was in committe, it took McConnell another trip to Washington on May 4th and 5th and intensive, skillful maneuvering by the "informal" committee to fend off the determined counterattack of the Corps of Engineers. In fact, it was necessary to resort again to the White House to convince all concerned that the Engineers' version of the bill did not suit the President's views. With the support of Sherman Adams, who made some alterations embodying Presidential policy, it was passed ultimately in a form acceptable to its supporters. After five years the Department of Agriculture was made what its officers called a partner in assisting local interests in developing a "balanced" program of conservation and flood prevention independent of the Corps, the Bureau of Reclamation and, it might be added, of the public works committee of the House and Senate.[44]

---

[43] "Cooperative Soil Conservation and Flood Prevention Projects," op. cit., p. 95. Among the many groups now supporting this legislation were the American Farm Bureau (which also supported the 50 per cent federal-local cost feature), the National Grange, the National Council of Farmer Cooperatives, the National Association of Soil Conservation Districts, the National Farmers Union, the National Reclamation Association (with some amendments regarding state water laws), the National Wildlife Federation, the Chamber of Commerce (with amendments in regard to local cost features) and many others. The "informal" committee did not testify before Senator Aiken's committee—supposedly as a result of pre-determined strategy.

[44] Actually the final bill enacted was H. R. 6788 with the Senate version substituted for the bill passed by the House. It became Public Law 566, 83d

This act incorporates the ingenious and disingenuous plea of its supporters, such as McConnell, that the initiative in planning and constructing works lie with "local organizations." The Secretary of Agriculture has blanket authority (subject to the support of appropriations) to commence a watershed management program in any area not exceeding 250,000 acres (though contiguous areas of this size may be in effect joined), provided that no funds for constructing a dam storing more than 2,500 acre feet of water shall be appropriated *without the consent of the House and Senate agriculture committees;* no dam may exceed 5,000 acre feet in capacity. The act provides no cost-sharing formula, but leaves this vital matter virtually to the discretion of the Secretary of Agriculture. The sole machinery for co-ordination provided in the act is the requirement that the Secretary of Agriculture submit any plan of works affecting irrigation or reclamation to the Secretary of the Interior, or affecting floodwater detention structures to the Secretary of the Army, for recommendations at least sixty days before any such plan is sent to Congress through the President. The lack of comments is no bar to the transmission of a plan. The President is authorized to issue regulations to effect co-ordination. The act also repeals the authority granted by the Flood Control Act of 1936 permitting the Secretary of Agriculture to make preliminary surveys for watershed management.[45]

Cong., 2d Sess., 68 *Stat.* 666, the "Watershed Protection and Flood Prevention Act, 1954," and was approved by the President August 4. The limitations of space make it impossible to relate more of the history of the act. It may, however, be found in 100 *Congressional Record* 1168, 3128-3152, 3164, 8496, 8595, 8619-8625, 9888, 9930, 10831, 11060, 11480, 11495, 11405, 11763. Cf. House Report No. 1140, Feb. 2, 1954; Senate Report No. 1620, June 18, 1954; and Conference Report No. 2297, July 20, 1954, 83d Cong., 2d Sess. The bill passed the Senate without debate or a record vote. In the House the "debate" was heavy with the redolence of roses as the dozen or so members most sympathetic with the legislation spent the day tossing bouquets to each other with only Rep. Saylor of Pennsylvania opposing in the discussion. Oddly enough, even the Public Works Committee had apparently made its peace with the Committee on Agriculture after a series of conferences which included Rep. Jones, Rep. Poage, and Rep. Cooley—the price was not revealed on the floor of the House.

[45] An account of the program contemplated under this act may be found in Gladwin E. Young, "Local Responsibilities for Watershed Protection Pro-

With the funds appropriated for the "pilot watershed" program a start was made on the soil conservation phase of the Salt-Wahoo project with the construction of works on the Roca sub-watershed of Salt Creek and the Swedeburg branch of the Wahoo Creek in the late autumn of 1953. Three weeks after the President signed the Watershed Protection Act of 1954, the Salt-Wahoo Watershed Association met in Lincoln with the Corps and the Soil Conservation Service to resume discussion of a joint plan. . . .

The history of the Salt-Wahoo project strikingly illustrates the price paid in our constitutional system for the fractionalization of power. It also demonstrates again need for instruments of co-ordination which can bridge the many gaps standing in the way of policy formulation. The machinery of government, moreover, does not supply sufficient initiative from within itself to foresee, much less to solve, many problems. Assuming at least for the moment, that both the Salt-Wahoo flood control project and the Watershed Protection Act of 1954 reflect desirable public policy, one may ask how they would have been put into being if adequate organized pressure had not been generated on their behalf by those directly interested in the outcome. The leaders of the Salt-Wahoo organization were told by a spokesman of the Soil Conservation Service that they would have to "push this thing" or they would not get what they wanted. The Soil Conservation Service offered a program which did not even have the hearty backing of the entire Department of Agriculture.[46]

It became one of the prime tasks of the Salt-Wahoo organization,

---

grams," *State Government,* XXVII, No. 12 (December, 1954), 255 ff. President Eisenhower issued regulations directing co-ordination in Executive Order 10584, December 18, 1954; *Federal Register,* Vol. 19, No. 246, pp. 8725-8726.

[46] Certainly the Department did not pressure for appropriations to support its program. The initiative came from the pressure groups and the idea for using the one year appropriation to start "pilot" projects came from Senator Wherry. The willingness of high Soil Conservation Service officers to gloss over their quarrel with the Corps has evoked snorts of disgust from the chief scribe of the watershed movement, Elmer T. Peterson, in his book, *Big Dam Foolishness: The Problem of Modern Flood Control and Water Storage* (New York: The Devin-Adair Company, 1954), pp. 37-49. Peterson has also frankly noted the implications of the watershed movement in regard to public power, pp. 101 ff.

and later of the informal citizens committee, to crusade with missionary zeal for the watershed program. Only the adroit maneuvering of organized opinion could have overcome the resistance of the Corps, the internal conflicts within the Department of Agriculture and the opposition of the public works committees in Congress. In the absence of satisfactory will or machinery for developing a program on the national level, the exponents of a relatively obscure project had to discover a similar interest elsewhere and amalgamate with it on a national basis. It may be presumed that the friends of the watershed movement belatedly have discovered what the members of the Rivers and Harbors Congress have long known, so that the National Watershed Congress which met in Washington in December, 1954, for its first annual meeting is now assured of a respectful and sympathetic Congressional audience. Moreover, its task has been simplified in so far as it may now deal only with the committees on agriculture.

In this instance the pressure group performed not only the representative function but an administrative one as well in seeking to coordinate the Corps and the Soil Conservation Service on the project level. Only when this effort failed because of reciprocal agency antagonism, did the Salt-Wahoo organization shift its rôle to the more common one of influencing legislation.[47]

The leaders of the Salt-Wahoo organization appeared to be guilty of duplicity in claiming that they were not anti-Engineers even though they were spokesmen for the SCS Program. Guilt in this instance may be more apparent than real. From the start of the project until after the passage of Watershed Protection Act of 1954 the Engineers claimed that small dams on the tributaries were unable to stop flooding after heavy rains. If there were any merit to the claims of SCS, there was need of proof by demonstration. Since

[47] It should be noted that the Salt-Wahoo organization attempted to formalize its co-ordinating rôle by securing a state enabling law in 1953 which permits the formation of watershed districts. Such a district is visualized as special unit or "local agency" of the sort mentioned in the Watershed Protection and Flood Prevention Act of 1954. For some details regarding the watershed district in Nebraska, see my article, "A New Voice in Government: The Watershed District," *State Government*, XXVI, No. 12 (December, 1953), 288 ff.

the Corps would not build tributary dams, it was necessary for the exponents of the watershed movement to support SCS or no demonstration would ever be made. The transparency of the Corps position is made apparent by the fact that the Army construction portion of the Salt-Wahoo project announced in November, 1954, includes at least *five* dams of a capacity well under 5,000 acre feet. In other words, the Corps now sees the virtue of small dams—if they are built by the Corps! Unfortunately the friends of the watershed movement were not willing to rest on the "pilot" program as a demonstration of the claimed value of the watershed technique. Instead, they pushed the Watershed Protection Act of 1954 through Congress before they had any sound basis for advocating it as a major addition to the present water resources programs.

The Salt-Wahoo organization claimed that its action supplied a democratizing element in administration by insuring that the program fashioned at its insistence was satisfactory to the home folks. But if this is so, it was democracy bearing a price tag which eventually must be siphoned out of the federal treasury. If it is proper to believe that federal programs must suit local interests, it is equally proper to seek assurances that the people of the nation get both a beneficial and an economical program for the pain in their pocketbooks. The adoption of the Watershed Protection and Flood Prevention Act of 1954, together with existing programs such as Pick-Sloan, can only continue a situation in which the weak, the timid, the hesitant—and even on occasion the deserving—may well be trampled in the cynical rush of the aggressive and acquisitive to the federal cornucopia.[48]

[48] During the House "debate" on H.R. 6788 Rep. Hill (R., Colo.) quoted the conference report, saying: ". . . under the policies established by the bill, plans and projects will not be handed down from the top as part of some overall development plan, but can be initiated only by the people of the localities most intimately involved . . ." 100 *Congressional Record* 3148. The Jones Committee observed that authorization overlaps permitted the Department of Agriculture to conduct its watershed projects under either flood control legislation or soil conservation legislation and thereby to co-ordinate with the Corps or not, as the Department saw fit, and to choose the committee which seemed to promise its blessing. House Committee Print No. 22, *op. cit.*, pp. 34-40. The "local initiative" authorized in the new law appears to be no different from that involved in projects which the Corps is invited to survey and construct.

In enacting the Watershed Protection and Flood Prevention Act of 1954 both Congress and the executive branch have once again demonstrated an apparent incapacity to deal with the problem of fashioning a comprehensive program of water resources conservation and development. It has been demonstrated that it is easier to yield to particular interests which are organized and articulate than it is to view a problem such as this from the standpoint of the entire nation. As long as reliance is placed on local initiative and pressure politics of the sort demonstrated in this case study, there will be no consideration of the national interest. A program can be developed but only if the initiative does not come solely from the bottom. Leadership must come from the top, from a President who will demonstrate that in resources policy there is not only an administrative way, but also a political will. Congress, faced with a problem of administrative fratricide rooted in well organized pressures, found that in this dispute the easiest solution was a settlement by divorce (as in the case of the Pick-Sloan Plan authorized by the Flood Control Act of 1944). As matters now stand both the Soil Conservation Service and the Corps will build dams. The precise point at which raindrops become floods has not been decided.

Interest Groups, Judicial Review, and Local Government*

CLEMENT E. VOSE

The doctrine of judicial review has placed the American judiciary at the center of public policy formation. Its decisions, the results of litigation, may confirm benefits for one group's aspirations and impede those of others. Professor Clement Vose examines the litigation of certain groups at the state and municipal level and the impact these decisions have for public policy-making at these two levels.

Past scholarship on judicial review of state and local government has been high on structure, power, and policy and low on process. The classic work of Dillon, McQuillin and McBain proved the power of courts in limiting municipal rule against state policy, and state action in many fields against federal constitutional limitations.[1] Rhyne has shown, in an up-to-date treatise, that judge-made doctrines continue to govern state and local practice.[2] The inferior position of these governmental units to both state and federal courts has long been illustrated in law school casebooks on municipal corporations and explained in political science texts on state and local government.

[1] John F. Dillon, *Commentaries on the Law of Municipal Corporations* (5th ed.; Boston: Little, Brown, 1911), 5 vols.; Eugene McQuillin, *A Treatise on the Law of Municipal Corporations* (2d ed.; Chicago: Callaghan, 1945), 7 vols.; Howard Lee McBain, *The Law and Practice of Municipal Home Rule* (New York: Macmillan, 1916).

[2] Charles Rhyne, *Municipal Law* (Washington: NIMLO, 1957).

* Clement E. Vose, "Interest Groups, Judicial Review, and Local Government," *Western Political Quarterly*, XIX (March, 1966), pp. 85-100. Reprinted by permission of the University of Utah, copyright owners.

The importance of courts is well understood; the ways in which these passive instruments of government are stimulated to action is not.[3] My attention to the details of litigation sponsored by organized interest groups flows from a central assumption that the important thing about appellate courts in the American system is that these courts govern by making policy. They may do this by deciding what is constitutional or unconstitutional and they may do it by the interpretation of statutes, administrative rules and regulations, the decisions of lower courts and so on. To say that courts are important in American government is to speak the obvious. But emphasis on their importance because of their policy-making function is not always the starting point in the textbook treatment of the judiciary. If it were, I believe there would be more attention to the ways cases are brought and to identify the true parties in such cases. Political scientists have not sufficiently moved off the dime of constitutional doctrine to describe the real gold of politics in the judicial process. This article looks at litigation conducted by action organizations and points to the importance of group agitation for judicial review of state and municipal public policy.

The Legitimacy of Interest Groups in Court Cases

The Supreme Court of the United States in 1963 vindicated the right of the most successful litigating organization of the day, the National Association for the Advancement of Colored People, to pursue its goals through the courts. In *NAACP* v. *Button*,[4] the

---

[3] The criticisms of Lawrence J. R. Herson in "The Lost World of Municipal Government," 51 *APSR* 330 (1957), that the texts neglected the political aspects of the judicial process have, to some extent, been remedied. Yet these texts have not yet incorporated the findings on group sponsorship of litigation as reported in the journals. The leading book in the new wave, Charles R. Adrian, *Governing Urban America* (2d ed.; New York: McGraw-Hill, 1961), includes a chapter on the law of municipalities, pp. 197-231, and another on intergroup activity and political power, pp. 119-46. Each is excellent—and I have often reread them—but the two subjects are largely unconnected to each other. A more recent text, Duane Lockard, *The Politics of State and Local Government* (New York: Macmillan, 1963), comes closer to an integration of the two subjects. He does this especially in chapters on the politics of constitutionalism, on the political process and on politics and the judiciary.
[4] 371 U.S. 415 (1963).

Court recognized the extent of group sponsorship of litigation and certified it against state legislation that aimed to severely limit cases brought by organizations. This was, of course, one way for a state government to protect its policies against judicial review. The failure of Virginia and other southern states to stop organizations from litigating, further legitimized judicial review and recognized the right of organizations to seek redresses in the judicial forum. This is what Mr. Justice Brennan said for the Supreme Court:

> . . . In the context of NAACP objectives, litigation is not a technique of resolving private differences; it is a means for achieving the lawful objectives of equality of treatment by all government, federal, state and local, for the members of the Negro community in this country. It is thus a form of political expression. Groups which find themselves unable to achieve their objectives through the ballot frequently turn to the courts. Just as it was true of the opponents of New Deal legislation during the 1930's, for example, no less is it true of the Negro minority today. And under the conditions of modern government, litigation may well be the sole practicable avenue open to a minority to petition for redress of grievances.

> • • •

> The NAACP is not a conventional political party; but the litigation it assists, while serving to vindicate the legal rights of members of the American Negro community, at the same time and perhaps more importantly, makes possible the distinctive contribution of a minority group to the ideas and beliefs of our society. For such a group, association for litigation may be the most effective form of political association.[5]

Academic categories of state and local government on the one hand and civil rights and civil liberties on the other have not kept organized interest groups from action. These are the propositions that link them together: (1) For some thirty years the Supreme Court has been nationalizing the constitutional rights of individuals. (2) In hundreds of decisions dealing with freedom of expression and religion, rights of defendants and rights of racial minorities

[5] *Id.*, at 425.

against segregation and discrimination the Supreme Court has spelled out new constitutional doctrine. (3) The bulk of these cases have questioned state and municipal public policy with the result that many, many state statutes, municipal ordinances, and other forms of state action have been invalidated. (4) National organizations have participated in practically 100 per cent of these cases by providing financial or legal assistance, by appearing as *amicus curiae,* or by giving strategic advice.[6]

The most active organizations include the following: the National Association for the Advancement of Colored People, the American Civil Liberties Union, the Commission on Law and Social Action of the American Jewish Congress, the American Committee for Protection of the Foreign Born, the Emergency Civil Liberties Commitee, the Watchtower Bible and Tract Society (Jehovah's Witnesses), American Jewish Committee, Japanese American Citizens League, Congress of Racial Equality, and Protestants and Other Americans United for the Separation of Church and State. Attorneys employed by these and other organizations provide the expertise that continuous attention to a problem brings to practitioners. Their persuasive powers are applied to the courts in long series of cases which spread over many years. That this has, at least, sometimes been true may be seen by looking briefly at some of the most celebrated Supreme Court reviews of state and local government policy in civil rights and liberties.

The School Segregation cases of 1954 and 1955 were themselves the product of litigation sponsored by the NAACP Legal Defense and Education Fund.[7] These five cases had been preceded by some fifty favorable Supreme Court decisions extending over the previous thirty years. Those decisions have been followed by a steady stream of litigation which has seen NAACP lawyers in an

[6] For a survey of the activity of organizations in the major cases of recent years, see Comment, "The South's Amended Barratry Laws: An Attempt to End Group Pressure Through the Courts," 72 *Yale L. J.* 1613-45 (Summer 1963). The great changes in the legal status of Negroes are explained in Jack Greenberg, *Race Relations and American Law* (New York: Columbia U. Press, 1959).

[7] *Brown* v. *Board of Education,* 347 U.S. 483 (1954), 349 U.S. 294 (1955).

average of ten appearances a year in the Supreme Court. The Association has also participated in numerous cases in the lower federal courts. Certainly some 90 per cent of this vast litigation has put in question a policy adopted by Southern states and municipalities. Much of it has dealt with the segregation of school pupils but, of course, local school arrangements are public policy.

The Flag Salute cases of 1940 and 1943[8] as well as the Prayer cases of 1961 and 1963[9] dealt also with public school policy and resulted in the invalidation of local law by the Supreme Court. Manwaring has shown that the flag salute question had stood unanswered for years because no organization would challenge the practice in the Courts. The Jehovah's Witnesses did so in the 1930's and after several tries gained review in the Supreme Court. They were finally successful in 1943 in having the obligatory flag salute for public school students invalidated.[10]

Individuals who conscientiously opposed the recitation of prayers in public school were parties to the recent cases on this question. This was necessary to establish standing as a party in the cases. But despite the national prominence of some successful parties in these cases—one thinks back to Mrs. Vashti McCollum as well as to Mrs. [Madalyn] Murray, perhaps America's two most prominent lady atheists—organized interest groups have not been far behind the scenes. *Amicus curiae* briefs were filed in the most recent prayer cases by the American Humanist Association, the American Ethical Union, the Synagogue Council of America and the National Community Relations Advisory Council, and the American Jewish Committee and Anti-Defamation League of B'nai B'rith.

The extent of interest group activity in litigation is certainly not yet realized. Nor has the data so far collected been accommodated to a political theory of democracy. This article focuses on cases which

---

[8] *Minersville School District* v. *Gobitis,* 310 U.S. 586 (1940), *West Virginia State Board of Education* v. *Barnette,* 319 U.S. 624 (1943).

[9] *Engle* v. *Vitale,* 370 U.S. 421 (1962). *Abington Township School District* v. *Schempp* and *Murray* v. *Curlett,* 374 U.S. 203 (1963).

[10] For a thorough review of methods of litigation used by The Witnesses, see David Manwaring, *Render Unto Caesar* (Chicago: U. of Chicago Press, 1962).

define the limits of state and local governmental power and insists that group activity in the litigation is both widespread and legitimate. The large number of cases sponsored by organizations is a function of the power of courts to act. This authority of the judiciary was beautifully set forth by Norman Williams, Jr., ten years ago, as follows:

> The main premises of American constitutional law repre-
> sents a codification and institutionalization of the primary
> values of a democratic society — equality of opportunity and
> equality of treatment, freedom of thought and considerable
> freedom of action, and fairness. Under the American system,
> a more or less independent mechanism of judicial review is
> established to provide an independent check on whether spe-
> cific governmental decisions conform to these standards.
> While controversy has often raged about judicial action in
> other areas, *it has always been recognized that it is an essen-
> tial part of the judicial function to watch over the parochial
> and exclusionist attitudes and policies of local governments,
> and to see to it that these do not run counter to national
> policy and the general welfare.*[11]

But courts are passive instruments of control and must be moved to decision by a party controverting government policy. The performance of this function has often been fulfilled by organized interest groups.

Interests opposed to each other in litigation are ordinarily not readily identifiable in the court reports. The parties are named and their counsel are listed but the parties are often there to give legal standing to the wider interests supporting a litigation. And the attorneys are representatives of those interests, often on a full-time basis. Little has been written on the function of interest groups in litigation. The current collection of examples will suggest something further about the variety of the phenomenon and show that group activity is not limited to celebrated cases on civil rights. Rather, litigation is a flow of pressure group activity that is old, common, and

[11] "Planning Law and Democratic Living," *Law and Contemporary Problems*, 20 (1955), 317.

essential to the judicial review of the most controversial policies of municipal government.

Public School Cases

Public education is important as a budget item and as a political issue in American communities. Many organizations have drawn the judiciary into the consideration of various aspects of local school affairs. Racial segregation was outlawed in cases initiated in this way and we are now well through the first decade of follow-up litigation to bring practice into conformity with constitutional doctrine. Court tests of school activities offensive to different religions have come up frequently in the past twenty years.

In 1933, well before this spate of cases on race and religion, an authority on the legal basis of school organization and administration wrote that "the relation of the school to civil society, on the one hand, and to the individual, on the other, is nowhere so well defined as in the great body of decisions rendered by the highest of our state and federal courts."[12] Since then, outside control of education has advanced as an activist judiciary has applied new tests to local practices. Of course, there is disagreement over whether these decisions are different from those in the first part of the century which Justice Holmes condemned because they prevented "the making of social experiments that an important part of the community desires, in the insulated chambers afforded by the several States."[13] Edward S. Corwin believed that these issues are alike. After the decision in the McCollum case in 1948 outlawing released time practices in the public schools of Champaign, Illinois, Corwin said: "In my opinion the Court would act wisely to make it clear at the first opportunity that it does not aspire to become, as Justice Jackson puts it, 'a super board of education for every school district in the nation.' "[14] Whatever one's view

[12] Newton Edwards, *The Courts and the Public Schools* (Chicago: U. of Chicago Press, 1933; 1955).
[13] *Truax* v. *Corrigan*, 257 U.S. 312, 344 (1921) (dissenting opinion).
[14] Edward S. Corwin, "The Supreme Court as a National School Board," *Law and Contemporary Problems*, 14 (Winter 1949), 22. The quotation of Justice Jackson is from *McCollum* v. *Board of Education*, 333 U.S. 203 (1948) (dissenting opinion).

may be there can be no denying that court decisions are having important ramifications in the educational life of American communities.

Interest Groups in Zoning Cases

The interest group approach follows the tradition of legal realism and emphasizes the political impulses behind litigation and the political results of judicial decisions rather than the arguments, reasoning and doctrines of law in cases. We are interested in the effect of judicial decisions on the distribution of power in communities. Take as an example the recent cases testing the authority of local zoning boards. In *Senior v. New Canaan Zoning Commission*[15] the Connecticut Supreme Court of Errors, in 1959, held constitutional the upgrading of lots in a residential semi-rural zone from two to four acre minimums. The decision met with mixed reaction throughout Fairfield County. The Court noted in its opinion that "the town of New Canaan, as of the 1950 census, had the highest per capita income of any town, village, or city in the United States." [16] It was not surprising to learn that the First Selectman of New Canaan described the ruling as beneficial. "It is good for the town to keep its prestige in a major suit of this kind," he said. There was general agreement that "the decision strengthened the power of zoning boards to decide the character of their communities." More recently *House and Home* has said that the U.S. Supreme Court's refusal to hear the arguments in the New Canaan Case "is seen as strengthening the power of zoning boards generally." [17] Civic groups in other communities were encouraged to fight further for similar zoning for minimum lot area. It was also recognized that such zoning worked hardships on lower-income groups and believed by some that it prevented an orderly population growth. The effect of the Court decision upholding four-acre minimum lots was also said to be an increase in price of existing two-

---

[15] *Senior v. New Canaan Zoning Commission,* 146 Conn. 531, 153 A.2d 415 (1959), appeal dismissed, 80 S. Ct. 1083 (1960).
[16] New York *Times,* July 5, 1959, p. 58.
[17] *House and Home,* July 1960, p. 41.

acre lots which were comparatively scarce. Quite certainly the courts which considered this case dealt with legal issues that touched not only the distribution of power within one community but in many similar suburban places and in central cities, as well. This was true for the Court of Common Pleas which, in the first instance, declared the zoning ordinance unconstitutional. It was also true for the Connecticut Supreme Court of Errors which reversed that decision and the United States Supreme Court which, on May 21, 1960, dismissed the appeal.[18]

The pressures for and against acreage, or snob, zoning (called "Ivy League socialism" by Dean Jefferson Fordham of the University of Pennsylvania Law School)[19] came to the surface in a case brought by a construction company against Easttown Township, a main-line suburb of Philadelphia.[20] There a 1940 ordinance provided that a minimum lot area in an "A" residential district should be one acre, with a minimum frontage of 150 feet. The court test was begun when the applicant sought to build a dwelling on a site slightly less than a half-acre, with a frontage of 100 feet. The Easttown Township Board of Adjustment refused to grant a variance and this decision was supported by the Chester County Court of Common Pleas. The Supreme Court of Pennsylvania first reversed the lower court, by a vote of 6 to 1 on June 28, 1957, then granted a rehearing, vacated its order, and in a final order, on May 27, 1958, reversed itself by a 4 to 3 vote, and ruled the order of the Board of Adjustment to be valid. By the time the case reached reargument the defense of acreage zoning by Easttown Township and its Devon Citizens Association was supported by the *amici curiae* briefs of Lower Merion Township, Willistown Township, the Pennsylvania Local Government Conference, the Pennsylvania Planning Association, and George Wharton Pepper, Esquire, a well-known citizen of Easttown. The opposing position of the Bilbar Construction Company was supported in briefs *amici curiae* by the

---

[18] The appeal was dismissed "for want of a substantial federal question," 80 S.Ct. 1083 (1960).

[19] *House and Home,* July 1960, p. 59.

[20] *Bilbar Construction Company* v. *Easttown Township Board of Adjustment,* 393 Pa. 62, 141 A.2d 851 (1958).

Home Builders Association of Philadelphia and the Home Life Insurance Company.[21]

In stressing the organizations in a case there is danger of neglecting other important considerations. This is the problem of any interpretation built around a single approach. But the objective is understanding, not a complete explanation that would satisfy all social scientists and lawyers at once. Very important new doctrine may be found in the Easttown Township decision when the Pennsylvania Supreme Court ruled that the regulation need only have a substantial or reasonable relation to health, safety, morals, or the general welfare. This seemingly went against Dillon's rule in holding that the presumption of constitutionality of an ordinance is as strong as that attending an act of the legislature.[22] With this and other decisions the importance of doctrine is assumed but the interest group environment in which these cases are decided is stressed.

Few major zoning disputes have been carried to the U.S. Supreme Court since the original case of *Euclid* v. *Ambler Realty Co.* was decided in 1926.[23] The Village of Euclid had as counsel a young man named James Metzenbaum who has said: "It has been my understanding that the railroads, the industrial plants and the realtors (*then* afraid of zoning; now strong champions of zoning*) paid the large fee to Mr. Newton D. Baker," [24] There is little question but what zoning cases are rife with organized interests.[25]

The National Institute of Municipal Law Officers

In exploring the group nature of the litigation which gives rise to

[21] David Craig, "Zoning," 20 *U. of Pitt. L. Rev.* 278 (1958).
[22] Theodore O. Rogers and others, *Zoning for Minimum Lot Area* (Philadelphia: U. of Villanova Press, 1959). See John M. Anderson, "Book Review," 34 *Notre Dame Law*, 603 (1959).
[23] *Euclid* v. *Ambler Realty Co.*, 272 U.S. 365 (1926). See James Metzenbaum, *The Law of Zoning* (3 vols.; New York: Baker, Voorhis, 1956). Editorial, New York *Times*, February 11, 1956.
[24] Interview of James Metzenbaum, Cleveland, Ohio, May 15, 1955; Letters of James Metzenbaum to author, September 22, 1955, and October 13, 1955.
[25] For valuable analyses of the important cases in this field, see the annual reviews of Norman Williams, Jr., "Recent Decisions in Planning Law," *American Institute of Planners Journal*, 27 (May 1961), 159; ibid., 28 (May 1962), 132; *ibid.*, 29 (May 1963) 127; *ibid.*, 30 (May 1964).

judicial decisions affecting municipal governments I shall first describe the side of government and, perhaps underplaying the role of
the attorney for a municipality, tell of some organizations which
stand behind him. Here is the defense of municipal power and the
policies favored by the majority. Considering the values of local rule
it is heartening to see that this defense is often well made. Then I
shall identify groups which have lost out in municipal decisions and
turn to the courts for relief. Considering that many of their cases are
brought to protect citizen rights it is impressive that these groups
bring zeal, skill, and money to litigation. Thus the place of courts in
municipal power struggles will be reached indirectly.[26]

Although the defense of actions by municipal corporations is
formally in the hands of their chief legal officer, titled variously corporation counsel, law director or city, town, village, borough or county
attorney, this work has been aided since 1935 by the National Institute of Municipal Law Officers. Known by its initials, NIMLO was
an offshoot of the United States Conference of Mayors though always
an independent organization. Its headquarters are in Washington
where a full-time legal staff is maintained under Charles S. Rhyne,
who has served as director since 1939. Its members are 1,200 American municipalities which rely on NIMLO as a collection center for
their varied legal experience. A description by NIMLO shows it to be
supported entirely by the annual membership fees paid by member
cities. Interestingly, this tells that "information collected and on file in
the Washington Office is never used by, nor made available to, any

---

[26] Bentley's proposition on the pressure of interests in the judiciary developed partly from his view of the Chicago traction company cases in which the
Supreme Court limited the rights of the franchise street railways as against
municipal control. *North Chicago City Railway Co. v. Blair*, 201 U.S. 399
(1906). He related the outcome in these cases to broad changes in public
opinion over the previous decade more than to the conscious efforts of organized interests or to the labors of the attorneys. Arthur F. Bentley, *The Process
of Government: A Study of Social Pressures* (Chicago: U. of Chicago Press,
1908), pp. 392-93. His conclusion was that Supreme Court justices are "a
functioning part of this government, responsive to the group pressures within
it, representative of all sorts of pressures, and using their representative judgment to bring these pressures to balance, not indeed in just the same way, but
on just the same basis, that any other agency does, and that in this Chicago
case they let a changing weight of group interests come very close to expression." *Ibid.*, p. 393.

person other than an attorney for a NIMLO member so that there is no possibility that this material will be employed against the cities which have collected it." [27]

NIMLO represents a kind of perfect expression of a paradoxical development—the nationalization of municipal law. It aids the busy municipal attorney "who needs the strength flowing from joint support of many municipalities in instances where the protest of a single municipality would be ineffective." Or, put another way by NIMLO, "furnishes an effective agency through which municipal attorneys can take joint cooperative action on Federal legislation and on any other matter of nationwide consequence to municipalities on matters in Washington, D.C., with great effectiveness." NIMLO offers many services but two activities may be identified as directly shaping the legal position of municipalities: drafting model ordinances and defending them by briefs in the Supreme Court of the United States.[28]

The very idea of model state constitutions and legislation, model city charters and ordinances has not been much explored. The phenomenon is very well known and accepted, for on its face it is easy to understand as necessary in a nation of fifty states and thousands of lesser governmental units. Yet the folklore of American government must yield a bit when it is realized that much modern local legislation has been drafted in Washington! At any rate, the *NIMLO Model Ordinance Service* is followed closely by most municipal law officers in advising local councils in the enactment of local legislation. The *Service* is in a loose-leaf binder to facilitate constant revision and supplementation and "each model ordinance has tried and proven provisions with citations to the special studies or leading court decisions upon which it is based." And it may be truly said that "many of

[27] The quotation is from a leaflet published by the National Institute of Municipal Law Officers, 839 17th Street, N.W., Washington 6, D.C. I am indebted to Mr. Brice W. Rhyne for information about NIMLO. Interview, Washington, D.C., March 25, 1960.

[28] The most important publication is Charles S. Rhyne, *Municipal Law* (Washington: NIMLO, 1957), said to be the only one-volume treatise on municipal law published since 1910. Regularly issued publications include NIMLO, *Municipal Law Review, NIMLO Model Ordinance Service, Municipal Ordinance Review, Municipal Law Court Decisions,* and the *Municipal Law Journal.*

these model ordinances have already been adopted by hundreds of municipalities."

If a "test case" is one whose outcome will affect interests beyond those of the parties in the dispute then NIMLO's frequent interest in municipal ordinance litigation is to be expected. In the bulk of instances cases involving model ordinances are settled at the state level and are prepared by the law officers of member municipalities. For example, in 1950 the NIMLO Model Sound Truck Ordinance, which had been adopted by the City of Allentown, Pennsylvania, was upheld by the Pennsylvania Superior Court.[29] The case for sustaining the ordinance was made by the city solicitor of Allentown. The lower court's holding was affirmed by the State Supreme Court and an appeal from this dismissed by the United States Supreme Court. When cases involving member municipalities come before the Supreme Court, NIMLO may take action in two ways. The organization may provide assistance to the city law officer in charge of the case by making suggestions on the brief or on the approach to the oral argument. On occasion Charles S. Rhyne, Director of NIMLO, may join as a joint author of a brief for a municipality.

The second form of NIMLO support in court cases is by *amici curiae* briefs, an activity which seems to be flourishing nowadays.[30] At least most of NIMLO's *amici* briefs have been in cases during the last three terms of the Supreme Court. There are nine cases which NIMLO has entered in this way. Of these, seven have supported city efforts to obtain lower gas and utility rates and two have involved municipal inspection practices.[31]

---

[29] *Commonwealth* v. *Guess*, 168 Pa.Super. 22, 76 A.2d 500 (1950), *affirmed* without opinion, 368 Pa. 290, 81 A.2d 553 (1912), *appeal dismissed*, 342 U.S. 912 (1952). See Rhyne, *Municipal Law*, p. 471, n. 28.

[30] See Samuel Krislov, "The Amicus Curiae Brief: From Friendship to Advocacy," 72 *Yale L. J.* 694 (April 1963).

[31] Among cases in which NIMLO has filed a brief as *amicus curiae* are the following: *Frank* v. *Maryland*, 359 U.S. 360 (1959); *City of Detroit* v. *Murray Corporation*, 355 U.S. 489 (1958); *Phillips Petroleum* v. *Wisconsin*, 347 U.S. 672 (1954); *District of Columbia* v. *Little*, 338 U.S. 866 (1949), in support of the petition for certiorari, and at 339 U.S. 1 (1950), on the merits; *Oklahoma Natural Gas Co.* v. *Federal Power Commission*, 358 U.S. 877 (1958), in support of petition for certiorari; *United Gas Pipe Line Co.* v. *Memphis Light, Gas & Water*, 355 U.S. 938 (1958), in opposition to cer-

NIMLO, as a kind of semi-governmental institution, acts with decorum and restraint in its work of ordinance design and defense. But, occasionally, an ally in extending and justifying municipal power may beseech the courts to act right by supporting a pet policy aim. A current example may be seen in criticisms of courts by supporters of urban renewal and slum clearance programs in American cities. In 1960 the *Cleveland Plain Dealer* addressed the courts editorially in this tone: "Frankly, we think the municipal judges who now try these cases have not given enough thought to the cancer which slums and rank overcrowding have created in this city. In our view, there consistently are too many postponements and too many suspended fines. . . . This wrist-slapping business must be stopped, for what's the use of hiring new inspectors and putting through a stricter housing code if the court doesn't follow up the good work?" [32] This point of view was applied to courts in other cities in the spring of 1960 by the National Association of Housing and Redevelopment which criticized judicial leniency in Cinncinati, Dayton, and St. Louis.[33] In those cities courts rejected evidence of violations obtained during inspections without search warrants. On June 20, 1960, a 4-to-4 tie vote in the United States Supreme Court let stand the arrest of a Dayton homeowner for refusing to admit a housing inspector without a warrant.[34] The defense of the Dayton ordinance permitting such inspections was led by Charles Rhyne in cooperation with the city attorney and NIMLO filed an *amicus curiae* brief in support, also. However, the tie vote has no force or precedent, so this particular problem is not yet ended.

NIMLO protects local law in the courts as a matter of routine and as a primary obligation. There are other organizations, established to serve the interests of local government, which participate in law suits only occasionally. Thus, the United States Conference of Mayors has

---

tiorari, 358 U.S. 103 (1958), on the merits; *Smith* v. *California*, 80 S.Ct. 399 (1960), in support of rehearing.

[32] Quoted in *Journal of Housing*, 17 (May 1960), 187-88.

[33] *Ibid.* The position of the National Association of Housing and Redevelopment was widely reported. See New York *Times*, July 10, 1960, p. 43; *Milwaukee Journal*, August 21, 1960.

[34] *Ohio ex rel. Eaton* v. *Price, Chief of Police*, 80 S.Ct. 1465 (1960).

been involved in only one case since its founding in 1934. As an organization of mayors of approximately 300 cities with a population of 50,000 or more the Conference in 1957 filed a brief *amicus curiae* supporting a petition by Mayor Hartsfield of Atlanta requesting the Supreme Court of the United States to consider the constitutionality of the Georgia County Unit Primary.[35] This brief contended that this system "represents a systematic discrimination against, and continuous debasement of, the political voice and position of municipalities and their citizens." And, "State Governments controlled by self-perpetuating rural minorities systematically discriminate against the interests of municipalities and their citizens." The Conference therefore entered its brief in order to place the Georgia County Unit Primary "in the larger context of urban underrepresentation." However, the Supreme Court denied review. It is fair to conclude that the United States Conference of Mayors ordinarily finds better expression of its goals than through litigation.

In contrast, the state leagues of municipalities act much more like NIMLO for, among many activities, they prepare codes of model ordinances appropriate in a single state and especially for smaller communities. These organizations also represent the interests of their member municipalities before state legislatures, administrative agencies and courts. In a typical state, for instance, the League of Wisconsin Municipalities filed eight *amici curiae* briefs in state supreme court cases during the past decade.[36] Ordinarily the preamble of such briefs explains that "the disposition of the matter before the court is of vital concern to all Wisconsin cities and villages." It is this judgment that the executive committee of the League applies in authorizing that a brief be submitted on behalf of its members. In Wisconsin the cities and villages which are members now number 492. State municipal leagues often decide whether to file briefs in cases partly on its view of

---

[35] *Hartsfield v. Sloan*, 357 U.S. 916 (1958). This information was obtained through a visit to the offices of the United States Conference of Mayors, 1707 H Street, N.W., Washington 6, D.C. See the pamphlet, *The United States Conference of Mayors: Its History, Organization, Activities, and Services* (Washington, 1953).

[36] This information is based, in part, on an interview with Mr. Robert D. Sundby, Legal Counsel, League of Wisconsin Municipalities, 30 East Johnson Street, Madison, Wisconsin, August 17, 1960.

the competence of the municipal corporation attorney for it continues to be a great irony of our judicial process that great principles affecting many interests not heard in a lawsuit may rise or fall in a quietly pursued litigation. The organizations that support the work of city law officers are understandable developments in this system of lawmaking.

Thus far I have assumed that municipal corporations have enough in common to join together in common defense when there are law suits questioning their powers, policies, and procedures. This view is supported by the program of the American Municipal Association, the national organization of the various state municipal leagues, which speaks of "the national municipal policy" which guides their activities. But while there are broad areas of agreement the differences in the size, location, financial condition and outlook among American communities are surely reflected in these organizations. Accordingly, the larger cities in a state are frequently at odds with the public position of their municipal league. And, no doubt, the American Municipal Association does not feel as strongly about the need for reapportionment as does the United States Conference of Mayors. Certainly the litigation in which these groups are active reflects their different constituencies and outlooks.

Turning to the single municipality and its attorney one finds some well-established differences. Litigation for a large city is proportionately much greater than for a smaller place though rate of growth is a factor of importance. Tax and liability cases bulk large in this work while annexation and related issues shows up in the legal business of a growing place. While national and state organizations of government officials often contribute to the defense of municipal corporations in the courts, municipal law officers do not depend solely on this support. Political scientists should give attention to this office and the political factors which condition its conduct.

To the extent that local government policy is set by organized interests in a locality then the defense of that policy in the courts is also a defense of those interests. There are many instances where this private interest is given ample chance to speak officially in support of the policy. In *Dean Milk Co.* v. *Madison*,[37] the city

[37] *Dean Milk Co.* v. *Madison*, 340 U.S. 349 (1950).

of Madison was represented throughout the litigation by the city attorney and an attorney for the Madison Milk Producers Association, as well. In *Zorach* v. *Clauson*,[38] the city of New York was represented by its own counsel and by an *amicus* brief by a city-wide committee of Protestants, Catholics, and Jews which favored released time from the schools, for religious instruction. When the Borough of Rutherford, New Jersey, wished to defend distribution of Bibles in the public schools it accepted the support of the Gideons International as intervenor to defend the policy in the courts and carry the costs.[39]

The frequent judicial defeat of states and municipalities a generation ago was attributed by Justice Brandeis to inferior public counsel. He felt over and over again that attorneys representing private interests were abler men than those representing cities and states. It is hard to make a comparison today. No doubt the organizations of public officials, especially the National Institute of Municipal Law Officers, the state leagues of municipalities, and the National Association of Attorneys General, have provided vital skill in support of individual public law officers in crucial legal tests. Private supporters also volunteer legal aid to governments in court cases. Abler men, larger staffs and bigger budgets today enable cities to defend themselves in the courts to balance adversary proceedings which tend to be lopsided when superior private counsel is employed.

American Trial Lawyers Association — Formerly National Association of Claimants' Counsel of America

Strong feelings of aggrieved parties, the devotion of able attorneys and associations of persons similarly situated go together in many of the best known actions against state and local government in recent years. In the city of New York, and elsewhere increasingly, a substantial part of the cost of operating the law department is due to the defense against "sidewalk injury cases." In 1959 the *NIMLO*

---

[38] *Zorach* v. *Clauson*, 343 U.S. 306 (1952).
[39] *Tudor* v. *Gideons International*, 14 N.J. 31, 100 A2d 857 (1953), *certiorari denied*, 348 U.S. 816 (1954).

Municipal Law Review reported that perhaps the most important problem of the municipal attorney is the question of tort liability. The report said: "This [condition] appears to be particularly true when consideration is given to the number of claims being presented, the large amounts now being awarded in damages, the often lack of funds with which to pay the same, the inability to secure adequate, if any, public liability insurance, and the removal by the courts and legislatures in various states of the municipalities' immunity from tort liability when acting in a governmental capacity."[40] The assault on the doctrine of municipal immunity from tort liability has been led by the National Association of Claimants' Counsel of America. The 7,500 members of this nation-wide bar association, known as NACCA, are no doubt, the most zealous, hardest working, best paid lawyers in the country. NACCA was founded in 1946. The National Association of Claimants' Counsel of America is made up of "attorneys specializing in the representation of injured persons."[41] Through national and regional conferences, reports and the *NACCA Law Journal,* the organization has stimulated and applauded a sensational trend toward bigger and better damage suits.[42] In 1965 the organization was renamed the American Trial Lawyers Association.

The opposing interests caught up by this trend were pointed up by the reaction of NACCA and NIMLO attorneys to the lifting of municipal immunity from tort liability by the Supreme Court of Florida in 1957 in the case of *Hargrove v. Town of Cocoa Beach.*[43] This was an action by a widow against the municipality for damage for the alleged wrongful death of her husband who died of smoke suffocation in an unattended jail. (The court report says the "husband was incarcerated in the town jail while in a helpless condition because of excessive intoxication.") The trial judge dismissed the complaint

[40] Comment of William E. Collins, Corporation Counsel, Rockford, Illinois, 22 *NIMLO Municipal L. Rev.* 357-58 (1959).
[41] *Encyclopedia of Associations,* 3rd ed.,: Vol. 1, *National Organizations of the United States* (Detroit: Gale Research Co., 1961), p. 266.
[42] Litigation is not the only form of activity for this organization. See the argument for juries by its President, Jacob D. Fuchsberg, "A Brief for the Jury in Civil Cases," *New York Times Magazine,* March 1, 1964, p. 34.
[43] 96 So.2d 130 (1957).

on the theory that the town was immune to liability for this type of tort. On appeal, the Florida Supreme Court reversed and receded from its prior decisions holding a municipal corporation immune from liability for the torts of police officers. Positively, the court held "that when an individual suffers a direct, personal injury proximately caused by the negligence of a municipal. employee while acting within the scope of his employment, the injured individual is entitled to redress for the wrong done."[44] The court reasoned that the immunity doctrine was inappropriate in a modern, urban democracy where the city "is in substantial measure a large business institution." In departing from the rule of municipal immunity, the Florida Supreme Court explained that its conclusion had "not been hastily formulated" and added: "The matter was thoroughly briefed and argued by counsel for the parties. At the invitation of the Court, the Florida League of Municipalities filed briefs and through counsel ably presented the matter *amicus curiae*."[45]

At the next annual convention of the National Institute of Municipal Law Officers, the city attorney of Pensacola reported that this opinion was most alarming and there was general concern that such judgments could "financially cripple any city or village at any time."[46] The Pensacola city attorney's comments were uttered with some humor and, while it may be unfair to take them at face value, a quotation will reveal something of the spirit of one official faced with the prospect of damage suits in the future.[47]

> . . . on leaving my home in Pensacola the other day I picked up a newspaper and read that in Miami a circuit court jury had returned a verdict in the sum of $23,000.00 because a man's arm was broken while he was being arrested. Of course, that's Miami. (Laughter.)
> . . . We look with a great deal of fear and trepidation to the decision in the *Hargrove* case in Florida particularly so in the Miami area where the verdicts are so fantastic. I hope

---

[44] *Ibid.*, 133-34.
[45] *Ibid.*, 136.
[46] Comment of F. Churchill Mellen, City Attorney, Pensacola, Florida, 22 *NIMLO Municipal L. Rev.* 450 (1958).
[47] *Ibid.*, p. 452.

that in the Northern part of Florida where the real South-
erners of Florida live that they will be much more practical
in their verdicts in the event that we have a such a thought-
less officer on our police department as to break a man's arm
when he is drunk. (Applause.)

In contrast, a note in the *NACCA Law Journal* praised the
decision of the Supreme Court of Florida in the Hargrove case as
"commendably repudiating the indefensible rule of municipal
immunity from tort liability."[48] Municipalities were described by
the claimant's compensation attorneys as "one of the best loss-dis-
tributing units of society." The note said simply, but in emotion-
charged words, that the immunity rule was "barefaced injustice."
The NACCA position may be summed up as follows: "It is better
that the losses due to the torts of city employees should fall upon
the cities and for the latter to bear the cost of such casualties than
upon the innocent victim of 'official' torts. Such losses should be
regarded as the social cost of administering government, spread over
the citizenry by the tax device, rather than have the cities partially
subsidized by the coerced contributions of their victims."[49] This
view appears to be gaining popular and judicial acceptance. Without
straining its implications too greatly one can see the obligations of
local government and the tax burden growing through this judicial
change of heart brought about, at least in part, by the zealousness
of NACCA, henceforth to be known as the American Trial Lawyers
Association.

Court Rules and Interest Group Access

Among all litigants those who challenge municipal action perhaps
have the easiest path. In conformity with "Dillon's rule," the powers
possessed by municipalities are ordinarily interpreted in a restrictive
way by the courts.[50] The troubles of municipal corporations are

[48] Case note by Thomas F. Lambert, Jr., 20 *Nacca L. J.* 241 (November
1957).
[49] *Ibid.,* pp. 236-37.
[50] "Dillon's Rule" was originally expressed as follows: "It is a general and
undisputed proposition of law that a municipal corporation possesses and can
exercise the following powers, and no others: First, those granted in express

increased by the procedures of state courts which make them far easier marks than federal courts. Friendly suits are common. Advisory opinions are rendered in many states. The declaratory judgment is more fully developed. Class actions are permitted more readily. The rules for *amicus curiae* and intervenors are less stringent. Above all, the "taxpayer's suit" stands as a symbol of the many procedures by which state courts have been brought to exert such power over local government. This device led Sayre and Kaufman, in their study of New York City, to conclude that courts "offer nongovernmental groups in the city a chance to influence officials in the other branches indirectly when they cannot do so directly."[51]

"Taxpayers' suits" satisfy the jurisdictional requirement that plaintiffs have standing to sue.[52] Normally, this requirement means that the plaintiff must sustain specific personal injury before he is allowed to go to court. However, municipal action in virtually every state may be tested under this relaxation of the "standing" doctrine where a plaintiff's status as a taxpayer "has been held sufficient to allow damage to him which is shared equally with all members of the public to form a judicially cognizable issue."[53] A taxpayer's suit has been defined as "a representative class action in equity, brought on behalf of all taxpayers against officials of the governmental unit challenged.[54] In practice, the word "taxpayer" has been treated so loosely that a group of persons wishing to question governmental action in the courts need only find the money and a nominal plaintiff to do so. This is why "taxpayers' suits" have functionally become "citizens' suits."[55]

---

words; second, those necessarily or fairly implied in or incident to the powers expressly granted; third, those essential to the accomplishment of the declared objects and purposes of the corporation—not simply convenient, but indispensable. Any fair, reasonable, substantial doubt concerning the existence of power is resolved by the courts against the corporation, and the power is denied." Dillon, *op. cit.*, I, 448.

[51] Wallace S. Sayre and Herbert Kaufman, *Governing New York City: Politics in the Metropolis* (New York: Russell Sage Foundation, 1960), p. 496.

[52] This section of my paper is drawn largely from Comment, "Taxpayers' Suits: A Survey and a Summary," 69 *Yale L. J.* 895-924 (April 1960).

[53] *Ibid.*, p. 898.

[54] *Ibid.*, p. 906.

[55] *Ibid.*

A *Yale Law Journal* survey shows that the objectives sought by plaintiff-taxpayers have varied widely with the following in order of importance:[56] (1) challenges to the use of the eminent domain power in connection with slum clearance, housing, highways, airport, and other public works projects; (2) attacks on the constitutionality of various methods of bond financing used by municipalities to circumvent limitations on indebtedness; (3) cases questioning the granting of franchises or licenses which represent public approval of privately owned but publicly used facilities; (4) efforts to withhold salary payments to civil servants who hold office in violation of statutory standards; (5) challenges to sales or donations of the public domain to private parties; (6) cases to achieve civil liberties objectives such as the prevention of expenditures for illegal methods of law enforcement or expenditures which would violate the separation of church and state; (7) suits to reapportion election or judicial districts.

Taxpayers' suits were first allowed by American courts just prior to the Civil War but did not reach a great volume until the end of the nineteenth century. Then in the Populist and Progressive periods a number of devices of democratic intent were fashioned to cope with entrenched officials and vested interests. In this connection the taxpayer's suit should be linked with the initiative, referendum, and recall as a symbol of the era. In this century the taxpayer's suit has been one of the chief weapons in the arsenal of the good government movement. The editor of the Madison, Wisconsin, *Capital Times,* whose roots are deep in the LaFollette movement, in 1960 established a special fund of $10,000 to be used, as he said, "in the protection of the public domain which is being raided periodically by private interests at the expense of the public interest." [57] He said that this fund would allow his newspaper "to start a taxpayer's suit where we believe that the state's lakes, rivers, streams, forests and parks are being taken over by private interests for private profit." [58] Similarly, the Citizens Union of the City of

---

[56] *Ibid.,* pp. 907-908.
[57] Madison, Wisconsin, *Capital Times,* February 22, 1960, p. 1.
[58] *Ibid.*

New York, described as "probably the most widely known and influential organization among the city's multitude of non-governmental groups,"[59] and with origins before 1900 in the good government reform movement, has begun numerous taxpapers' actions throughout its history. Its activity in the courts has also taken other forms and has varied with the character of the local government. During the administrations of Mayors John F. Hylan (1918-25) and James J. Walker (1926-32) the Citizens Union brought some nineteen lawsuits to restrain illegal expenditures of public funds and was successful in about twelve. The present counsel of the Citizens Union said recently that in the last few years he had "brought some half dozen suits to restrain various governmental actions which we believed to be illegal. In addition, the Citizens Union occasionally intervenes, by leave of the court, as *amicus curiae* or friend of the court, in suits brought by others." [60] This use of taxpayers' suits by one newspaper and one civic organization is indicative of practices throughout the country.

The situation created by this easy access to the courts has been described by the *Yale Law Journal* in the following way:

> . . . Such litigation allows the courts, within the framework of traditional notions of "standing," to add to the controls over public officials inherent in the elective process the judicial scrutiny of the statutory and constitutional validity of their acts. Taxpayers' suits also extend the uniquely American concept of judicial review to legislative action by allowing minorities ineffective at the ballot box to invalidate statutes or ordinances on constitutional grounds. . . . Taxpayers' suits thus create an army of potential private attorneys general acting on whatever private incentives may induce them to spend the time and money to bring a taxpayer's suit. . . . And since group financing of such litigation is not

[59] Sayre and Kaufman, *Governing New York City*, see note 38, above, p. 497.
[60] Letter of Samuel D. Smoleff to author, July 7, 1960. Citizens Union cases include the following: *Childs* v. *Moses*, 290 N.Y. 828, 50 N.E. 2d 235; *Bergerman* v. *Murphy*, 303 N.Y. 762, 103 N.E. 2d 545; *Bergerman* v. *Gerosa*, 3 N.Y. 2d 855, 166 N.Y. Supp. 2d 306; *Bergerman* v. *Byrnes*, 305 N.Y. 811, 113 N.E. 2d 557; *Bergerman* v. *Wagner*, 2 N.Y. 2d 908, 161 N.Y. Supp. 2d 434.

infrequent, taxpayers' suits also mobilize various voluntary associations seeking private, economic, or social objectives to further law enforcement and prevention of corruption in government.[61]

The objections to the widespread use of taxpayers' suits are numerous. Even when unsuccessful the delay occasioned by such actions "may unduly obstruct the completion of public projects." [62] These suits may harrass officials and immobilize local government thereby inhibiting progressive community action. But most important of all, "taxpayers' suits may push the concept of judicial review of legislative and executive action too far." [63] The common complaints about judicial review merit repeating:

> By calling upon the courts to sit in judgment of decisions taken by the political branches of government, when no one is sufficiently injured thereby to have standing as an individual, taxpayer litigation may undermine the independence and prestige of the judiciary, impairing its ability to perform more traditional judicial functions. Since the courts are not designed, as are the political branches, to harmonize divergent views within the community and take action in accordance with the broadest possible concensus, such reviews may exceed their proper function. Moreover, placing the courts in the role of a "super legislature" may encourage irresponsibility and lack of creativity on the part of the political branches because they will be aware that decisions taken by them are always subject to judicial reversal.[64]

This should suggest that the concept of judicial review, which is usually thought of merely in terms of Supreme Court review of acts of Congress and of state legislatures deserves consideration from the viewpoint of the government of communities, as well. The vast array of state and federal courts which may review the actions of community governments means that the scope of local power is always open to challenge by litigating interest groups.

[61] Comment, op. cit., p. 904.
[62] Ibid.
[63] Ibid., p. 910.
[64] Ibid.

IV
PRESSURE GROUPS
AND REGULATION

Pressure Groups:
A Threat to Democracy?

H. R. MAHOOD

There has been an increase in the amount, tempo and intensity of pressure group activity in recent decades. Many and various reasons may be given for this. Certainly the advantages of organization have become obvious to workers, farmers, Negroes and others in the attainment of their respective goals.[1] Population increase has given rise to more and newer aspirations which are encompassed and furthered by new ogranizations. Technological advances on many fronts have produced new and highly differentiated economic and social groupings with problems which may or may not be completely resolved through existing organizations. Also, the appearance of new organizations has threatened and endangered older ones bringing about realignments and consolidations among them. Finally governmental policy-making has contributed to the creation of groups. The Tennessee Valley Authority, for example, gave rise to various groups in the Tennessee River Valley on both the state and local level which benefited from the program. Likewise, the Rural Electrification Administration and its programs of public power stimulated a myriad

[1] V. O. Key, *Politics, Parties, and Pressure Groups,* 5th ed. (New York: Thomas Y. Crowell, 1964), develops the establishment and growth of some of the leading pressure groups in American politics and their activities.

of professional and business organizations connected with public power.[2] Such factors as these, then, have been generative in the proliferation of pressure groups and their activities in American politics.

The multiplication and differentiation of pressure groups have been matched by a refinement of various techniques and greater use thereof to maximize political effectiveness. Groups are turning, for example, to more extensive use of television along with wider use of radio and the press. Coupled with these are greater use of the mails, attendance at a variety of organization conventions, dissemination of auto bumper stickers, wider personal contacts with public and private officials, use of billboards and any other media to both convince and exploit those susceptible to pressures. More and more of group budgets are expended not only on public media but also for the hiring and retention of certain functional specialists such as writers, researchers and public relations specialists.

Pressure groups have also continued to exploit the American political system which bestows certain advantages on them vis-á-vis government in their continuing competition for public power and support.[3] As previously mentioned, pressure groups have ready access to communications and other media. This access is more privileged and available to them than it is to government. Pressure groups also have more continuity both in policy and personnel, better paid personnel, more secrecy in operation and lower public visibility. They also have less public accountability and freer selection of targets for their pressures than government and its agencies have.

These events have greatly contributed to the growing political power and significance of pressure groups in the political system and their influence on the workings of that system. With their position and importance established, it is only natural that they have become subjects of controversy. By being able to influence policies which not

---

[2] For a brief discussion of the impact of the Tennessee Valley Authority and the Rural Electrification Administration and their political stimulation on the local level, see Arthur M. Schlesinger, Jr., *The Politics of Upheaval* (Boston: Houghton-Mifflin, 1960), pp. 362-384.

[3] Donald C. Blaisdell, *American Democracy Under Pressure* (New York: The Ronald Press, 1957).

only affect their own members but also non-members and rival groups, they are alternately criticized and praised or viewed with suspicion, mistrust or approbation.

Some of the more serious criticisms leveled at pressure groups and their activities are first, that they are not democratically organized. Critics charge that the rank and file members have little to do with the selection of group officers and leaders and even less with policy-making. A small clique, it is argued, dominates the group hierarchy and operates at times in a manner totally indifferent to the hopes and aspirations of the membership as a whole.[4] Group meetings and conventions are rigged by leadership so as to allow little time and opportunity for the general membership to question policies or leaders. Little is known by the members in regard to total membership, financial affairs or operating procedures.

Second, groups are severely criticized because they put their own interests above the "public" interest. They tend to operate on the "Me First Principle." They are so blinded by their own narrow interests that they are totally incapable of realizing other legitimate interests may exist. They are simply incapable of rising above their own selfishness and working for the good of the entire nation.[5]

A third criticism of groups is their use of certain techniques. It is often expressed by group critics that they use questionable methods —bribing, deceiving, cheating, falsifying—in obtaining their objectives. By engaging in such unethical tactics, they engender suspicion and fear in the minds of public officials. Their use of pressure mail, telephone calls, telegrams and personal visits is further evidence of the lengths to which groups will go in order to get what they want.

In the eyes of their detractors, these criticisms add up to a powerful indictment of pressure groups and their value to the American political system. They do more harm than good by dividing the American people through their tactics, continually confusing them

[4] Grant McConnel, "The Spirit of Private Government," *American Political Science Review* (September, 1958), pp. 754-770.
[5] Stuart Chase, *Democracy Under Pressure* (New York: The Twentieth Century Fund, 1945), p. 4.

with their slanted propaganda, and inhibiting effective governmental action by constantly badgering and harrassing public officials with conflicting claims.

Various proposals and remedies, both formal and informal, have been offered by critics to deal with the problems of pressure groups. The most prominent of the formal type, perhaps, has been regulation. Laws have existed on both the national and state levels for some time dealing with libel, bribery, slander and fraudulent use of mails. Also, toward the end of the nineteenth century, more and more states passed laws regulating lobbying activities by various private organizations. In 1874, Alabama outlawed bribery, and in 1877, Georgia wrote into its constitution a provision that "lobbying was a crime." In the 1890's, Massachusetts legalized public exposure of pressure tactics, and soon Wisconsin and New York followed its lead. Today other states such as Illinois, California, and Texas have enacted recent legislation regulating pressure activities in their own particular way.[6]

National regulation of pressure groups did not begin until 1946 when Congress passed the Congressional Reorganization Act (P.L. 79-601). Title III of this act called for regulation of certain types of political activity by pressure spokesmen. This law applied to "any person who solicits, collects, or receives money to be used principally to influence Federal legislation." Thus a lobbyist (or pressure spokesman) was required to register with the Clerk of the House of Representatives and the Secretary of the Senate and file financial statements and other information regarding their employers and the lobbying they engaged in. Penalties were provided for non-compliance.

This law, however, did not impose any restrictions on the general activities of groups or their representatives. Nor did it impose any financial restrictions. It was simply making as a matter of public record many of the behind-the-scenes legislative operators, including lawyers, former congressmen and former federal officials who were

---

[6] A recent approach to the regulation of pressure groups on the state level is that of California. For the recommendations of the California investigations see, California Legislative Assembly, Interior Committee on Governmental Efficiency and Economy, *Federal and State Laws on Lobbying* (Sacramento, 1950). Also the Reports of this Committee, 1955-57.

LOBBY SPENDING FOR YEARS 1961-1965*

CATEGORY	1961 REPORTING GROUPS	1961 AMOUNT SPENT	1962 REPORTING GROUPS	1962 AMOUNT SPENT	1963 REPORTING GROUPS	1963 AMOUNT SPENT	1964 REPORTING GROUPS	1964 AMOUNT SPENT	1965 REPORTING GROUPS	1965 AMOUNT SPENT
Business	171	$1,672,259	170	$1,836,126	153	$1,521,600	147	$1,361,427.81	154	$1,472,863.72
Citizens	52	494,175	50	531,002	51	707,333	57	1,065,197.29	64	836,113.02
Employee and Labor	40	892,569	37	945,206	36	1,130,124	33	945,071.32	31	1,094,782.86
Farm	22	367,238	22	412,524	21	405,849	23	365,471.81	25	419,633.65
Military and Veterans	10	133,735	6	141,991	5	140,180	6	154,493.05	7	167,634.81
Professional	17	426,120	19	344,455	20	318,519	21	331,616.11	23	1,493,384.96
Total	312	$3,986,096	304	$4,211,304	286	$4,223,605	287	$4,223,277.39	304	$5,484,413.02

* Congressional Quarterly Service, "Legislators and Lobbyists," (Washington, D.C.: Congressional Quarterly Service), p. 39. Figures for 1964 and 1965 were added to the original table.

perceptive in the ways of influencing legislation. It turned the public spotlight on many individuals who had operated either covertly and/or discretely through contacts with various key congressmen influential in the legislative process. Both the public and some congressmen had little knowledge as to who these persons were and even less of the money being spent by them and who they represented.

Although the passage of this law was helpful to the public and many congressmen in revealing certain lobbying techniques of pressure groups, it was not in force long before it became clear to many that the law was defective. Its vague phraseology, for example, raised questions as to who should register as a lobbyist. Further, the act made no provision for a central enforcement agency which would supervise compliance, investigate the accuracy of statements filed and publicize this information. In practice, both the Clerk of the House of Representatives and the Secretary of the Senate act as little more than depositories for filed statements. These offices have neither the facilities nor the staffs to properly analyze, verify and catalogue the filed information. Finally, recent criticism claims the law did not go far enough. In light of expanded activities by pressure groups before executive agencies, critics charge that the law should have originally covered executive lobbying. Because of these statutory shortcomings, it is small wonder that the lobbying law soon became involved in litigation. The definitive court interpretation of the law came in 1954 in the case *United States* v. *Harriss*.[7]

Another formal approach to the problems of pressure groups consists of measures to strengthen governmental organization. It is claimed by their critics, that pressure groups have become significantly influential because various governmental institutions have neither the

---

[7] 347 U.S. 612 (1954). This case grew out of certain lobbying activities by a New York cotton broker, Robert M. Harriss. Harriss was charged in violation of the law being neither registered nor reporting his lobbying activities to influence legislation. A lower federal court ruled the lobbying law unconstitutional on the grounds that it was too vague and indefinite to meet the requirements of due process, that the registration and reporting requirements violated the First Amendment and that certain of the penalty processes violated the constitutional right to petition Congress. On appeal, the Supreme Court ruled in 1954 that the lobbying law was constitutional though construing it narrowly.

strength nor the know-how to neutralize pressure penetration. Some congressmen are especially susceptible to group activities while others are not; some pressure groups have extensive legislative influence while others do not; and certain legislative procedures help some groups and hurt others. Congress needs proper re-organization and equipment to do a proper job in dealing with pressure activities. Countervailing powers within the legislature are needed to minimize pressures and protect the public interest

Actually, some basic changes have already been made, for example, in congressional machinery. In 1946, recommendations in the Legislative Reorganization Act produced long-needed congressional reforms and reorganization.[8] Committee reorganization, professional staffing, public hearings and improved bill-drafting are indicative of congressional modernization and streamlining. Also, such thorny legislative problems as seniority, party discipline and filibustering are also under periodic review. Whether or not Congress, incorporating all these and other contemplated changes, would be a formidable and effective barrier against incessant group pressures can only be an object of conjecture. (For Congressmen's views on lobbying, see questionnaire pp. 304-305.)

At the same time pressure groups are active before the national legislature, they may also be bringing pressure on the executive. Like Congress, the executive branch has also undergone reorganization and strengthening since the end of World War II.[9] Recruitment policies have been changed and improved and salaries have been raised continuously to make them more competitive with private industry. The civil service system has continued to be extended. These policies have upgraded public service and thereby, attracted higher caliber people to government service. Is this type of establishment, however, to be completely impervious to group demands or merely designate which group demands can be incorporated into executive policies and which cannot?

[8] Joint Committee on the Organization of Congress, *Report*, 79th Cong., 2nd Sess., September 2, 1946.
[9] See the two reports of a special commission chaired by the late President Herbert Hoover. Commission on Organization of the Executive Branch of the Government (Washington, D. C.: Government Printing Office, 1949, 1955).

One other formal approach to the pressure group problem is functional representation. This is an essentially positive approach whereas regulation and the strengthening of governmental institutions are essentially negative. The functional approach emphasizes the utility of pressure groups within the political system and the contribution they can make to it. Functional representation does exist today in France. An Economic and Social Council exists within the French governmental framework which represents the most important economic and social pressure groups within the nation. The Council has consultative and advisory powers on economic and social legislation.[10]

If functional representation was adopted in some form within our system, government and pressure groups would be tied more closely together. Pressure groups would have a definite role to play and have a greater stake in the success or failure of various public policies. Their activities would be on a more regularized and open basis and they would be able to provide needed information and ideas for the legislative process.[11] At the present time, however, there appears to be little public sentiment for such a radical governmental change.

An informal method of pressure group management is the principle of "countervailing power" or the development of counterpressures. As illustrated by John Kenneth Galbraith, this principle operates within the business community.[12] According to Galbraith, the gradual concentration of American business created not only strong producers (or sellers) but also strong buyers who act as a countervailing force on the sellers. The strong buyers and sellers are a check on each other. Pressures stimulate counterpressures. This has become a significant pattern within our economic and social

[10] See E. Drexel Godfrey, Jr., *The Government of France* (New York: Thomas Y. Crowell, 1961), p. 58.

[11] This type of representation was tried by Franklin Roosevelt during the days of the New Deal. The National Industrial Recovery Act attempted to incorporate economic groups more completely into government and give them responsibilities. See, for example, Arthur M. Schlesinger, Jr., *The Coming of the New Deal* (Boston: Houghton-Mifflin, 1958), pp. 87-118.

[12] John Kenneth Galbraith, *American Capitalism: The Concept of Countervailing Power* (Boston: Houghton-Mifflin, 1952).

communities. Diverse and competing centers of private power are engaged in an eternal power struggle. Sometimes, for example, labor may countervail agriculture, or private utilities may counterbalance public utilities, or Negro activities may oppose those of Southern whites.

It is a mistake, however, to believe that countervailing power applies universally. Some groups, such as veterans, find little opposition to their activities. On the other hand, organized labor in southern states and communities has not been an effective counterforce to business, and organization drives have not produced the results labor leaders have sought. Local attitudes and the political environment have been factors minimizing the applicability of countervailing power.

There is probably no single best approach to pressure group control. Certainly, existing statutory regulation is vague and too difficult to enforce to be meaningful. Any attempt, however, to write a stringent law might run afoul of First Amendment freedoms inherent in freedom of association. No consensus exists as to the threat posed by pressure groups to democracy and our governmental processes. Perhaps what is needed is a more positive approach to pressure groups and a government that is both receptive and discriminating to group demands. Pressure groups make important contributions to the American political process by (a) stimulating and formalizing the desires of thousands of American citizens, (b) transmitting these collective desires and aspirations to government at the appropriate level, (c) presenting needed and specialized information to national policy-makers, and (d) maintaining surveillance of policy-making centers so as to protect the interests of their memberships. The total effect of pressure groups and their activities upon government is one of amelioration.

Political pluralism has contributed to America's greatness. Our progress in economic, social, technological and cultural fields has been stimulated and expanded by pressure groups. Their operation is sometimes chaotic and sometimes selfish, but by the very fact that groups may pursue their interests so freely and openly is a sign that our political processes are in a healthy state.

CONGRESSMEN'S VIEWS ON LOBBYING*

What do Members of Congress think of the activities of lobbyists belonging to what often is termed the "Third House of Congress?"

A 1957 Congressional Quarterly poll of Senators and Representatives revealed that Congress found lobbyist helpful to the legislative process. The 122 Congressmen answering the poll generally agreed they:

Received enough information to identify lobbyists who pressured them.

Felt little unreasonable pressure from the lobby corps.

Received valuable information on complicated issues from the lobbyists.

Questionnaire

A total of 122, or 23 percent, of the 528 Congressmen polled returned their questionnaires with these results (figures will not total since many Members checked more than one item):

84, or 69 percent: "I am receiving enough information to enable me to identify lobbyists who contact me."

15, or 12 percent: "I am not receiving enough information about lobbyists and therefore favor provisions in the pending bill (S 2191) to direct the General Accounting Office to collect and distribute such information."

76, or 62 percent: "Most lobbyists are helpful to me because they supply detailed facts on complicated legislative questions." (Nine other Congressmen, or 7 percent, checked the question after amending it to read "some" lobbyists instead of "most" lobbyists.

4, or 3 percent: "Most lobbyists confuse the issue because they distort the facts."

50, or 41 percent: "Lobbyists help Congress to legislate with maximum intelligence."

* Congressional Quarterly Service, "Legislators and Lobbyists," p. 12.

6, or 5 percent: "Congress would be better off without lobbyists."

21, or 17 percent: "Lobbyists neither help nor hinder me in my work."

13, or 11 percent: "I often have felt unreasonable pressure from lobbyists."

25, or 21 percent: "I sometimes have felt unreasonable pressure from lobbyists."

40, or 33 percent: "I have never felt unreasonable pressure from lobbyists."

11546   138

PUBLISHED BY CHARLES SCRIBNER'S SONS, NEW YORK

PRESIDENTIAL ELECTIONS
STRATEGIES OF AMERICAN ELECTORAL POLITICS

By Nelson W. Polsby and Aaron B. Wildavsky

MEMBER OF THE HOUSE
LETTERS OF A CONGRESSMAN

By the late Congressman Clem Miller
Edited, with additional text, by John W. Baker